OECD DOCUMENTS OCDE

FROM HIGHER EDUCATION TO EMPLOYMENT

VOLUME II: Canada, Denmark, Spain, United States.

DE L'ENSEIGNEMENT SUPÉRIEUR A L'EMPLOI

VOLUME II : Canada, Danemark, Espagne, Etats-Unis.

ORGANISATION FOR ECONOMIC CO-OPERATION AND DEVELOPMENT
ORGANISATION DE COOPÉRATION ET DE DÉVELOPPEMENT ÉCONOMIQUES

ORGANISATION FOR ECONOMIC CO-OPERATION AND DEVELOPMENT

ORGANISATION DE COOPÉRATION ET DE DÉVELOPPEMENT ÉCONOMIQUES

Pursuant to Article 1 of the Convention signed in Paris on 14th December 1960, and which came into force on 30th September 1961, the Organisation for Economic Co-operation and Development (OECD) shall promote policies designed:

— to achieve the highest sustainable economic growth and employment and a rising standard of living in Member countries, while maintaining financial stability, and thus to contribute to the development of the world economy;
— to contribute to sound economic expansion in Member as well as non-member countries in the process of economic development; and
— to contribute to the expansion of world trade on a multilateral, non-discriminatory basis in accordance with international obligations.

The original Member countries of the OECD are Austria, Belgium, Canada, Denmark, France, Germany, Greece, Iceland, Ireland, Italy, Luxembourg, the Netherlands, Norway, Portugal, Spain, Sweden, Switzerland, Turkey, the United Kingdom and the United States. The following countries became Members subsequently through accession at the dates indicated hereafter: Japan (28th April 1964), Finland (28th January 1969), Australia (7th June 1971) and New Zealand (29th May 1973). The Commission of the European Communities takes part in the work of the OECD (Article 13 of the OECD Convention). Yugoslavia has a special status at OECD (agreement of 28th October 1961).

En vertu de l'article 1er de la Convention signée le 14 décembre 1960, à Paris, et entrée en vigueur le 30 septembre 1961, l'Organisation de Coopération et de Développement Economiques (OCDE) a pour objectif de promouvoir des politiques visant :

— à réaliser la plus forte expansion de l'économie et de l'emploi et une progression du niveau de vie dans les pays Membres, tout en maintenant la stabilité financière, et à contribuer ainsi au développement de l'économie mondiale ;
— à contribuer à une saine expansion économique dans les pays Membres, ainsi que les pays non membres, en voie de développement économique ;
— à contribuer à l'expansion du commerce mondial sur une base multilatérale et non discriminatoire conformément aux obligations internationales.

Les pays Membres originaires de l'OCDE sont : l'Allemagne, l'Autriche, la Belgique, le Canada, le Danemark, l'Espagne, les Etats-Unis, la France, la Grèce, l'Irlande, l'Islande, l'Italie, le Luxembourg, la Norvège, les Pays-Bas, le Portugal, le Royaume-Uni, la Suède, la Suisse et la Turquie. Les pays suivants sont ultérieurement devenus Membres par adhésion aux dates indiquées ci-après : le Japon (28 avril 1964), la Finlande (28 janvier 1969), l'Australie (7 juin 1971) et la Nouvelle-Zélande (29 mai 1973). La Commission des Communautés européennes participe aux travaux de l'OCDE (article 13 de la Convention de l'OCDE). La Yougoslavie a un statut spécial à l'OCDE (accord du 28 octobre 1961).

© OECD 1992
OCDE

Les demandes de reproduction ou de traduction totales ou partielles de cette publication doivent être adressées à :
Applications for permission to reproduce or translate all or part of this publication should be made to:
M. le Chef du Service des Publications, OCDE
Head of Publications Service, OECD
2, rue André-Pascal, 75775 PARIS CEDEX 16, France

AVANT-PROPOS

L'OCDE a conduit une activité intitulée "Enseignement supérieur et Emploi", qui comportait trois projets distincts : "Les sorties des enseignements supérieurs et les entrées dans la vie active" ; "Le cas des lettres et des sciences sociales" ; et "Les développements récents de la formation professionnelle continue".

Ce volume relève du premier de ces trois projets. De nombreux pays Membres ont préparé des contributions, à partir d'une note d'orientation détaillée rédigée par le Secrétariat. Ces contributions ont souvent exigé un important effort conceptuel pour rassembler des données d'origines très diverses. Elles reflètent l'état des connaissances dans chaque pays et, en même temps, des approches, des méthodologies et même des philosophies très différentes.

Le premier volume rassemblait les contributions de l'Allemagne, de l'Australie, de l'Autriche et de la Belgique. On présente dans ce second volume celles du Canada, du Danemark, de l'Espagne, des Etats-Unis. Les contributions des autres pays seront présentées dans les volumes suivants.

Il faut noter que ce projet met l'accent sur les flux plutôt que sur les catégories d'établissements ; on appelle "enseignements supérieurs" les formations suivies par ceux qui ont terminé des études secondaires ou de niveau équivalent. Ceci peut ne pas correspondre avec la définition plus restrictive qui en est donnée dans certains pays.

Ce projet a été conduit par Eric Esnault, du Secrétariat. Les idées exprimées par les auteurs n'engagent la responsabilité ni de l'OCDE, ni des autorités nationales intéressées. Ce volume est publié sous la responsabilité du Secrétaire général de l'OCDE.

FOREWORD

The OECD activity on Higher Education and Employment covers three discrete projects: "The flows of graduates from higher education and their entry into working life"; "The case of the humanities and the social sciences"; and "Recent developments in continuing professional education".

This report is devoted to the first of these three projects. Many Member countries submitted contributions in response to detailed guidelines prepared by the Secretariat. These contributions constitute a major conceptual effort to assemble information from many sources. They reflect the state of the art and illustrate a variety of approaches, methodologies and even philosophies.

The first volume contained contributions from Germany, Australia, Austria and Belgium. Presented here are those from Canada, Denmark, Spain and the United-States. Contributions from other countries will be presented in the succeeding volumes.

It should be noted that the emphasis is on flows rather than institutions. "Higher education" is defined as the education and training experience of those who have completed upper secondary education or its equivalent. This may not coincide with the more restrictive connotation of the term in some countries.

This project was led by Eric Esnault, of the Secretariat. The views expressed by the authors do not commit either the OECD or the national authorities concerned. This volume is published on the responsibility of the OECD Secretary-General.

CONTENTS
TABLE DES MATIERES

CANADA/CANADA	5
DANEMARK/DENMARK	59
ESPAGNE/SPAIN	87
ETATS-UNIS/UNITED STATES	129

CANADA

Ramona McDowell, Gilles Jasmin

Department of the Secretary of State of Canada

La version française de ce document est disponible auprès du Secrétariat

TABLE OF CONTENTS

I.	Postwar developments in post-secondary education in Canada	7
II.	Post-secondary education in Canada	8
III.	The post-secondary student population	10
IV.	Graduates from community colleges	12
V.	Graduates from universities	15
VI.	Women and post-secondary education	20
VII.	Graduates who continue their education	24
VIII.	Non-graduates outflows from post-secondary education	26
IX.	Labour market conditions facing graduates	27
X.	Transition into the labour force	28
XI.	Articulation between education and jobs	35
XII.	Employment destinations of post-secondary graduates	41
XIII.	Issues facing post-secondary education in Canada	47

Annex 1: Disciplines included in major fields of study at the post-secondary, non-university level — 49

Annex 2: Disciplines included in major fields of study at the university level — 51

Annex 3: Occupational categories included in major classifications — 53

Annex 4: Industrial categories included in major classification — 55

Bibliography — 56

THE FLOW OF GRADUATES FROM HIGHER EDUCATION AND THEIR ENTRY INTO WORKING LIFE

RAMONA MCDOWELL
Research and Information on Education Directorate
Department of the Secretary of State of Canada

I. POST-WAR DEVELOPMENTS IN POST-SECONDARY EDUCATION IN CANADA

Following World War II, Canada entered a period of rapid urbanization and industrialization. By the 1960s, the expansion of educational opportunities and the development of the requisite facilities had come to be regarded as a necessary social investment for future economic growth. The Economic Council of Canada, influenced by human capital theory, was one of many voices urging the expansion of post-secondary education.

Government articulated a policy of universal accessibility, with equal opportunities for all Canadians to acquire as much education and training as they desired (Dennison and Gallagher, 1986). The result of this philosophy, coupled with a buoyant economic climate in the 1960s, was the development in many provinces of a publicly funded community college system, the construction of new institutions of post-secondary education, the expansion of the numbers and scope of programs offered at the post-secondary level and the provision of government financial assistance for less advantaged students.

The rapid growth in funding slowed in the 1970s, and in the early 1980s Canada, like many western countries, experienced economic stagnation, recession, inflation and unemployment. Fiscal difficulties for governments resulted in policies of constraint in many fields including post-secondary education (Decore and Pannu, 1986).

While governments are pressured by both financial difficulties and taxpayers to reduce spending on education, the Economic Council identifies as imperative the need to pursue a standard of excellence in highly educated individuals and to raise the national level of literacy, numeracy and analytical competence to cope with an information based society (Economic Council of Canada, 1990).

Government, faced with conflicting priorities, urges fiscal restraint in post-secondary education. Educators, with a limited growth in resources, are trying to cope with rapidly increasing enrolments. Increases in tuition fees are unpopular with students and their families, and proposals for cutting back on educational services such as computer and research facilities draw criticism from potential employers and graduates who fear an erosion in the quality of education.

While post-secondary graduates from some fields of study are facing increasing levels of unemployment or underemployment and a decreasing financial return on their educational investment, some employers, particularly in the high technology sector are experiencing difficulty filling existing positions on their workforce.

In the face of these difficulties, some have called for the definition of common goals and cooperative action to maximize the positive role that post-secondary education can play in meeting individual and economic goals. No national policy on post-secondary education has been articulated in Canada. Authoritative planning of the labour force is not a realistic alternative, given a social and political commitment to freedom of choice and open accessibility to education. Instead, the flow and quality of information concerning the opportunities available those undertaking post-secondary education and the labour market conditions awaiting graduates must be improved so that society and the individual maximize the benefits received in partnership from post-secondary education.

II. POST-SECONDARY EDUCATION IN CANADA

Canada's constitution places the primary jurisdiction over all levels of education with the provinces, resulting in a complex system with ten distinct provincial and two territorial structures. Most post-secondary institutions are public, funded in large part by the government of the province in which they are located. While universities enjoy almost total autonomy in academic activity, the non-degree sector in each province is much more closely regulated and is typically managed as single system (Skolnik, 1990).

All provinces distinguish between the degree and non-degree granting sectors of post-secondary education. The universities offer undergraduate, graduate studies and professional programs and are involved in research. The non-degree sector provides career training below the professional level to graduates from secondary school and in some provinces also provides university transfer programs.

School attendance is compulsory until age 15 or 16, and the course of elementary and secondary education lasts 12 years in most provinces, and 11 in Quebec. Admission to community colleges and universities is generally granted on the basis of secondary school graduation. In Quebec, admission to university requires completion of a two year program at a collège d'enseignement général et professionel (CÉGEP).

Universities awarding secular degrees are public institutions which operate according to an approximately common standard. In the face of a strong commitment to equality of access, universities are not hierarchically differentiated and the bulk of funding is supplied on a per capita basis (Skolnik, 1990).

A university Bachelor's degree may be obtained after three or four years study, with the more specialized Honours program requiring four years. Graduates may enter a Master's program, requiring one or two more years depending on the speciality. Entrance into a Doctorate program normally requires a Master's degree. Doctoral studies usually require one or two years full-time residency and a dissertation, and typically take three to four years beyond the Master's level. In addition to degrees, various diploma or certificate programs requiring a shorter period of study are available at the university level.

Although university degree programs do not generally require related work experience, cooperative programs which combine academic work with supervised periods of related employment are growing in popularity. Correspondence courses and distance education through the use of television are increasingly offered by universities in an effort to improve accessibility to higher education, particularly for part-time adult learners.

Thirty years ago post-secondary education was offered almost exclusively by universities, but in the 1960s, many provinces began structuring publicly funded community college systems to reach students interested in career-oriented technical programs. Although non-university post-secondary education has long been available in Nova Scotia, the province has only recently established institutions which it would classify as community colleges such as those developed in other parts of Canada (Dennison and Gallagher, 1986).

Community colleges also offer continuing education for adults, retraining and basic education skills. College level certificate and diploma programs are now offered by a variety of institutions: CÉGEPs, colleges of applied arts and technology, community colleges, and specialized technological colleges and institutes in areas such as agriculture and nursing. Private colleges also exist, particularly in business and commercial or service career areas, but public colleges account for the vast majority of students in the non-degree sector (Skolnik, 1990).

Unlike the university systems which are similar from province to province, the community college systems differ in organization and purpose on the basis of the individual circumstances which brought about their establishment. In Ontario, community colleges provide a distinct alternative to universities with vocational-technical curriculums. In Quebec, the CÉGEPS link secondary schools with both universities and the workforce with university preparatory training and technological career programs. British Columbia's community colleges offer both career programs and university transfer programming (Dennison and Gallagher, 1986).

III. THE POST-SECONDARY STUDENT POPULATION

The number of graduates from Canadian secondary schools peaked at a high of 305,900 in 1982, and has been declining since that date. This decline is due largely to demographics; declining birthrates have decreased the size of the school age population. The graduation rate has remained steady over the last decade, and more Canadians are staying in school past the compulsory age level of 15 or 16.

TABLE 1

Secondary School Graduates, Canada, 1980 to 1987.

Source: Statistics Canada, Education in Canada A Statistical Review, 1983–1984 and 1987–1988.

YEAR	NUMBER OF GRADUATES	SENIOR ENROLMENT GRADUATING
1980	296,200	80%
1981	305,100	81%
1982	305,900	81%
1983	289,100	78%
1984	290,400	78%
1985	278,400	76%
1986	276,900	78%
1987	268,300	76%

Contrary to expectations, this decline in the number of secondary school graduates has not led to a decline in post-secondary enrolments. Increases in the proportion of secondary graduates continuing on to post-secondary studies as well as increased participation on the part of previously underrepresented groups have resulted in growth, although growth in enrolments have levelled at the community colleges.

The increase since 1980 in the proportion of young women continuing their education is particularly marked. In 1979-80, 42% of young women graduating from secondary school continued directly to post-secondary education. By 1987-88, the proportion had increased to 56%.

In 1979-80, approximately 13% of the 18-21 age cohort was enroled full-time in community colleges, with the proportion rising to 17% in 1983-84 and 20% in 1987-88. Participation in undergraduate university programs by this age cohort rose from 18% to 21% and ultimately to 27% over the same period.

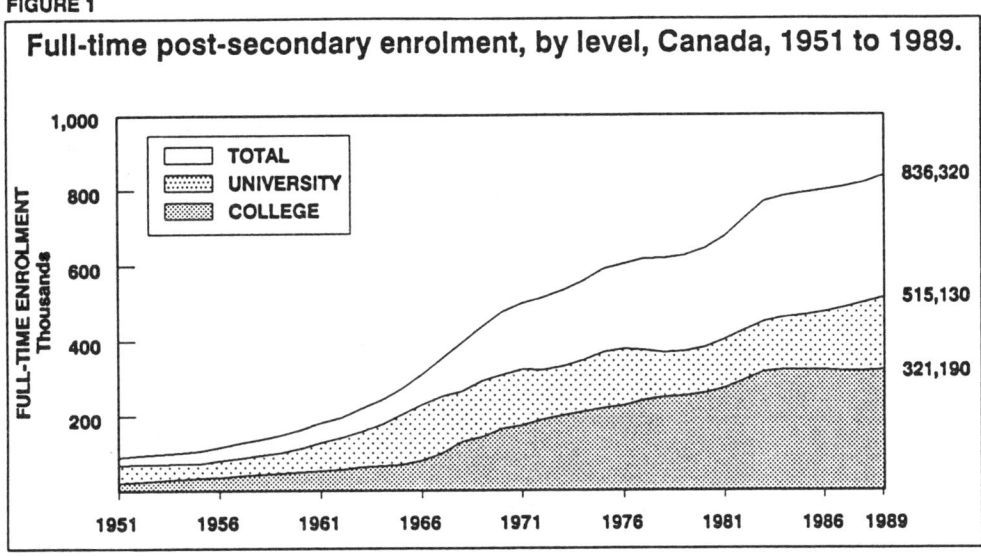

FIGURE 1
Full-time post-secondary enrolment, by level, Canada, 1951 to 1989.

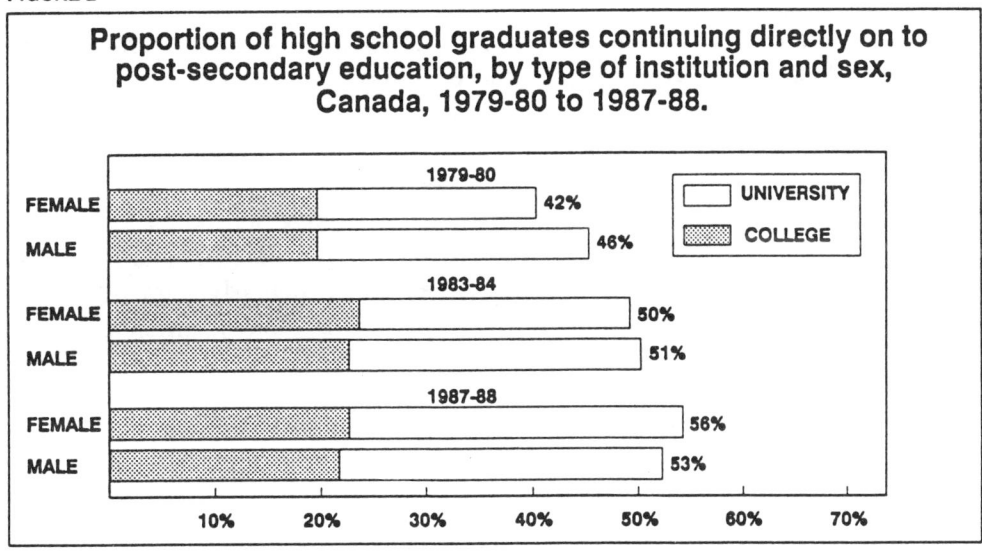

FIGURE 2
Proportion of high school graduates continuing directly on to post-secondary education, by type of institution and sex, Canada, 1979-80 to 1987-88.

Although the expansion of the post-secondary sector has facilitated participation by increasing numbers of Canadians, economic factors have also played a role. Professional and managerial occupations have expanded and employers increasingly rely on formal qualifications as a screening device when hiring or promoting. These factors provide incentive to secondary school graduates to continue and for those already in the labour force or returning to it to upgrade their education.

Demographic shifts have reduced the size of the cohort under age 24. While the large majority of students at community colleges and universities are still under 24 years of age, there has been an increase in the numbers of Canadians over the age of 30 pursuing further education.

FIGURE 3

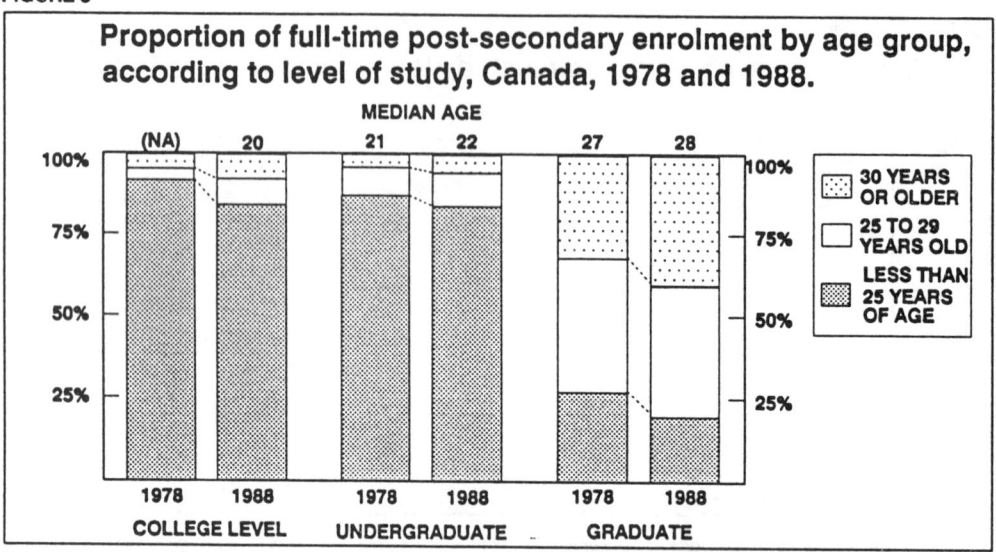

Research done in Quebec indicates that of every 100 Quebecers entering primary school, 38 will attend university before age 30, and an additional 25 will enrol sometime after their thirtieth birthday (La Haye and Lespérance, 1989).

Part-time enrolments are also increasing, particularly in career programs at community colleges where full-time enrolments have been declining slightly since 1985 (Statistics Canada, 1989). University undergraduate programs have experienced an 89% increase in part-time enrolments since 1970 and graduate part-time enrolments have increased by 162% (Statistics Canada, 1990). Part-time studies are particularly attractive to those already in the labour force who are interested in upgrading their qualifications and are unable or unwilling to attend school full-time.

IV. GRADUATES FROM COMMUNITY COLLEGES

A. Methodological note

Community college career programs provide an education preparing a student to enter an occupation above the level of a skilled tradesman, but below that of a professional. Ontario, Newfoundland, Prince Edward Island, Nova Scotia and New Brunswick offer only career programs at the community colleges. In other provinces, community colleges also offer university transfer courses.

Students who complete university transfer programs are not included in the graduate counts used in this report, since they have not completed their full post-secondary education, but only a portion of the requirements for a degree which will eventually be granted at the university level. The general programs at Quebec colleges are classed as university transfer programs.

Diplomas may be earned in career programs in seven main fields of study. The Arts include such subject areas as theatre arts, graphic and commercial art and interior design. The Humanities encompass journalism, library and archive science among other fields. The Health Sciences include nursing and medical technologies. Engineering/Applied Sciences include chemical, electronic and transportation technologies, and computer sciences. Natural Sciences/Primary Industries encompass agriculture, resource processing and environmental and conservation technologies. The Social Sciences/Services include subject areas such as social services, recreation, and correctional services. Business/Commerce include secretarial and administrative work, marketing and the areas of food preparation and hospitality.[1]

In some tables in this report two major fields of study, Business/Commerce and Engineering/Applied Science have been divided into subgroupings. Mechandising/Sales is considered separately from the other disciplines in Business/Commerce, while the disciplines remaining appear under the heading Management/Administration. Chemical/Industrial Engineering Science includes: Chemical Technology, Drafting, Industrial Technology and Surveying. Electrical Engineering Science includes Electrical Engineering, Mathematics and Computer Science. Mechanical/Construction Sciences include Construction, Mechanical and Transportation Technologies.

B. Statistical overview

In 1987, 58,500 diplomas were awarded in career programs, an increase of 53% over eleven years earlier. The rate of increase in the number of graduates is slowing however, with the reduction in size of the 18-21 age population group which forms the bulk of students at Canadian community colleges. This decrease is offset in large part at present by the increased participation on the part of this "baby-bust" generation and the growth in part-time enrolment by older groups.

Regional variations occur in enrolments in community colleges. In Ontario, college enrolments are declining, while the universities are full to capacity (Skolnik, 1990). In Quebec and British Columbia college enrolments are up. Perhaps applied programs which offer little opportunity for an eventual transfer to university, such as those offered by the community colleges of Ontario, are becoming less attractive in some areas as students and employers become increasingly credential conscious.

As well as a change in the number of graduates, the proportions graduating from different fields of study have changed since 1976. In that year, the proportions graduating from the three most popular fields, Health Sciences, Business/Commerce and Engineering/Applied Sciences, were: 31%, 21% and 19% respectively, for a total of

---

1. See Annex 1 for a complete list of subject areas in each program field.

slightly over seven out of ten of all graduates. In 1987, graduates in the Health Sciences accounted for one-third less of the total (19%) which could be a result of the combined impact of a tightening of the labour market, and of the greater availability of university level programs in nursing and other applied Health Sciences. Business/Commerce graduates increased their share to 27% and Engineering/Applied Sciences to 24%, these three fields comprising a total of seven out of ten graduates. The proportion for all other programs did not change substantially.

Despite a decline in the number of Engineering/Applied Sciences diplomas awarded, it still remains one of the most popular fields for graduates from community colleges. It is unlikely that the high demand for these skills will decline in the near future.

It would appear that the majority of community college graduates, apart from those with diplomas in Engineering/Applied Sciences, are headed for jobs in the service sector, where nearly all of the new job creation in the Canadian economy is taking place (Economic Council of Canada, 1990).

TABLE 2

Graduates of Community College Career Programs by Field of Study, Canada, 1976, 1981, 1984 and 1987.

Source: Statistics Canada, Community colleges and related institutions: postsecondary enrolment and graduates.

FIELD OF STUDY	THOUSANDS OF QUALIFICATIONS AWARDED			
	1976	1981	1984	1987
Health Sciences	11.5	9.5	10.5	11.0
Business/Commerce	8.0	13.0	16.0	16.0
Engineering/Applied Science	7.0	11.0	16.0	14.0
Social Sciences/Services	5.5	7.0	8.0	8.5
Arts	2.5	4.0	4.5	4.5
Natural Sc./Primary Industries	2.0	3.0	3.5	3.0
Humanities	0.5	0.5	1.0	1.0
Other Fields	0.0	0.0	0.5	0.5
Not Reported	0.5	0.0	0.0	0.5
Total Number of Graduates	37.5	48.0	60.0	59.0

FIGURE 4

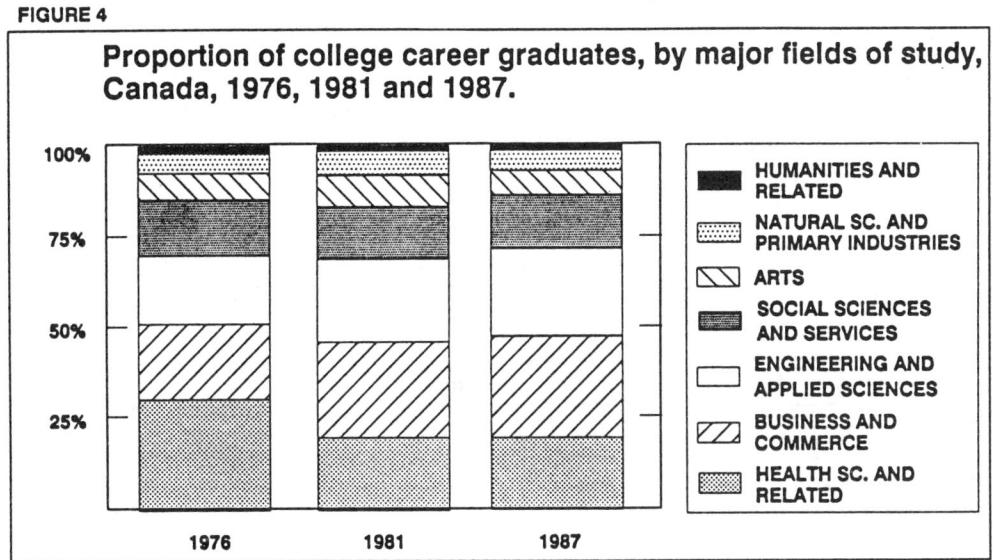

V. GRADUATES FROM UNIVERSITIES

A. Methodological note

Although individual Canadian universities vary considerably in size and in the range of disciplines in which a degree may be obtained, the major fields of study are: Education, Fine/Applied Arts, Humanities, Social Sciences which includes Business and Commerce,[2] Agriculture/Biological Sciences, Engineering/Applied Sciences, Health Professions and Mathematics/Physical Sciences which includes Computer Science.[3]

Bachelor's level graduates include those earning undergraduate degrees, diplomas or certificates and first professional degrees in law, medicine, dentistry, theology and education. The Master's of Divinity degree is considered a first professional degree. Only earned doctorates are included in the statistics on Doctorates. Undergraduate diploma and certificate programs have entry conditions similar to those for Bachelor degree candidates, but are typically of shorter duration. Graduate diplomas or certificates may be awarded after a Master's degree or after a first degree in the same field of study (Statistics Canada, 1989).

B. Statistical overview

In 1988, over 143,000 university qualifications were granted in Canada, an increase of

---

2. Business/Commerce account for a sizeable proportion of graduates in the Social Sciences, and are treated as a separate field of study in many of the tables in this report.
3. See Annex 2 for a complete list of subject areas in each program field.

39% since 1975 and 2% over the previous year. This increase reflects a decade which saw the proportion of 18-24 year old Canadians enroled at university increase from 12% to 17% as well as higher levels of participation by other groups. Almost 86% of the degrees, diplomas and certificates were granted at the Bachelor's level, with 11% at the Master's level and 2% at the Doctoral level.

TABLE 3

University Degrees, Diplomas and Certificates Granted by Field of Study, Canada, 1975, 1980, 1985 and 1988.

Source: Statistics Canada, Universities: Enrolment and Degrees.

FIELD OF STUDY	THOUSANDS OF QUALIFICATIONS AWARDED			
	1975	1980	1985	1988
Education	25.5	25.1	22.0	23.5
Social Sciences*	28.6	36.7	48.7	55.6
Humanities	12.9	12.5	14.5	17.3
Engineering/Applied Sc.	6.5	9.3	11.3	10.4
Health Professions	6.6	7.9	9.3	10.9
Agriculture/Biological Sc.	6.1	6.7	6.6	8.8
Mathematics/Physical Sc.	5.4	5.7	9.7	9.7
Fine/Applied Arts	2.5	3.2	3.8	4.4
Other Fields/Not Reported	8.9	7.6	7.0	3.1
Total Number Granted	103.0	114.7	132.9	143.7

* includes Business and Commerce

In 1988, 28% more Bachelor's and first professional degrees were granted than in 1975. The number of degrees granted increased in each field of study except Education. In Business/Commerce the number more than doubled.

The proportion of Bachelor's graduates awarded a degree in Education decreased from 27% to 18% over the period, perhaps anticipating a softening of demand for elementary and secondary teachers following of the declining birth cohorts of the 1970s and 1980s. Twenty-six percent of university graduates earned a degree in the Social Sciences in 1988, a five percent increase over 1975. Business/Commerce also increased their proportional share of graduates by 5% over the period.

It is at the Master's level that the growth in the number of degrees awarded has been most marked, an increase of 50% over 1975. This may be due to actual or perceived increases in the educational prerequisites of desirable jobs or diminishing employment prospects for graduates with undergraduate degrees. While a greater number of degrees were awarded in each field of study, proportionately fewer degrees were awarded in the Humanities in 1988 (13% of the total) than in 1975 (19% of the total).

TABLE 4

Bachelor's and First Professional Degrees Granted by Field of Study, Canada, 1975, 1980, 1985 and 1988.

Source: Statistics Canada, Universities: Enrolment and Degrees.

THOUSANDS OF QUALIFICATIONS AWARDED

FIELD OF STUDY	1975	1980	1985	1988
Education	18.4	16.9	15.4	16.2
Social Sciences	17.2	18.3	22.2	26.6
Humanities	9.9	9.5	9.9	12.3
Business/Commerce	5.7	8.7	11.9	12.6
Agriculture/Biological Sc.	5.4	5.5	5.1	7.2
Health Professions	5.1	5.8	6.2	7.4
Engineering/Applied Sc.	4.8	7.3	8.4	8.0
Mathematics/Physical Sc.	4.2	4.4	7.6	7.2
Fine/Applied Arts	2.2	2.7	3.0	3.6
Other Fields/Not Reported	7.7	7.4	7.8	2.7
Total Number Granted	80.6	86.5	97.5	103.8

TABLE 5

Master's Degrees Granted by Field of Study, Canada, 1975, 1980, 1985 and 1988.

Source: Statistics Canada, Universities: Enrolment and Degrees.

NUMBERS OF QUALIFICATIONS AWARDED

FIELD OF STUDY	1975	1980	1985	1988
Social Sciences	2,480	2,710	3,150	3,350
Education	2,160	2,830	2,920	2,980
Humanities	2,080	1,790	2,010	2,200
Business/Commerce	1,630	1,900	2,730	2,940
Engineering/Applied Sc.	960	1,110	1,610	1,570
Mathematics/Physical Sc.	830	770	1,030	1,160
Agriculture/Biological Sc.	490	620	700	790
Health Professions	300	500	730	910
Fine/Applied Arts	130	200	290	350
Other Fields/Not Reported	NA	10	20	20
Total Number Granted	11,060	12,440	15,190	16,270

The number of Doctorates granted increased 30% between 1975 and 1988. There were substantial increases in the number of graduates from all fields of study except Humanities and Fine/Applied Arts.

TABLE 6

Doctoral Degrees Granted by Field of Study, Canada, 1975, 1980, 1985 and 1988.

Source: Statistics Canada, Universities: Enrolment and Degrees.

| | NUMBERS OF QUALIFICATIONS AWARDED ||||
FIELD OF STUDY	1975	1980	1985	1988
Mathematics/Physical Sc.	420	330	390	470
Social Sciences	350	390	390	460
Humanities	280	240	250	290
Agriculture/Biological Sc.	240	210	250	320
Engineering/Applied Sc.	230	190	280	350
Education	170	210	210	230
Health Professions	120	140	180	230
Business/Commerce	20	20	30	40
Fine/Applied Arts	10	10	10	10
Other Fields/Not Reported	NA	10	20	10
Total Number Granted	1,840	1,750	2,010	2,410

FIGURE 5

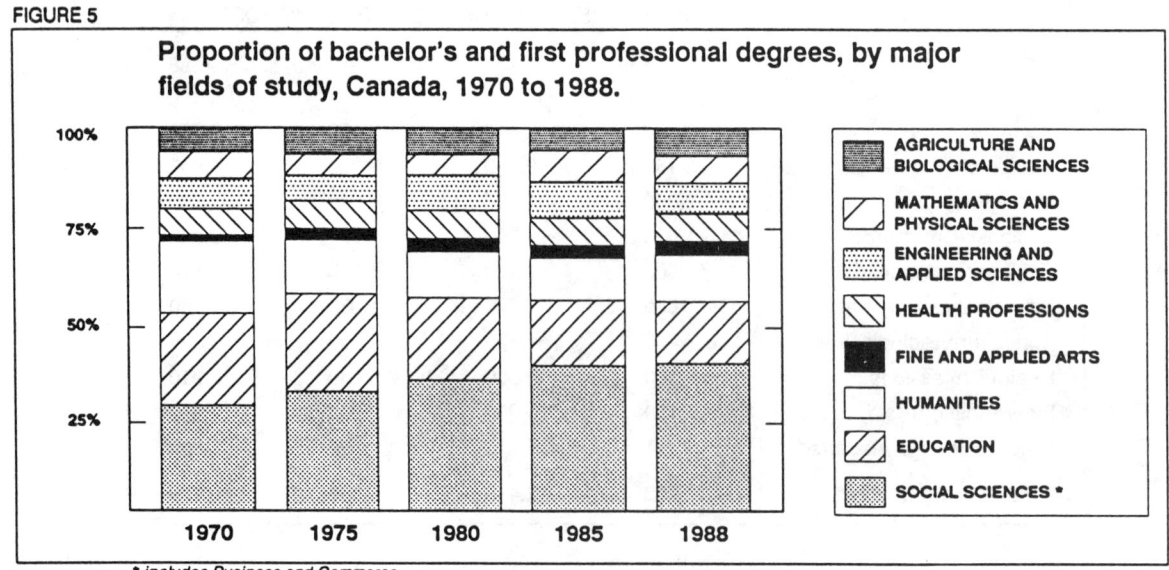

Proportion of bachelor's and first professional degrees, by major fields of study, Canada, 1970 to 1988.

* includes Business and Commerce

FIGURE 6

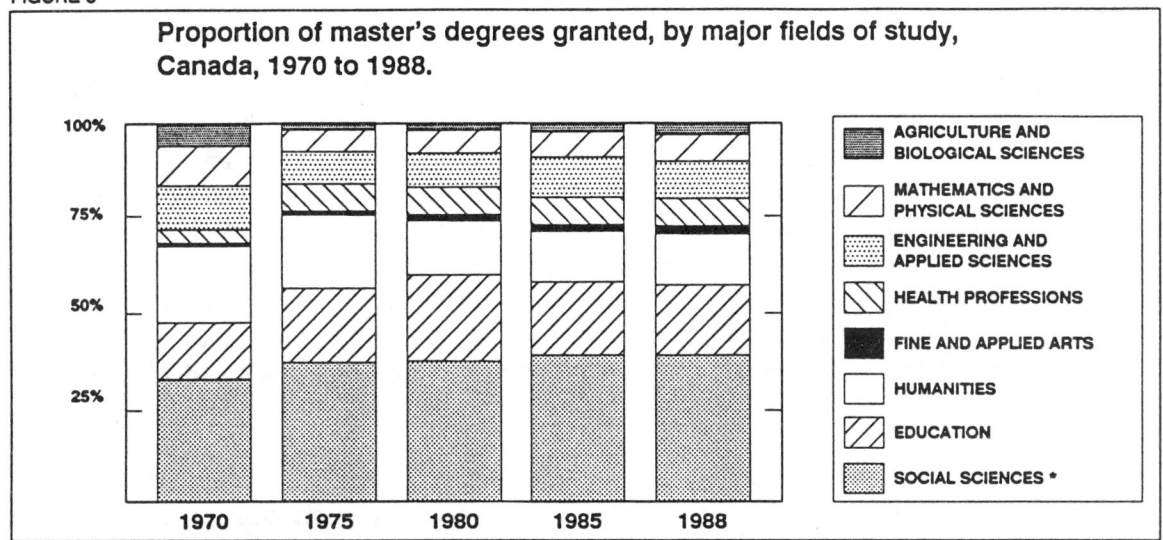

* includes Business and Commerce

FIGURE 7

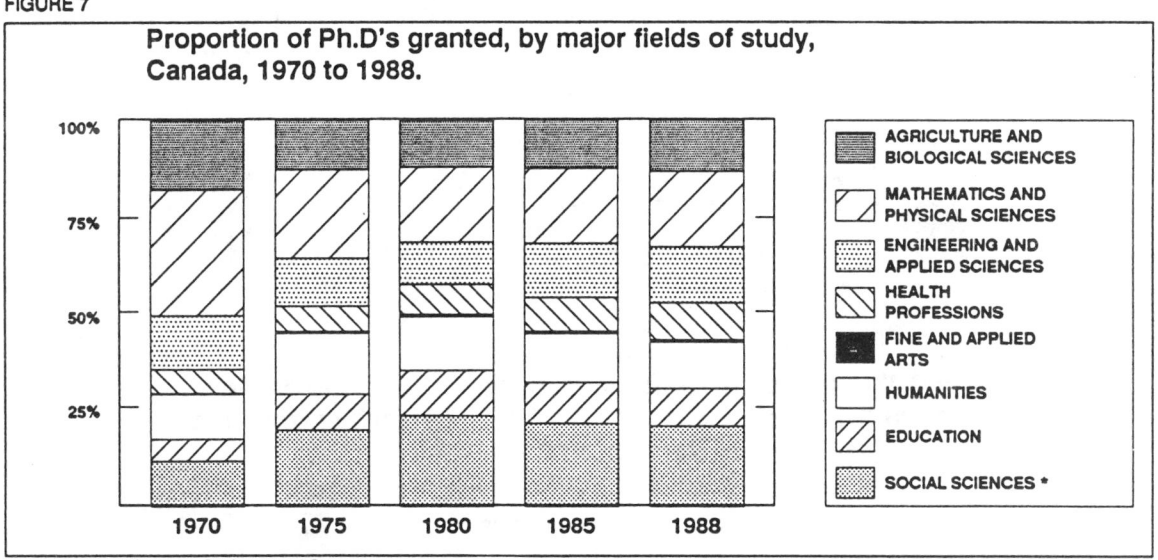

* includes Business and Commerce

VI. WOMEN AND POST-SECONDARY EDUCATION

Historically, men and women have averaged similar numbers of years of formal education in Canada. This spurious equality occurred because women have been more likely than men to complete secondary school, while men have been more likely than women to continue on to the post-secondary level. Recently however, women's access to higher education has increased dramatically. Indeed, the increasing number of women entering higher education is one reason that student numbers at the university level have not declined although the peak of the baby boom has now passed through the post-secondary system. The influence of sex on participation patterns within higher education has not been erased yet however, with gender tracking still evident in some disciplines.

Women pursing a post-secondary education at the community college, undergraduate or graduate level are more likely than men to come from middle or upper class backgrounds with parents who possess high levels of education. Why this is the case has not been ascertained. More educated parents may be the first to recognize the importance of their daughters attaining higher qualifications. Perhaps having themselves experienced post-secondary education they are more likely to encourage daughters. They are also more likely to be able to offer financial help to all their children, rather than just sons who traditionally received it (Guppy and Pendakur, 1989).

FIGURE 8

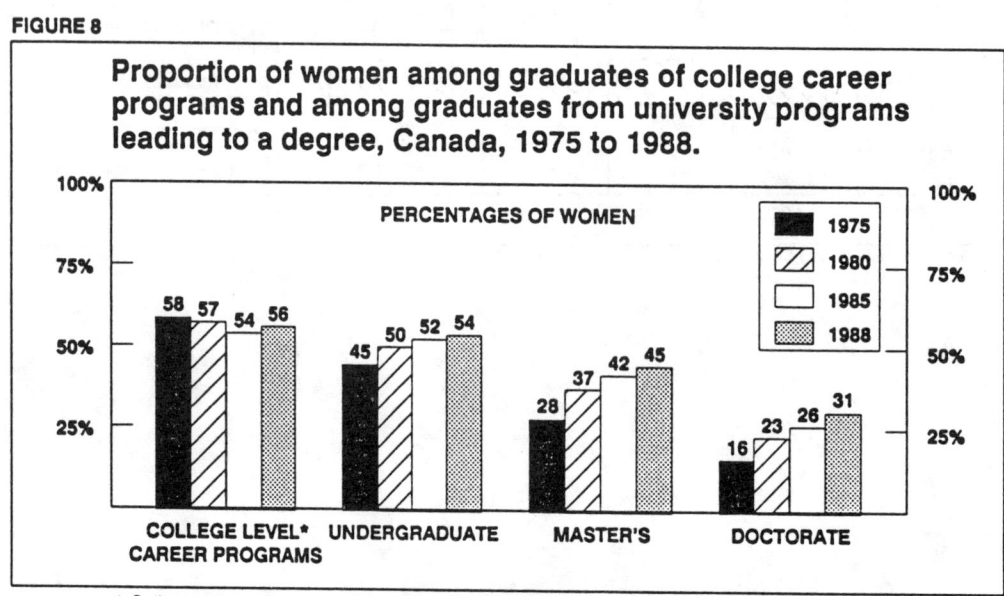

Proportion of women among graduates of college career programs and among graduates from university programs leading to a degree, Canada, 1975 to 1988.

* College data are those for 1976, 1980, 1985 and 1987.

A. Women in community colleges

Prior to the 1970s, the training of teachers and nurses took place in non-university institutions which were attended predominantly by women. Even the absorption of teacher education into the universities and the establishing of university level nursing programs not altered the position of women in the non-university post-secondary sector. Women have accounted for approximately six of ten graduates of post-secondary career programs since the mid-seventies (Gilbert and Guppy, 1988).

Over the period between 1976 and 1987 the number of women graduating from career programs increased by 44% to an absolute total of 33,100 in 1987. Over the same period, the number of men graduating increased 66% to 25,200.

Despite equal overall participation rates, the distribution of men and women by fields of study varies greatly. In 1987, half of men graduated in Engineering/Applied Sciences and one-fifth from Business/Commerce. Women graduates were more evenly distributed, primarily in Business/Commerce (32%), where they dominate the secretarial field, Health Sciences (29%), where they dominate nursing, and Social Sciences/Services (19%), where they dominate in education and counselling.

TABLE 7

Graduates of Community College Career Programs by Field of Study and Sex, Canada, 1987.

Source: Statistics Canada, Community colleges and related institutions: postsecondary enrolment and graduates.

FIELD OF STUDY	NUMBER OF GRADUATES	
	MALE	FEMALE
Engineering/Applied Science	11,700	2,300
Business/Commerce	5,300	10,600
Social Sciences/Services	2,400	6,200
Natural Sciences/Primary Industries	2,100	1,000
Arts	1,900	2,600
Health Sciences	1,500	9,600
Humanities	200	600
Other Fields of Study	100	200
Total Number of Graduates	25,200	33,100

B. Women in universities

In 1988, women received 53% of all degrees, diplomas and certificates awarded by Canadian universities. Except in Business/Commerce, Engineering/Applied Science and Mathematics/Physical Science, more women earned degrees than men. While there is movement towards a more even sex distribution in these historically male dominated areas, men are not increasing their relative participation in teaching and nursing where women have traditionally been in the majority (Gilbert and Guppy, 1988).

TABLE 8

University Graduates by Field of Study and Sex, Canada, 1988.

Source: Statistics Canada, Universities: Enrolment and Degrees.

FIELD OF STUDY	NUMBER OF GRADUATES	
	MALE	FEMALE
Social Sciences	13,500	16,900
Engineering/Applied Science	9,100	1,300
Business/Commerce	9,000	6,500
Education	7,400	16,100
Mathematics/Physical Sciences	7,100	2,600
Humanities	6,500	10,800
Agriculture/Biological Sciences	4,100	4,700
Health Professions	3,400	7,500
Fine/Applied Arts	1,500	2,900
Other Fields of Study	1,200	1,900
Total Number of Graduates	62,800	71,200

Women have increased their share of undergraduate qualifications from earning 45% of the total in 1975 to earning 55% in 1988. By 1988, women had increased their representation in all fields of study, although the gains in Mathematics/Physical Science were quite small. Nor did they greatly improve their representation in the Fine/Applied Arts where they already earned a substantial majority of the degrees awarded in 1978.

Although the participation rate of women is steadily increasing at the graduate level, in 1988 women received only 45% of Master's degrees and 31% of Doctorates. At the Master's level, women earned over half of qualifications in the Health Professions, Fine/Applied Arts, Humanities and Education. The proportion of Master's degrees in Engineering/Applied Sciences granted to women has doubled over the last decade, but they still represent only a tiny fraction of the total. Only in the field of Education are women granted half of Doctorates.

FIGURE 9

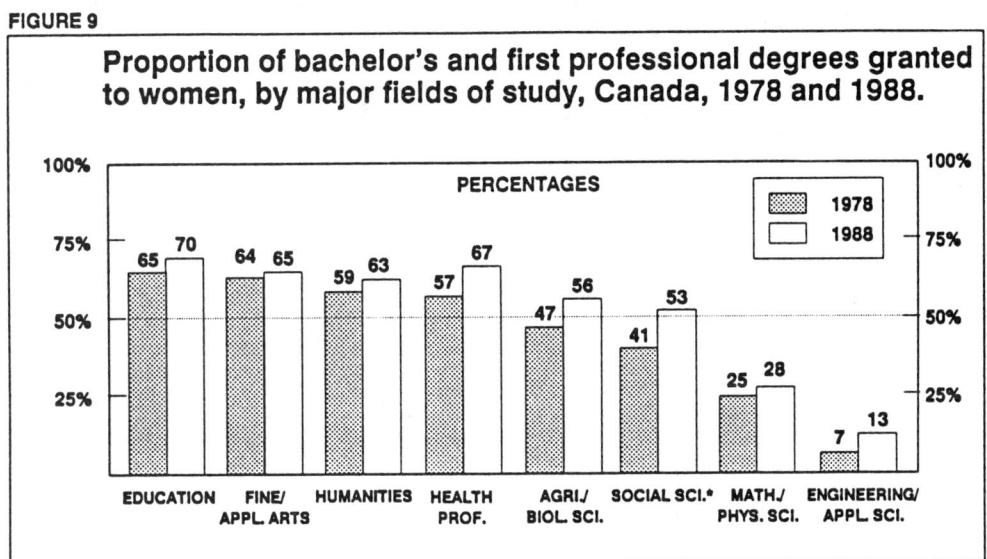

* includes Business and Commerce

FIGURE 10

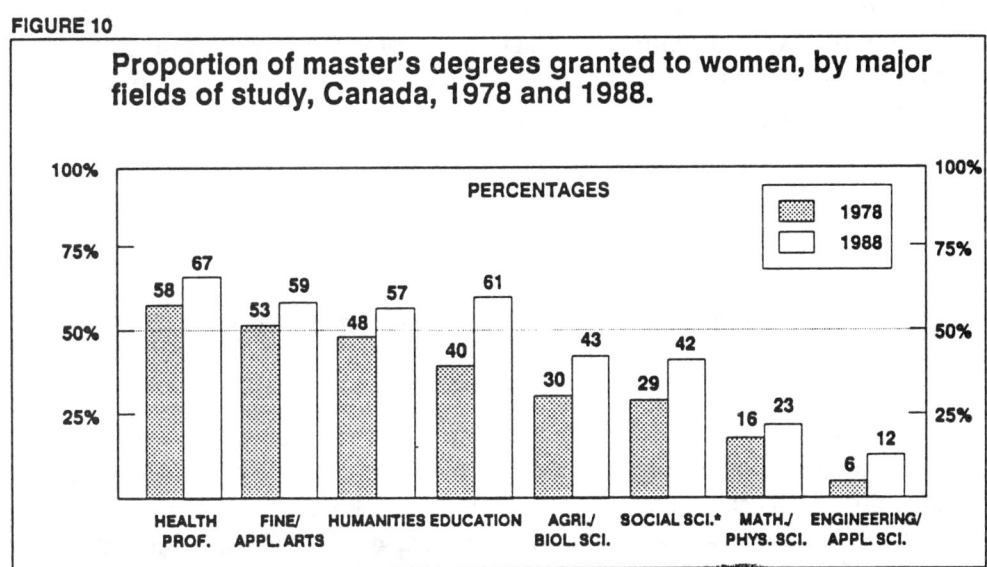

* includes Business and Commerce

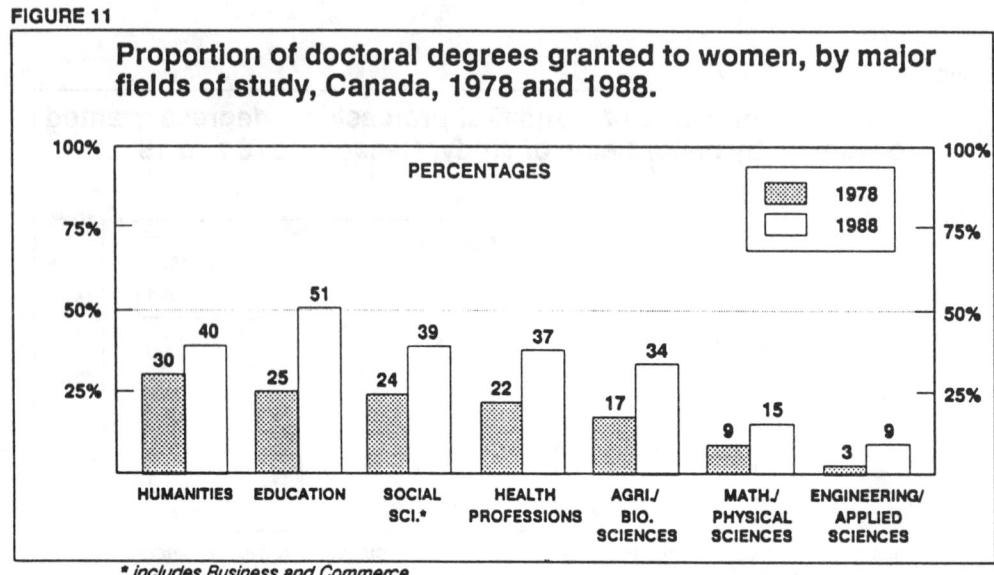

FIGURE 11

Proportion of doctoral degrees granted to women, by major fields of study, Canada, 1978 and 1988.

* includes Business and Commerce

The women's movement and the growth of professional and managerial jobs in the 1960s and 1970s have resulted in increased numbers of women graduating from colleges and universities. While women represent a small minority in engineering, mathematics and related disciplines and at the graduate level in universities they are pursuing studies in these areas in increasing numbers. Men, however, are not moving into secretarial work, nursing or teaching which have been dominated by women in the past.

VII. GRADUATES WHO CONTINUE THEIR EDUCATION

A small proportion of students, having received a first degree or diploma, remain to study for higher or parallel qualifications. However, not all of those studying for advanced qualifications can be assumed to be recent graduates from more junior levels of education. Increasingly Canadians over the age of 30 and part-time students are attracted to continuing education programs at the college level and graduate programs at the universities, swelling the pool of potentially highly qualified workers.

The 1984 National Survey of the Graduates of 1982 identified those 1982 graduates who were again enroled in an educational institution in January 1983. One-fifth of college graduates, more than one-third of Bachelor's degree holders, one-quarter of Master degree holders and one-tenth of Doctorates were continuing their education.

This trend was even more pronounced in a recent cohort. Approximately half of the 1986 community college graduates and university Bachelor's graduates were studying again two years after graduation, as were one-third of Master's and almost one-sixth of

Doctorate degree holders.

TABLE 9

Post–Secondary Graduates Enroled in an Educational Institution One Year After Graduation for 1982 Graduates and Two Years After Graduation for 1986 Graduates, Canada, 1983 and 1988.

Source: Secretary of State and Statistics Canada, The Class of 82, 1986.
Special tablulations produced by Statistics Canada for the Secretary of State, 1990.

GRADUATE'S INITIAL QUALIFICATION	1982 GRADUATES AGAIN ENROLED IN 1983	1986 GRADUATES AGAIN ENROLED IN 1988
College Diploma*	20%	49%
University Bachelor's Degree	37%	51%
University Master's Degree	27%	35%
University Doctorate Degree	11%	15%

*includes university transfer programs

Factors influencing the decision to remain in school longer include the labour market outlook for graduates, the educational prerequisites of available or desirable jobs, students' perceptions of the added value of increased education and of the cost-benefits of remaining in school as opposed to entering a difficult job market (Clark et al., 1979). In addition, in some provinces the post-secondary education system provides students with several channels facilitating the movement from the community college to the university level.

In Ontario this is generally not the case, since the community college system was designed as a distinct entity leading to the workforce rather than further education. Community college graduates receive little or no credit for their qualifications if admitted to university, although there is growing pressure to establish some standard of equivalencies (Premier's Council of Ontario, 1990).

While the proportion of university degrees awarded at the graduate level remained fairly constant, the number of Master's and Doctorate degrees awarded almost doubled between 1970 and 1988. Many of the new jobs created over this decade are expected to require at least five years of post-secondary education (Mulder, 1990), so graduate enrolments may be expected to continue to rise. In Ontario, companies are already competing to hire Ph.D. and Master level graduates to fill their need for highly educated personnel (Premier's Council of Ontario, 1990).

VIII. NON-GRADUATE OUTFLOWS FROM POST-SECONDARY EDUCATION

It is estimated that two-thirds of all jobs created in Canada in the 1990s will require more than a secondary school diploma (Mulder, 1990). Yet there is little doubt that the emphasis on maximizing accessibility to post-secondary education has negatively affected retention rates, making attrition a serious problem in the post-secondary education system.

Unfortunately, no national system exists for ascertaining how many post-secondary students leave the system before completing their course of studies or why they do so. Although some research work on attrition has been done at the provincial level, most provincial research has focused on secondary rather than post-secondary retention rates. The available research indicate that dropout rates at the community colleges vary by field of study, gender, and academic qualifications before beginning a course of study.

QUEBEC
Thirty-eight percent of the 1980 career program entrance cohort at Quebec CÉGEPs had not received their diploma by the end of the decade. Approximately 17% left the program which they had initially chosen, but graduated from another one. Forty-five percent of the incoming cohort graduated from their initial choice of program and field of study.

Men were somewhat more likely than women to leave school without completing their education. They were also less likely than women to graduate from their initial chosen field of study. Non-completion rates also varied by field of study from a high of almost half (49%) among those studying Applied Arts to a low of one-quarter (25%) among those studying Health Sciences (Lévesque and Pageau, 1990).

ONTARIO
In Ontario, only half of students who enrol in the community colleges graduate either from the program they initially chose or from some other program. Attrition rates are highest in the first year of a program, raising concerns about the academic preparation of incoming students. Certainly, dropout rates are one and a half higher for students who enter with a grade 12 diploma than with grade 13, the prerequisite for university admission. Men are more likely to leave than are women, and students in Applied Arts, Business and Technology fields of study are more likely than students in Health Sciences to leave without completing their program. The former occupational areas are easier to enter without a diploma than are occupations in the health field, where a diploma is frequently a strict requirement (Premier's Council of Ontario, 1990).

Wastage is not attributable to any one specific factor; motivation, personal factors and involvement in part-time work all contribute to departure from the system (Chénard, 1989). Even students with the academic qualifications and other social or personal characteristics usually associated with success and perseverance in school drop out in large numbers (Gomme and Guppy, 1984). Financial difficulties do not seem to be a major causal factor in determining persistence or departure from the educational system in Canada (Gilbert and Auger, 1988).

IX. LABOUR MARKET CONDITIONS FACING GRADUATES

In recent years, the industrial and occupational structure of Canada's labour force has changed. As in many other industrialized countries, there has been a shift from the natural resources and manufacturing sectors to the service sector. The public administration component of the service sector expanded rapidly during the 1950s, followed by social service areas such as education, health and welfare in the 1960s, and the "commercial" fields of the service sector in the 1970s (Myles, 1988).

Seven out of ten employed Canadians now work in the service sector and only three out of ten in the goods producing sector. Recent growth in the goods producing sector has only been sufficient to replace losses during the 1981 to 1983 recession (Gower, 1990).

During the 1980s, four occupational groups have accounted for 97% of employment growth in Canada: managerial/administrative, medicine/health, sales, and service occupations. An ever increasing share of these jobs have high skill or educational requirements.

Declines in the number of jobs in many blue-collar occupations which began in the 1970s continued in the 1980s. Even in the goods producing sector, the shift to a service dominated labour market is evident, with technological and organizational change increasing the importance of credentialed occupations.

The size of the labour force has expanded to fill the new jobs, in the postwar period though immigration, but in recent years through increasing labour force participation by women, who filled 72% of new jobs created over the decade. In Canada 57% of women of working age are in the labour force. Among OECD countries, only the United States and the Scandinavian countries have higher female participation rates (Economic Council of Canada, 1989).

Despite these positive indicators, problems face recent graduates and other Canadians looking for work. The growth of consumer service industries, especially food and accommodation services, over the past decades are producing a bifurcated labour market at least in the commercial sector (Myles, 1988). Many of the new jobs are lowing paying, part-time or seasonal in nature. A polarization is occurring, with a decreasing percentage of workers in the middle of the income distribution, earning the median income plus or minus 25%. Increasing numbers of highly skilled, well-remunerated Canadians earn in excess of that. At the same time the proportion of the labour force in relatively dead-end jobs and poorly paid increases.

Unemployment during the late 1980s has not dropped to the pre-recession levels of the early 1970s. Long term unemployment of six months or more is declining very slowly, affecting almost a quarter of those out of work. Seasonal employment and unemployment are particularly persistent problems for 16-24 year olds, those with little formal education and residents in the Atlantic provinces of Canada (Economic Council of Canada, 1989).

Part-time employment is increasingly a characteristic of the Canadian labour force. One in five workers is employed part-time. Women are more likely than men to work less than 30 hours a week; one-quarter of employed women in Canada worked part-time in 1988 compared to 8% of men (Parliament, 1990). The choice of part-time work may be voluntary or involuntary. It is known, however, that the proportion of Canadians who work only part-time because they are not able to find full-time employment, the "disguised" unemployed, is growing (Gower, 1990).

X. TRANSITION INTO THE LABOUR FORCE

Labour force participation rates increase with educational attainment, while a lack of formal qualifications appears to impede labour force participation. College and university graduates are more than twice as likely to be in the labour force as Canadians with less than nine years of schooling. Over the last decade, those with little formal education have become less likely to be in the labour force while participation rates for those with at least some post-secondary education increased.

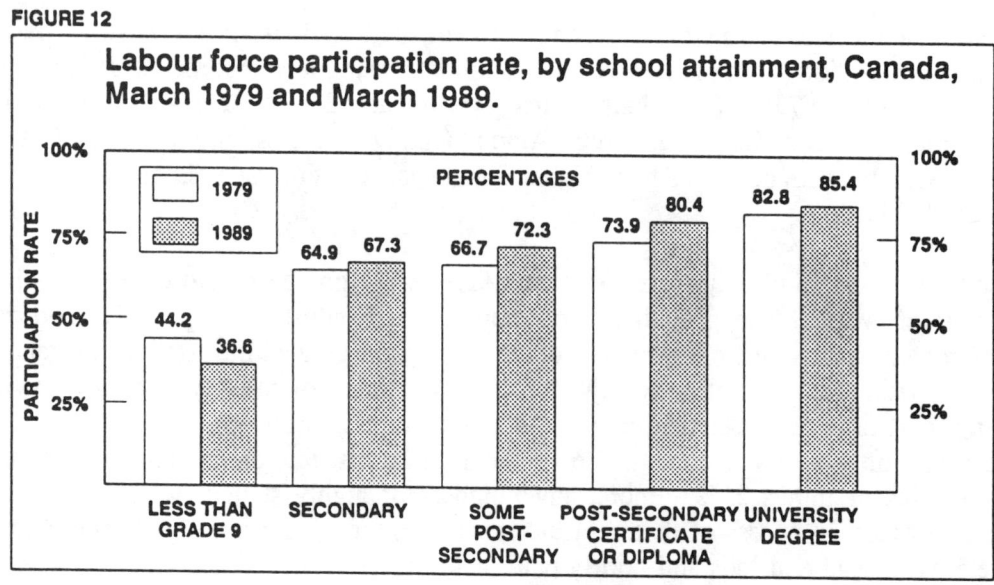

FIGURE 12

Labour force participation rate, by school attainment, Canada, March 1979 and March 1989.

Not only are Canadians with post-secondary education more likely to be in the labour force than other groups, they are also more likely to be successful in finding employment. Unemployment rates decline as the level of education increases. University degree holders experience levels of unemployment significantly below the national average. These highly qualified Canadians have an unemployment rate only one-quarter that of workers without secondary schooling. Even among the young, who have persistently higher levels of unemployment than other workers, post-secondary qualifications reduce the likelihood of being unemployed.

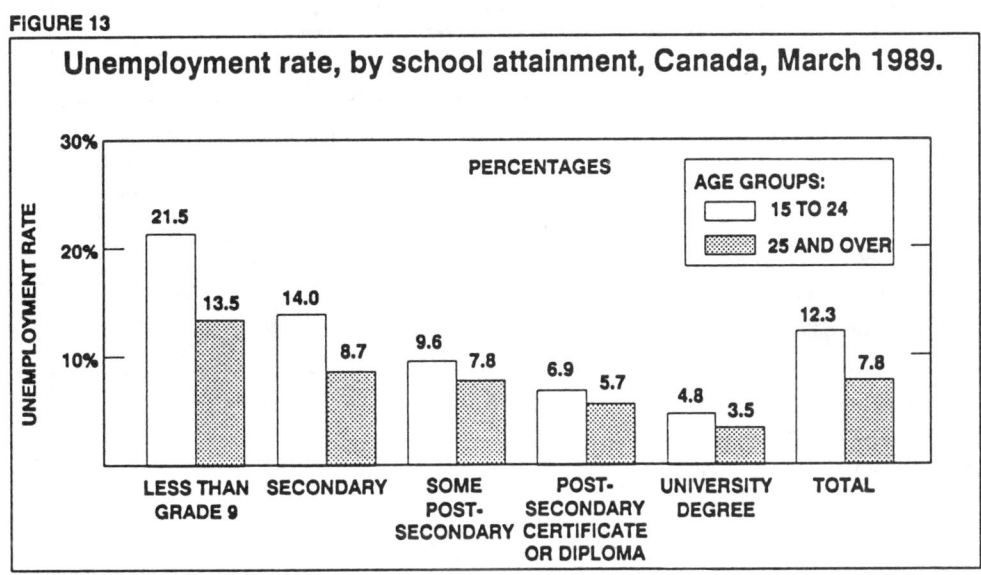

FIGURE 13
Unemployment rate, by school attainment, Canada, March 1989.

A. Labour force status of community college graduates

Community colleges in Canada were established to provide an education responsive to the requirements of the labour market. Career-oriented programs facilitate graduates' links to particular occupations, potentially minimizing unemployment.

The *1988 National Survey of the Graduates of 1986* showed that the majority of graduates of community colleges and related institutions, regardless of field of study, had not experienced significant periods of unemployment in the two years since obtaining their diploma. Available comparative data for the year 1987 show that periods of unemployment were endemic among 16-24 year old Canadians as a whole.

About one-quarter of graduates trained in technologies related to Electrical, Chemical/Industrial Engineering, Natural Sciences/Primary Industries had experienced short-term unemployment, that is of six months or shorter duration. Chemical/Industrial Engineering, Natural Sciences/Primary Industries graduates were also more likely to suffer long-term or chronic periods of unemployment than other college graduates. The low frequency of short and long term unemployment among Health Sciences graduates indicates that they make a relatively rapid transition from school into the labour force.

TABLE 10

Periods of Unemployment Experienced by 1986 Community College Graduates in the Two Years After Graduation by Field of Study, Canada, 1988.

Sources: Special tabulations produced by Statistics Canada for the Department of the Secretary of State, 1990.
Statistics Canada, Canada's Youth: A Profile of Their 1987 Labour Market Experience.

	1986 GRADUATES IN 1988		
FIELD OF STUDY	Unemployed 1 Month or Less	Unemployed 2 to 6 Months	Unemployed 7 Months or More
Health Sciences	86%	10%	4%
Social Sciences/Services	78%	15%	7%
Merchandising/Sales	76%	19%	5%
Management/Administration	75%	19%	5%
Mechanical/Construction Sc.	71%	20%	8%
Electrical Engineering Sc.	67%	25%	8%
Chemical/Industrial Engineering Sc.	65%	23%	12%
Natural Sc./Primary Industries	63%	24%	13%
Total Reported Graduates	79%	15%	6%
All Canadians aged 16-24	*42%*	*47%*	*11%*

Data for Arts and Humanities graduates not available.
Data for all Canadians are for the year 1987.

Two years after graduating, nine out of ten 1986 community college graduates were employed. Health Science graduates had the lowest unemployment or non-participation rates of all college level graduates. In May 1988, the unemployment rate for 15-24 year old Canadians holding post-secondary certificates or diplomas was 7.3%. At that point in time at least, a community college diploma provided them with an advantage in obtaining employment when compared to young Canadians with a secondary school diploma (unemployment rate of 13.4%) or only some post-secondary education (unemployment rate of 12.8%).

Among those community college graduates who were employed, full-time employment was the norm. The size of the minority working part-time varied greatly by discipline, being highest among graduates in Social Sciences and Health Sciences. Graduates who worked less than 30 hours per week most frequently cited an inability to obtain full-time employment as their reason for doing so.

TABLE 11

Labour Force Status of Community College Graduates Two Years After Graduation, Canada, 1988.

Source: Special tabulations produced by Statistics Canada for the Department of the Secretary of State, 1990.

	1986 GRADUATES IN 1988		
FIELD OF STUDY	Employed	Unemployed	Not in Labour Force
Health Sciences	94%	4%	2%
Electrical Engineering Sc.	91%	7%	2%
Management/Administration	89%	7%	4%
Social Sciences/Services	89%	8%	3%
Merchandising/Sales	89%	8%	3%
Mechanical/Construction Sc.	89%	8%	3%
Chemical/Industrial Engineering Sc.	86%	10%	3%
Natural Sc./Primary Industries	84%	13%	3%
Total Reported Graduates	90%	7%	3%

Data for Arts and Humanities graduates not available.

TABLE 12

Labour Force Status of Employed Community College Graduates Two Years After Graduation, Canada, 1988.

Source: Special tabulations produced by Statistics Canada for the Department of the Secretary of State, 1990.

	1986 GRADUATES IN 1988	
FIELD OF STUDY	Employed Full-time	Employed Part-time
Mechanical/Construction Science	98%	2%
Natural Sciences/Primary Industries	97%	3%
Electrical Engineering Science	97%	3%
Chemical/Industrial Engineering Science	96%	4%
Management/Administration	94%	6%
Merchandising/Sales	93%	7%
Social Sciences/Services	89%	11%
Health Sciences	85%	15%
Total Reported Graduates	92%	8%

Data for Arts and Humanities graduates not available.

TABLE 13

Periods of Unemployment Experienced by 1986 University Graduates in the Two Years After Graduation by Field of Study, Canada, 1988.

Source: Special tabulations produced by Statistics Canada for the Department of the Secretary of State, 1990.

	1986 GRADUATES IN 1988		
FIELD OF STUDY	Unemployed 1 Month or Less	Unemployed 2 to 6 Months	Unemployed 7 Months or More
Health Professions	92%	6%	2%
Education	81%	13%	6%
Mathematics/Physical Science	79%	15%	6%
Agriculture/Biological Science	78%	14%	8%
Business/Commerce	77%	15%	7%
Social Sciences	76%	17%	7%
Engineering/Applied Science	75%	19%	6%
Humanities	75%	18%	7%
Fine/Applied Arts	70%	20%	10%
Total Reported Graduates	78%	15%	7%

QUEBEC

In Quebec, 92% of the 1985 bachelor's level graduates who were in the labour force were employed in 1987. Fine/Applied Arts graduates were the least likely to be employed (78%), while Health Sciences and Mathematics graduates were the most likely to have jobs (98%). Nine out ten of those employed were working full-time, with a variation by discipline from 68% among Fine/Applied Arts to 99% in Engineering and Computer Sciences. The majority of those working part-time were doing so because they had been unable to obtain full-time employment (Audet, 1989).

ONTARIO

In 1986 the Ontario government conducted an employment survey of 1985 Ontario university graduates. Unemployment rates for those who were in the labour force one year after graduation varied by field of study from 2% for those who had studied in the Health Professions to 13% for graduates in the Fine/Applied Arts with a provincial average of 7%. Graduates in Education and Fine/Applied Arts had relatively high levels of part-time employment compared to graduates from other fields of study (Denton et al., 1987).

Data from the 1987 Follow-up Survey of the Graduates of 1982 allow a comparison of recent university graduates and a those with as much as five years of labour market experience. Since the surveys took place only one year apart, variations are substantially free of variations in external market conditions.

SASKATCHEWAN
Results of a survey by the province of Saskatchewan of 1988 graduates from certificate or diploma programs offered by provincial Institutes of Applied Arts and Technology show trends similar to the National Graduate Survey. Six months after graduation, 84% of the respondents were employed, and 12% were unemployed. More than three-quarters of those who were unemployed at the time of the survey had worked at some time since completing their training. At the time of the survey graduates in Health programs had the highest employment rates (94%), while those in Industrial programs experienced the lowest employment rates (76%). Part-time work was most common among graduates from Health and Service fields (Saskatchewan Education, 1989).

BRITISH COLUMBIA
British Columbia's 1989 survey of graduates from 1988 occupational career programs found 81% to be employed one year after graduation. Graduates from Health programs were the most likely to be employed and those from Natural Resource/Transportation and Fine/Performing Arts were the least likely to have found work (Province of British Columbia, 1989).

B. Labour force status of university graduates

As is the case with community college graduates, most university graduates are making the transition to the labour force without significant periods of unemployment. Results of the <u>1988 National Survey of the Graduates of 1986</u> indicate that Health Professions graduates are substantially more likely to find immediate employment than graduates from other fields of study. Only a fraction, just 2%, had experienced chronic unemployment. Fine/Applied Arts graduates were the least likely of all university graduates to have found immediate, steady employment and the most likely to have suffered short or long term unemployment.

Two years after graduation, graduates in the Health Professions had the lowest level of unemployment among university graduates. In the Health field, formal qualifications are usually a prerequisite for employment, eliminating "outside" competition for jobs from graduates from other fields at the college or university levels. High employment levels observed among Education graduates may also be due to the controlled access to the teaching profession. Provincial data on the labour force status of graduates appear to confirm the national survey results.

Unemployment declines as time in the labour market increases. The groups with relatively high initial levels of unemployment show the greatest gains in employment levels. Graduates in Agriculture/Biological Sciences still have the lowest levels of employment relative to those with degrees in other fields of study.

TABLE 14

Labour Force Status of University Graduates, Five Years After Graduation for 1982 Graduates and Two Years After Graduation for 1986 Graduates, Canada, 1987 and 1988.

Source: Special tabulations produced by Statistics Canada for the Department of the Secretary of State, 1990.

LABOUR FORCE STATUS

	1986 GRADUATES IN 1988			1982 GRADUATES IN 1987		
FIELD OF STUDY	Employed	Un-employed	Not in Labour Force	Employed	Un-employed	Not in Labour Force
Education	92%	5%	3%	93%	3%	4%
Health Professions	91%	4%	5%	94%	2%	4%
Business/Commerce	90%	7%	3%	93%	3%	4%
Mathematics/Physical Sc.	85%	7%	8%	87%	4%	9%
Engineering/Applied Sc.	85%	7%	8%	91%	3%	6%
Humanities	78%	13%	9%	85%	4%	11%
Social Sciences	78%	12%	10%	86%	5%	9%
Fine/Applied Arts	75%	16%	9%	85%	4%	11%
Agriculture/Biological Sc.	64%	12%	19%	77%	5%	18%
Total Reported Graduates	84%	9%	7%	89%	5%	7%

While unemployment levels decline as time spent in the labour market increases, the proportion of graduates employed part-time employment does not. Graduates in Engineering/Applied Science and Business/Commerce are almost universally employed full-time, while Fine/Applied Arts graduates remain the most likely to work part-time even five years after graduation.

High levels of joblessness are not inextricably linked with part-time employment. Education graduates, who have high levels of employment also are more likely than average to be employed part-time both two and five years after graduation. While many occupations formally offer only full-time employment, in the teaching profession supply teaching is a formally recognized alternative albeit a less secure one to full-time, permanent employment.

TABLE 15

Labour Force Status of Employed University Graduates, Five Years After Graduation for 1982 Graduates and Two Years After Graduation for 1986 Graduates, Canada, 1987 and 1988.

Source: Special tabulations produced by Statistics Canada for the Department of the Secretary of State, 1990.

LABOUR FORCE STATUS

	1986 GRADUATES IN 1988		1982 GRADUATES IN 1987	
FIELD OF STUDY	Employed Full-time	Employed Part-time	Employed Full-time	Employed Part-time
Engineering/Applied Sc.	98%	2%	98%	2%
Business/Commerce	97%	3%	97%	3%
Mathematics/Physical Sc.	94%	6%	96%	4%
Health Professions	90%	10%	86%	14%
Social Sciences	89%	11%	89%	11%
Agriculture/Biological Sc.	88%	12%	90%	10%
Humanities	86%	14%	87%	13%
Education	86%	14%	86%	14%
Fine/Applied Arts	77%	23%	80%	20%
Total Reported Graduates	90%	10%	90%	10%

Two main reasons were given by graduates for working part-time. The inability to obtain full-time employment and unavailability for full-time employment because the respondent was going to school were cited with equal frequency in the 1988 survey. In 1987 however, the inability to find a full-time job was mentioned most frequently.

XI. ARTICULATION BETWEEN EDUCATION AND JOBS

The occupational structure in Canada has been transformed by the decline in the economic importance of primary industries, and by growth in the service sector. Entry-level jobs now require greater cognitive and verbal skills, and advanced levels of education are increasingly being used as an allocative criterion for jobs. This has led to a generally closer articulation of the educational system and the labour market (Hunter, 1988).

Although concern has been expressed over the lack of fit between the demand for workers in some fields and the supply of graduates (The Canadian Labour Market Productivity Centre, 1990), a fair degree of articulation does seem to exist between the output from education and the input to employment. The National Graduate Surveys indicate that most graduates find work which is at least partly related to their field of study within a short period after graduating.

College diploma holders and university graduate degree holders tend to enter occupations for which their studies provide specific preparation. This link is particularly strong in the case of disciplines leading to regulated professions, where quotas on entry into study programs are imposed, through either limiting the number of spaces for new entrants or through imposing very high admission requirements.

Many who hold university undergraduate degrees come from study programs that are not designed to qualify them for any specific profession. Although they possess knowledge and skills that can be applied to a wide array of occupations both at the entry level and all through their working life, they may take longer initially to achieve a successful placement in the labour market than do those whose field of study is closely connected to an occupation or profession.

A. Match between education and jobs for community college graduates

The 1988 National Survey of the Graduates of 1986 asked employed community college graduates to assess the degree of relatedness of their current job to their field of study. More than eight out of ten said that their jobs were directly or partly related to their field of study.

Graduates in the Health Sciences field were far more likely than other recent graduates to have found employment which they considered to be directly related to their field of study. Only a fraction of those employed were working in jobs unrelated to the Health Sciences (3%), while as many as one fifth of graduates from other fields were in jobs with no connection to their academic qualifications.

TABLE 16

Relationship of Job to Education for Employed Community College Graduates Two Years After Graduation, Canada, 1988.

Source: Special tabulations produced by Statistics Canada for the Department of the Secretary of State, 1990.

FIELD OF STUDY	1986 GRADUATES IN 1988		
	Directly Related	Partly Related	Not Related
Health Sciences	88%	9%	3%
Social Sciences/Services	66%	19%	15%
Merchandising/Sales	61%	26%	13%
Mechanical/Construction Sc.	59%	27%	14%
Chemical/Industrial Engineering Sc.	58%	27%	15%
Natural Sc./Primary Industries	57%	24%	19%
Electrical Engineering Sc.	51%	31%	18%
Management/Administration	50%	30%	20%
Total Reported Graduates	63%	23%	14%

Data for Arts and Humanities graduates not available.

Results from two provincial studies, although not identical in format, lend support to the findings of the national survey.

SASKATCHEWAN
Nine out of ten employed Saskatchewan community college graduates from the class of 1988 were in training-related occupations six months after graduation. Graduates from Health Sciences (99%) almost universally had found training related employment while Industrial (81%) program graduates were the least likely to be using all or some of the skills acquired in their program (Saskatchewan Education, 1989).

BRITISH COLUMBIA
A 1989 survey of 1988 career program graduates from British Columbia colleges found that 91% of those who looked for work had found a job related to their training and 79% of these graduates were still in such a job. Health Science programs graduates (90%) were the most likely to be employed in jobs which utilized their training and Fine/Performing Arts graduates (59%) were the least likely to have been in related employment current to the time of the survey (Province of British Columbia, 1989).

Results of the National Graduate Survey indicate that by 1988, almost no 1986 community college graduates had moved into jobs with entry requirements exceeding their qualifications. Slightly over half of employed community college graduates were employed in positions requiring a diploma. Two years after graduation four out of ten were working in jobs for which a college diploma was not a requirement. This may be indicative of a degree of imbalance in the supply of and demand for graduates, forcing some to accept jobs which do not require their formal qualifications.

Graduates in the Health Sciences were the most likely to find jobs commensurate with their level of training. Half or more of graduates from technologies related to Electrical Engineering, Chemical/Industrial Engineering, Mechanical/Construction Science or Social Sciences had achieved a match between the entry requirements of their current job and their academic qualifications. More than half of graduates from Natural Sciences/Primary Industries, Management/Administration and Merchandising/Sales were underemployed by this measure.

TABLE 17

Academic Qualifications Compared to Hiring Requirements of Current Job for Community College Graduates Two Years After Graduation, Canada, 1988.

Source: Special tabulations produced by Statistics Canada for the Department of the Secretary of State, 1990.

	1986 GRADUATES IN 1988		
FIELD OF STUDY	Less than Required	Same as Required	More than Required
Health Sciences	1%	84%	15%
Electrical Engineering Science	1%	63%	36%
Chemical/Industrial Engineering Science	1%	58%	41%
Social Sciences/Services	1%	55%	44%
Mechanical/Construction Science	1%	51%	48%
Natural Sciences/Primary Industries	2%	48%	50%
Management/Administration	2%	42%	56%
Merchandising/Sales	1%	41%	58%
Total Reported Graduates	1%	58%	41%

Data for Arts and Humanities graduates not available.

B. Match between education and jobs for university graduates

Two years after graduation, nearly half (47%) of 1986 university graduates were working in jobs directly related to their field of study, making them considerably less likely than community college graduates to be in study-related careers at that point in time. Over one-third (36%) of university graduates rated their current employment as partly associated with their education. The proportions of university and college graduates in jobs not connected to their field of study were similar.

Although 83% of all 1986 graduates were working in jobs that were to some extent related to their academic qualifications, there were substantial differences between the fields of study. More than nine out ten graduates in the Health Professions, Education and Engineering/Applied Science evaluated their jobs as partly or directly study-related. Less than three-quarters of graduates from programs in Agriculture/Biological Science, Humanities, Social Sciences and Fine/Applied Arts graduates were employed in an associated job.

TABLE 18

Relationship of Job to Education for Employed University Graduates Two Years After Graduation, Canada, 1988.

Source: Special tabulations produced by Statistics Canada for the Department of the Secretary of State, 1990.

FIELD OF STUDY	1986 GRADUATES IN 1988		
	Directly Related	Partly Related	Not Related
Health Professions	74%	20%	6%
Education	65%	26%	9%
Engineering/Applied Science	56%	36%	8%
Mathematics/Physical Science	53%	34%	13%
Business/Commerce	46%	39%	15%
Agriculture/Biological Science	36%	39%	25%
Humanities	33%	41%	26%
Fine/Applied Arts	31%	38%	31%
Social Sciences	30%	44%	26%
Total Reported Graduates	47%	36%	17%

QUEBEC

In Quebec in 1986, 70% of employed 1985 Bachelor's level graduates had obtained work related to their principal field of studies. This figure represents a slight improvement over the situation of 1982 graduates surveyed in 1984 (66%) but is similar to that of 1980 graduates surveyed in 1982 (69%). Given that the Canadian economy was only beginning to emerge from a recession in 1984, it would appear that the proportion of seven out of ten university graduates finding study-related employment is fairly representative of the province of Quebec.

Graduates most frequently mentioned the lack of jobs available (38%) as an explanation for not working in an area related to their field of study. The limited opportunities offered by the study-related jobs available (16%) was another commonly cited explanation. Only 5% of employed graduates said that they had never intended to look for work in their field of specialization (Audet, 1989).

ONTARIO

The *1985 Ontario Graduate Employment Survey* included several measures of the relationship between university graduates' qualifications and the jobs they held in 1986. While almost nine out of ten graduates reported that the general skills required by their jobs were somewhat or very related to their field of study, results vary considerably according to the qualifications of respondents. Holders of first professional degrees (91%) and one year Bachelor of Education degrees (which are earned following completion of an initial Bachelor's degree) (74%) were the most likely to state that their jobs were "very" related to their major field of study. Only one-third (34%) of graduates from three year Bachelor programs and slightly over half (56%) of graduates from four *year Honours programs reported working in jobs "very related" to their educational program.*

The specific content of their jobs were judged to be somewhat related or very related to their programs of studies by three-quarters of 1985 graduates. Again, graduates from first professional (91%) and Teaching (74%) degree programs were the most likely to report a very close match between the program content of their job and their qualifications. Only one-fifth (21%) of graduates with three year Bachelor's and half (47%) with four years Honours degrees had jobs the specifics of which were closely related to their field of study (Denton et al., 1987).

Two years after graduating, the majority of 1986 Canadian university graduates were employed in jobs for which a university level degree was an entrance requirement. However, a sizeable minority, more than four out of ten, possessed greater academic qualifications than required for their job. Underemployment varied widely by field of study. Over half of graduates with degrees in the Humanities or the Fine/Applied Arts were underemployed, but only one-quarter of those with degrees in Engineering/Applied Sciences.

Underemployment appears to decrease as graduates gain experience in the labour market. Five years after graduating, six out ten employed graduates held jobs commensurate with their academic qualifications while approximately one-third were overqualified. The greatest progress in terms of finding appropriate employment occurred in those fields where graduates' initial levels of underemployment had been relatively high.

The positions of groups of graduates with regard to one another do not vary greatly between the national surveys of graduates two and five years after graduation; Engineering/Applied Science graduates being the most likely in both cases to have jobs appropriate to their level of education while Fine/Applied Arts graduates are the least likely. The career-oriented disciplines appear to have some advantage in finding jobs which match their academic qualifications, but underemployment seems to be commonplace.

TABLE 19

Academic Qualifications Compared to Hiring Requirements of Current Job for University Graduates, Five Years After Graduation for 1982 Graduates and Two Years After Graduation for 1986 Graduates, Canada, 1987 and 1988.

Source: Special tabulations produced by Statistics Canada for the Department of the Secretary of State, 1990.

QUALIFICATIONS COMPARED TO REQUIREMENTS

FIELD OF STUDY	1986 GRADUATES IN 1988 Less than Required	Same as Required	More than Required	1982 GRADUATES IN 1987 Less than Required	Same as Required	More than Required
Engineering/Applied Sc.	3%	73%	24%	3%	73%	24%
Mathematics/Physical Sc.	4%	65%	31%	4%	71%	25%
Education	4%	57%	39%	3%	63%	34%
Health Professions	6%	54%	40%	9%	68%	23%
Agriculture/Biological Sc.	5%	52%	43%	5%	63%	32%
Business/Commerce	5%	49%	46%	4%	58%	38%
Social Sciences	5%	47%	48%	5%	55%	40%
Humanities	5%	43%	52%	5%	52%	43%
Fine/Applied Arts	2%	37%	61%	4%	52%	44%
Total Reported Graduates	4%	53%	43%	4%	61%	35%

ONTARIO

A survey of 1985 graduates of Ontario universities found that one year after graduation the proportion of graduates whose level of educational attainment matched their employer's requirements varied among those with undergraduate qualifications from 69% for holders of diplomas to 74% for holders of Bachelor's degrees with Honours. One year Bachelor of Education (87%) and first professional degree holders (97%) were the most likely to have obtained a job appropriate to their level of education, even more likely than graduates with a Master's degree (62%) or a Doctorate (81%). Qualification for a controlled access profession gives Ontario graduates at least a distinct advantage in finding employment both related and appropriate to their education (Denton et al., 1987).

XII. EMPLOYMENT DESTINATIONS OF POST-SECONDARY GRADUATES

Although there exists a strong correlation between educational attainment and occupational placement, many other factors influence graduates' employment destinations. The period of job search and experimentation is influenced by structural factors such as demographic change and fluctuations in the economy and by individual factors such as employment contacts, interpersonal skills and aspirations.

As a result, the labour market destinations of graduates from the same field of study may be dispersed across a range of occupations and industries[4]. The extent of this range varies with the degree of closeness between the academic field of study and certain occupations or industries in the labour market, or with the number of alternative opportunities to graduates from any given field.

The occupational and industrial structure of the Canadian labour market is changing. The public administration sector, which formerly hired many Canadian graduates from higher education, has been stagnating or at best growing slowly in recent years. It accounted for approximately 7% of non-agricultural employment in Canada in 1988, unchanged from 1970. The service sector is expanding rapidly, and increasing its share of the non-agricultural workforce from 28% to 34% over the same period (Statistics Canada, 1989). The high technology sector outperforms the rest of the economy and is the source of many new jobs. Already many firms in this sector are faced with shortages of skilled trades, technical, scientific and professional staff (Canadian Labour Market and Productivity Centre, 1990)

A. Occupational destinations of community college graduates

Given the explicit career orientation of college programs, it is not surprising to note patterns of occupational concentration among community college graduates. Two years after completing their study program, graduates from any given field of study tended to be concentrated in one or two occupational categories.

Graduates from Health Sciences programs were overwhelmingly employed in Health related occupations (88%). Those with diplomas in the various Engineering technologies: Chemical/Industrial, Electrical, and Mechanical/Construction, were primarily employed in Science/Engineering and Fabricating/Assembling/Repairing occupations. More than half of graduates from the Natural Sciences/Primary Industries fields of study worked in jobs classified as Science/Engineering (33%) or Primary Industry/Agriculture (24%). A sizeable proportion of Social Science/Service graduates were employed in Service occupations (42%). Merchandising/Sales graduates frequently worked in Managerial/Administrative (33%) or Sales (20%) positions. Managerial/Administrative work also occupied a large portion of graduates from Management/Administration studies (44%).

---

4. Annex 3 provides a detailed list of occupational categories referred to in this report. Annex 4 provides a detailed list of industrial categories.

TABLE 20

Most Common Current Occupations for Community College Graduates Two Years After Graduation, Canada, 1988.

Source: Special tabulations produced by Statistics Canada for the Department of the Secretary of State, 1990.

MOST COMMON OCCUPATIONS IN 1988

FIELD OF STUDY	Science/ Engineering	Managerial/ Administrative	Fabricating/ Assembling/ Repairing	Service	Clerical
Health Sciences	0%	6%	0%	0%	0%
Chem./Indust. Eng. Sc.	40%	7%	14%	2%	2%
Electrical Engineering Sc.	33%	7%	23%	4%	7%
Mechanical/Construction Sc.	26%	11%	24%	3%	3%
Natural Sc./Primary Indust.	33%	6%	3%	6%	3%
Social Sciences/Services	3%	6%	3%	42%	3%
Merchandising/Sales	0%	33%	0%	13%	13%
Management/Administration	4%	44%	2%	6%	18%
Total Reported Graduates	22%	15%	12%	8%	7%

FIELD OF STUDY	Sales	Construction	Health	Processing/ Machining	Primary Industry/ Agriculture
Health Sciences	0%	0%	88%	0%	0%
Chem./Indust. Eng. Sc.	5%	7%	0%	9%	0%
Electrical Engineering Sc.	6%	11%	1%	1%	1%
Mechanical/Construction Sc.	5%	8%	3%	5%	3%
Natural Sc./Primary Indust.	3%	6%	3%	9%	24%
Social Sciences/Services	3%	3%	3%	3%	0%
Merchandising/Sales	20%	7%	0%	7%	0%
Management/Administration	14%	4%	2%	2%	2%
Total Reported Graduates	7%	7%	7%	4%	4%

Data for Arts and Humanities graduates not available.

B. Occupational destinations of university graduates

Teaching[5], and Managerial/Administrative positions are occupational destinations for a number of Canadian university graduates, but the distribution of graduates by field of

---

5. The proportion of university graduates employed in Teaching was five times as great as for community college graduates. A university degree is required to teach above the preschool level in Canada.

study is not easily characterised. Two years after graduation some fields appear closely linked with one occupational grouping while graduates from other fields are employed in a fairly broad range of occupations.

TABLE 21

Most Common Current Occupations for University Graduates Two Years After Graduation, Canada, 1988.

Source: Special tabulations produced by Statistics Canada for the Department of the Secretary of State, 1990.

MOST COMMON OCCUPATIONS IN 1988

FIELD OF STUDY	Teaching	Managerial/ Administrative	Science/ Engineering	Health	Social Sciences
Agriculture/Biological Sc.	19%	14%	15%	17%	4%
Business/Commerce	3%	48%	6%	1%	15%
Education	73%	8%	0%	2%	5%
Engineering/Applied Sc.	4%	13%	68%	0%	1%
Fine/Applied Arts	29%	13%	3%	1%	7%
Health Professions	5%	5%	1%	83%	2%
Humanities	27%	14%	3%	2%	10%
Mathematics/Physical Sc.	15%	21%	48%	1%	1%
Social Sciences	16%	19%	5%	7%	21%
Total Reported Graduates	23%	21%	13%	10%	10%

FIELD OF STUDY	Clerical	Sales	Service	Construction	Primary Industry/ Agriculture
Agriculture/Biological Sc.	7%	7%	5%	1%	6%
Business/Commerce	12%	10%	2%	0%	0%
Education	3%	2%	2%	0%	0%
Engineering/Applied Sc.	1%	2%	1%	2%	1%
Fine/Applied Arts	12%	5%	5%	1%	0%
Health Professions	2%	1%	0%	0%	0%
Humanities	16%	4%	5%	1%	1%
Mathematics/Physical Sc.	5%	4%	1%	1%	1%
Social Sciences	15%	6%	5%	1%	0%
Total Reported Graduates	8%	5%	3%	1%	1%

The articulation of field of study and career was evident between Health Professions and Health occupations (83%), between Education and Teaching (73%) and between Engineering/Applied Sciences and Science/Engineering occupations (68%). Almost half of employed Business/Commerce graduates held Managerial Administrative positions (48%), and a similar proportion of Mathematics/Physical Sciences graduates were working in Science/Engineering occupations (48%).

Teaching was a major source of employment not only for Education graduates but also for those in the fields of Agriculture/Biological Sciences (19%), Fine/Applied Arts (29%), and Humanities (27%) and the Social Sciences (16%). Graduates from the latter two fields of study were distributed across a range of occupational groups besides Teaching; sizeable proportions were employed in Managerial/Administrative, Clerical and in the Social Science categories.

ONTARIO
The most commonly held occupations for 1985 Ontario university graduates in 1986 were: computer programmer (6%), accountant, auditor or financial officer (6%), elementary school teacher (6%), and secondary school teacher (3%). Comparisons of the occupations of 1982 and 1985 Ontario university graduates show increases in the percentages of graduates employed as computer programmers, managers and administrators, social workers and welfare or community service workers. The percentage employed as accountants, auditors or financial officers decreased (Denton et al., 1987).

C. Industrial sector destinations of community college graduates

Community college graduates survey in 1984 and 1988 were employed across the industrial spectrum, in both the public and the private sector. In Canada, health and social services, and education are largely within the public sector, as are government services. Manufacturing and Business are predominently composed of private sector enterprises.

The degree of dispersion of community college graduates is indicative of the wide diversity of training available at the post-secondary non-university level. However, graduates from each field of study show a tendency to employment in certain sectors over others.

The 1986 Health Sciences graduates are almost universally employed in the Health/Social Services Sector (92%). This degree of concentration is unequalled among other groups of graduates.

Graduates with diplomas in the technologies of Chemical/Industrial Engineering Science, Electrical Engineering Science and Mechanical/Construction Science are concentrated in Manufacturing (21%-37%) and to a lesser extent in Business Services (16%-19%). Management/Administration graduates are also clustered in the Manufacturing (15%) and Business Services (15%) sectors.

Social Sciences/Services graduates are predominantly employed in the public sector: Health/Social Services (36%), Government Services (22%) and Educational Services

(9%). Graduates from Technological programs related to Natural Science/Primary Industries or Management/Administration are employed in industries in both the public and private sectors.

TABLE 22

Most Common Industrial Sectors of Employment for Community College Graduates Two Years After Graduation, Canada, 1988.

Source: Special tabulations produced by Statistics Canada for the Department of the Secretary of State, 1990.

FIELD OF STUDY	MOST COMMON INDUSTRIES OF EMPLOYMENT IN 1988				
	Health/ Social Services	Manufac- turing	Business Services	Govern- ment Services	Educational Services
Health Sciences	92%	1%	1%	1%	2%
Chemical/Indust. Eng. Sc.	2%	37%	19%	10%	2%
Electrical Engineering Sc.	4%	21%	16%	9%	4%
Mechanical/Construction Sc.	5%	28%	16%	7%	-
Natural Sc./Primary Indust.	2%	13%	13%	13%	2%
Social Sciences/Services	26%	4%	4%	22%	9%
Merchandising/Sales	12%	11%	16%	8%	5%
Management/Administration	4%	15%	15%	8%	3%
Total Reported Graduates	27%	13%	11%	9%	4%

Data for Arts and Humanities graduates not available.

D. Industrial sector destinations of university graduates

The relationship between field of study and industry of employment is not as marked as the relationship between field of study and occupation. Almost one-quarter are employed in Educational Services (23%), but Business Services (14%), Health/Social Services (13%), Government Services (10%) and Manufacturing (9%) also hire substantial proportions of university graduates. This distribution is almost identical to that of 1982 university graduates surveyed in 1984.

Nevertheless, graduates of some programs are more likely to be employed in one sector than any other. More than three-quarters of employed graduates in the Health Professions work in the Health/Social Services sector (77%). Similarly, the majority of Education graduates are employed in the Educational Services sector (71%).

Graduates from other fields of study are more dispersed, although there is a tendency for graduates from the disciplines of Fine/Applied Arts, Humanities, and Social Sciences to be employed in the Educational Services industry (20%-32%) or Government Services (8%-16%). Graduates from the disciplines of Business/Commerce, Engineering/Applied Sciences, and Mathematics/Physical Sciences are more likely to have found employment in Business Service (23%-30%) or Manufacturing sectors (10%-34%).

TABLE 23

Most Common Industrial Sectors of Employment for University Graduates Two Years After Graduation, Canada, 1988.

Source: Special tabulations produced by Statistics Canada for the Department of the Secretary of State, 1990.

MOST COMMON INDUSTRIES OF EMPLOYMENT IN 1988

FIELD OF STUDY	Educational Services	Business Services	Health/ Social Services	Government Services	Manufacturing
Agriculture/Biological Sc.	25%	5%	15%	13%	10%
Business/Commerce	3%	30%	4%	11%	10%
Education	71%	2%	7%	5%	1%
Engineering/Applied Sc.	5%	23%	1%	8%	34%
Fine/Applied Arts	29%	8%	4%	8%	4%
Health Professions	8%	1%	77%	5%	2%
Humanities	32%	8%	6%	10%	8%
Mathematics/Physical Sc.	15%	29%	2%	11%	13%
Social Sciences	20%	8%	20%	16%	5%
Total Reported Graduates	23%	14%	13%	10%	9%

ONTARIO
The distribution of 1985 Ontario university graduates in 1986 shows a similar pattern. Seven out of ten graduates were located in the same five industrial divisions: Manufacturing, Business Services, Government Services and Health/Social Services. The proportion of graduates employed in the public sector had decreased slightly when compared to 1982 graduates; from 46% from 49% (Denton et al., 1987).

XIII. ISSUES FACING POST-SECONDARY EDUCATION IN CANADA

Post-secondary education in Canada has changed greatly over the past four decades. Government funded expansion has increased the number of universities as well as the array of programs at all levels of study. In addition, the establishment of community colleges has provided non-university, career oriented training to students who otherwise might not receive a post-secondary education. The number of Canadians enroled in post-secondary programs has increased from 90,600 in 1951 to 856,500 in 1990. Almost one-quarter of the population 15 years and over now possesses post-secondary qualifications.

Despite this investment in human capital, increasing numbers of recent graduates are unemployed or underemployed. The economic rate of return is decreasing for an undergraduate degree. The qualification is coming to be regarded as a basic requirement for employment, and in those fields of study without strong occupational linkages, only as a basis for further study. At the same time, shortages exist or are predicted in other areas of the Canadian labour market force for workers with community college or university qualifications.

There have been calls, especially from the business sector, for human resources planning to channel students into areas of study where there are shortages of qualified workers and away from areas where the supply of graduates in the marketplace exceeds the demand. However, given an ethic of individual choice in a country large in size with strong regional identities and a relatively decentralized federal government, manpower planning on the large scale is not likely to be effective.

Clearly, structural unemployment results in a loss not only to the individual, but society as well. However, obtaining a job, although an important factor, is not the sole aim of post-secondary education. Even graduates from fields of study with above average levels of underemployment or unemployment are likely to say that they would repeat their course of study if given the opportunity.

Should Canada be providing young people with an inclusive education in the Arts and Sciences to develop well-rounded generalists adaptable to the changing requirements of the labour market? Is a more specialized training, producing graduates ready to enter specific occupations and professions of greater utility? The choice need not be for one or the other, rather it is matter of optimally balancing priorities.

It would seem, however, that students are aware of and react to changes in the labour market. Nursing programs at the community college level, for example, are declining in popularity as students increasingly opt for the university level Bachelor's degree in Nursing as a basis for a career or to upgrade their qualifications. This freedom of choice is facilitated by the fact that post-secondary education in Canada, although not free, is relatively inexpensive. Tuition fees represent only about one-tenth of total university income, approximately 90% of funding coming from federal and provincial governments and other sources.

There are increasing cooperative efforts on the part of educational institutions, government and business to aid graduates in making the transition from school to the labour market. Canada will require a well educated labour force to remain competitive in a global economy, while continued economic restraint translates into reductions in the funds available for education. The quantity and quality of information available on the labour market conditions facing graduates should be improved so that all parties involved can the best possible choices.

ANNEX 1: DISCIPLINES INCLUDED IN MAJOR FIELDS OF STUDY AT THE POST-SECONDARY, NON-UNIVERSITY LEVEL

ARTS

Applied Arts
Commercial Arts
Communications
Design
Graphic Arts
Performing Arts
Related disciplines

BUSINESS/COMMERCE

Administration and Management
Food Services
Marketing
Merchandising/Sales
Secretarial Science
Related disciplines

ENGINEERING/APPLIED SCIENCES

Chemical Technology
Construction Technology
Drafting
Electrical Engineering
Industrial Technology
Mathematics and Computer Science
Mechanical Technology
Surveying
Transportation Technology
Related disciplines

HEALTH SCIENCES

Equipment Technology
Health Technology
Medical Technology
Nursing
Related disciplines

HUMANITIES

History
Journalism
Languages
Library Science
Religion
Related disciplines

NATURAL SCIENCES/PRIMARY INDUSTRIES

Agriculture
Conservation Technology
Horticulture
Resource Processing Technology
Veterinary Technology
Related disciplines

SOCIAL SCIENCES/SERVICES

Corrections Technology
Counselling Services
Criminology
Early Childhood Education
Recreation Leadership
Social Services
Tourism
Related disciplines

ANNEX 2: DISCIPLINES INCLUDED IN MAJOR FIELDS OF STUDY AT THE UNIVERSITY LEVEL

AGRICULTURE/BIOLOGICAL SCIENCES

Agricultural Science
Biochemistry
Biology
Botany
Household Science
Veterinary Medicine
Zoology
Related disciplines

FINE/APPLIED ARTS

Art Studies
Design
Graphic Arts
Music
Performing Arts
Related disciplines

EDUCATION

Education Administration
Educational Evaluation
Educational Psychology
Kinanthropology
Teacher Training
Related disciplines

HEALTH PROFESSIONS

Clinical Sciences
Dentistry
Medicine
Nursing
Optometry
Pharmacy
Surgery
Related disciplines

ENGINEERING/APPLIED SCIENCES

Architecture
Aeronautical Engineering
Chemical Engineering
Civil Engineering
Electrical Engineering
Forestry
Mechanical Engineering
Related disciplines

HUMANITIES

Classics
History
Journalism
Languages
Library Science
Literature
Philosophy
Religion and Theology
Related disciplines

MATHEMATICS/PHYSICAL SCIENCES

Chemistry
Computer Science
Geology
Mathematics
Metallurgy
Meteorlogy
Physics
Related disciplines

SOCIAL SCIENCES

Administration
Anthropology
Archaeology
Business and Commerce
Canadian Studies
Economics
Geography
Law and Jurisprudence
Political Science
Social Work
Sociology
Related disciplines

ANNEX 3: OCCUPATIONAL CATEGORIES INCLUDED IN MAJOR CLASSIFICATIONS

CLERICAL

Clerks
Office Machine Operators
Secretaries
Stenographers
Tellers
Typists
Occupations related to the above

HEALTH

Dentists
Dietitians
Nurses
Optometrists
Pharmacists
Physicians and Surgeons
Veterinarians
Occupations related to the above

CONSTRUCTION

Surfacing Occupations
Utility Construction Trades
Building Trades Occupations
Occupations related to the above

MANAGERIAL/ADMINISTRATIVE

Administrators
Financial Officers
Government Officials
Inspectors
Managers
Personnel Officers
Occupations related to the above

FABRICATING/ASSEMBLY/REPAIRS

Assembling Occupations
Mechanics
Product Fabricating Occupations
Repairing Occupations
Occupations related to the above

PRIMARY INDUSTRIES/AGRICULTURE

Farming Occupations
Fishing, Trapping
Forestry, Logging Occupations
Horticulture
Oil and Gas Field Occupations
Mining
Occupations related to the above

PROCESSING/MACHINING

Chemical Processing Occupations
Food Processing Occupations
Machining Occupations
Mining and Milling Occupations
Wood Processing Occupations
Occupations related to the above

SALES

Commercial Travellers
Sales Clerks
Street Vendors
Insurance Agents
Real Estate Salespersons
Buyers
Occupations related to the above

SCIENCES/ENGINEERING

Architects
Computer Programmers
Draughtsmen
Engineers
Life Scientists
Mathematicians
Physical Scientists
Systems Analysts
Occupations related to the above

SERVICES

Food Preparation Occupations
Launders and Dry Cleaners
Maintenance Workers
Occupations in Lodging
Personal Service Occupations
Protective Services Occupations
Occupations related to the above

SOCIAL SCIENCES

Archivists
Economists
Librarians
Occupations in Law
Other Social Scientists
Psychologists
Social Workers
Sociologists
Occupations related to the above

TEACHING

University Teachers
Elementary School Teachers
Secondary School Teachers
Other Teaching Occupations
Occupations related to the above

ANNEX 4: INDUSTRIAL CATEGORIES INCLUDED IN MAJOR CLASSIFICATIONS

BUSINESS SERVICES

Computer Services
Accounting Services
Engineering
Architecture
Scientific and Technical Services
Legal Services
Management Consulting
Related services

EDUCATIONAL SERVICES

Elementary Education
Secondary Education
Post-secondary, Non-university Education
University Education
Libraries
Museums and Archives
Related services

GOVERNMENT SERVICES

Defence and Protective Services
Courts of Law
Human Resource Administration
Economic Resource Administration
Foreign Affairs
Related services

HEALTH/SOCIAL SERVICES

Hospitals
Private Medical Practices
Medical Laboratories
Rehabilitation Services
Non-hospital Institutions
Day-care Services
Counselling Services
Related services

MANUFACTURING

Foods and Beverages
Textiles and Clothing
Wood Products
Printing and Publishing
Metal Products
Electrical and Electronic Products
Non-metallic Mineral Products
Chemical Products
Related manufacturing

BIBLIOGRAPHY

Association of Universities and Colleges of Canada. *Trends: The Canadian University in Profile.* Ottawa, 1990.

Audet, M. *Qu'advient-il des diplômés et diplômées universitaires?* Québec: Ministère de l'Enseignement supérieur et de la Science, 1989.

British Columbia. Ministry of Advanced Education, Training and Technology. *1988 Former Students Outcomes Report.* Victoria, 1989.

Canada. Department of the Secretary of State of Canada. *Profile of Higher Education in Canada 1988-1989.* Ottawa, 1989.

Canada. Department of the Secretary of State of Canada. *Profile of Higher Education in Canada 1990 Edition.* Ottawa, 1991.

Canada. Statistics Canada. *Community College Student Information System.* Ottawa, n.d.

Canada. Statistics Canada. *University Student Information System User Manual.* Ottawa, 1983.

Canada. Statistics Canada. *Education in Canada. A Statistical Review for 1987-88.* Ottawa, 1989.

Canada. Statistics Canada. *Community colleges and related institutions: post-secondary enrolment and graduates.* Ottawa, 1989.

Canada. Statistics Canada. *Historical Labour Force Statistics - actual data, seasonal factors, seasonally adjusted data.* Ottawa, 1989.

Canada. Statistics Canada. *Universities: Enrolment and Degrees.* Ottawa, 1990.

Canada. Statistics Canada and the Department of the Secretary of State of Canada. *The Class of 82.* Ottawa, 1986.

Canadian Labour Market and Productivity Centre. *High-Tech Sector A Growing Source of Skilled Jobs.* Ottawa, 1990.

Chénard, Pierre. *L'interruption des études à l'Université du Québec.* Ste. Foy: Université du Québec, 1989.

Clark, W. et al. *The Class of 2001 - The school-age population - Trends and Implications - 1961 to 2001.* Ottawa: Statistics Canada, 1979.

Decore, A. and Pannu, R. "Educational Financing in Canada 1970-71 to 1984-85: Who Calls the Tune, Who Pays the Piper?" *Canadian Journal of Higher Education,* 26, 2: 27-49.

Dennison, J. and Gallagher, P. *Canada's Community Colleges A Critical Analysis.* Vancouver: University of British Columbia Press, 1986.

Denton, M. et al. *Employment Survey of 1985 Graduates of Ontario Universities.* Toronto: Ontario Ministry of Education, 1987.

Economic Council of Canada. *Legacies, Twenty-Sixth Annual Review.* Ottawa, 1989.

Economic Council of Canada. *Good Jobs, Bad Jobs Employment in the Service Economy.* Ottawa, 1990.

Gilbert, S. and Guppy, N. "Trends in Participation in Education by Gender", in *Social Inequality in Canada Patterns, Problems and Policies.* ed. J. Curtis et al. Scarborough: Prentice-Hall, 1988.

Gomme, I. and Gilbert, S. "Paying the Cost: Some Observations on the Problem of Post-secondary Student Attrition." *The Canadian Journal of Higher Education,* 14, 3: 95-99.

Gower, D. "Labour Force Trends in Canada and the United States", in *Canadian Social Trends*. edited by C. McKie and K. Thompson. Toronto: Thompson Education Publishing, 1990.

Guppy, N. and Pendakur, K. "The Effects of Gender and Parental Education on Participation Within Post-Secondary Education in the 1970s and 1980s." *The Canadian Journal of Higher Education*, 19, 1: 49-62.

Hunter, A. "Formal Education and Initial Employment: Unravelling the Relationship Between Schooling and Skills Over Time." *American Sociological Review*, 53, 5: 753-765.

La Haye, J. and Lespérance, A. *Accès à l'université. Description de la situation à partir des donneés de 1984-1985.* Québec: Ministère de l'Enseignement supérieur et de la Science, 1989.

Lévesque, M., and Pageau, D. *La Persévérance aux études. Le choix des collégiennes et des collégiens dans les années 80.* Québec: Ministère de l'Enseignement supérieur et de la Science, 1990.

Mulder, N. "Learning and Earning in the Nineties." *Orbit*, 21, 2: 3.

Myles, J. "The expanding middle: some Canadian evidence on the deskilling debate." *Canadian Review of Sociology and Anthropology*, 25, 3: 335-364.

Parliament, J. "Women Employed Outside the Home", in *Canadian Social Trends*. edited by C. McKie and K. Thompson. Toronto: Thompson Education Publishing, 1990.

Premier's Council of Ontario. *People and Skills in the New Global Economy.* Toronto, 1990.

Québec. Conseil supérieur de l'éducation. *Rapport annuel 1988-1989 sur l'état et les besoins de l'éducation.* Québec, 1989.

Rush, J., et al. *Making the Match volume 3.* London: University of Western Ontario, 1989.

Rush, J., et al. *Making the Match volume 4.* London: University of Western Ontario, 1990.

Saskatchewan. Education, Policy and Planning Branch. *Employment Statistics Report. 1988 Graduate Follow-up Survey.* Regina, 1989.

Skolnik, M. *How Ontario's College System Might Respond to Pressures for the Provision of More Advanced Training.* background paper, Ontario Ministry of Colleges and Universities, 1990.

Skolnik, M. *"Higher Education Systems in Canada."* draft paper, Ontario Ministry of Colleges and Universities, 1990.

DANEMARK

DENMARK

Hanne Traberg, Poul Bache

***Ministry of Education and Research
Department of Higher Education***

Contents

I.	Higher Education in Denmark	61
II.	Changes in the output of higher education	63
III.	The structures of the outflows from higher education	68
IV.	Young women in the general structure of outflows	73
V.	Changes in the transition to working life	75
VI.	The labour market situation of new graduates	78
VII.	Conclusions	82
Annex		84
References		86

I. HIGHER EDUCATION IN DENMARK

In this paper, the term "higher education" is defined as tertiary education in general, i.e. all formal education based on 12 years of primary and secondary education. The main qualifications giving access to higher education are shown in Table 1.

Table 1

**Examinations qualifying for admission to higher education
(numbers of students qualified, 1990)**

Studentereksamen from a gymnasium (3-year academically oriented upper secondary school)	24 100
HF (higher preparatory examination)	5 000
HHX (higher commercial examination)	8 900
HTX (higher technical examination)	1 100

Source: Ministry of education

These examinations qualify for admission to higher education in general, but additional qualifications may be required in some cases. Persons without one of the four "qualifying" examinations can also gain admission to higher education, usually on the basis of an evaluation of their individual competences. Approximately 60 per cent of the applicants to higher education hold the *studentereksamen*, whereas almost 20 per cent of the applicants do not hold any of the above mentioned qualifying examinations.

The numbers of persons completing the qualifying examinations has been increasing constantly since the 1960's. A short decrease in the middle of the 1980's has been followed by another increase due to the expansion of the *HHX* and *HTX* courses.

The numbers of young people qualifying for admission to further and higher education are shown in Table 2. The proportion of a youth cohort with a qualifying examination has increased from 38.6 per cent in 1982 to 48.2 per cent in 1990. s. It is expected that the number of people with qualifying examinations will decrease in the second half of the 1990's due to the demographic development.

Table 2

Number of young people qualifying for admission to further and higher education in percent of a youth cohort of 19 year olds

	1982	1985	1988	1990	2000	2010
Upper sec. exam.	19 922	20 938	18 231	19 319	14 737	16 991
Higher prep. exam.	4 429	5 290	4 879	4 993	4 018	4 309
Higher comm. exam.	5 238	7 079	8 117	9 419	7 810	8 286
Higher techn. exam.	0	48	283	741	715	759
Total	29 589	33 355	31 510	34 472	27 280	30 345
A youth cohort of 19-year-olds	76 532	84 440	74 846	71 373	58 822	64 697
Percent of a youth cohort of 19-year-olds	38.66	39.50	42.10	48.30	46.38	46.90

In the Danish education system, three levels of higher education can be identified (see Table 3):

- <u>Short-cycle courses</u> (KVU), i.e. courses of education of 1 or 2 years' duration, including very often a period of practical training.

- <u>Medium-cycle courses</u> (MVU), i.e. courses of education of 3 or 4 years' duration, e.g. teacher training, engineering, social work or business studies.

- <u>Long-cycle courses</u> (LVU), i.e. courses of education with an officially stipulated time of study of 5 years' duration leading to the *kandidat*-degree (roughly equivalent to a US/UK master's degree). Graduates from these courses can go on to postgraduate programmes leading to the Ph.D.-degree.

All higher education in Denmark is financed by the Ministry of Education, and students enrolled in full-time courses do not pay any fees. Some higher education institutions are private or chartered institutions, others are state institutions, but they are all funded and administered according to the same regulations.

Table 3

Higher education institutions in Denmark

University	College	Vocational
Long-cycle	Medium-cycle	Short-cycle
Research	No research	No research
Relatively large institutions in the larger towns	Many relatively small institutions all over Denmark	Many institutions of various size
High degree of autonomy in academic matters	Less autonomous	Increasing autonomy
Governed by bodies, elected by staff and students	Various forms of governance	Governed by boards dominated by labour market organisations

II. CHANGES IN THE "OUTPUT" OF HIGHER EDUCATION

The output of graduates

The size of the total output of higher education graduates has been relatively constant throughout the 1980's. On a yearly basis, approximately 9 000 have graduated from the short-cycle courses, 7 000 from the medium-cycle courses, and 6 000 from the long-cycle courses.

Table 4

Output of higher education graduates (1982-88)

	1982	1985	1988
Short-cycle	8 990	9 456	8 708
Medium-cycle	6 642	6 832	6 940
Long-cycle	5 873	5 916	5 801
Total	21 505	22 204	21 449

Source: (1)

As there has been a considerable increase in the input to higher education in the second half of the 1980's, the output of graduates will be rising in the beginning of the 1990's.

Table 5

Input to higher education (1982-88)

	1982	1985	1988
Short-cycle	12 565	11 466	12 222
Medium-cycle	8 480	10 968	12 661
Long-cycle	12 524	14 346	16 535
Total	33 569	36 780	41 418

Source: (1)

When comparing tables 4 and 5, one can see an almost unchanged output of graduates from the medium-cycle and long-cycle courses in spite of an increased input. As far as the medium-cycle courses are concerned, the explanation is on the one hand that as from 1984 the business-language courses have been extended from being short-cycle to medium-cycle courses and on the other hand that there has been an increasing dropout from part-time business studies (HD). At the long-cycle courses, the explanation is first and foremost that students spend a very long time -- often 8 or 9 years -- to complete their studies.

Persons holding a *studentereksamen* (upper secondary school leaving examination) or an *HF*-examination constitute by far the greatest part of the input to higher education. There is also however, particularly to the short-cycle level, a relatively large input of persons with other qualifications.

The number of completed upper secondary school leaving examinations and *HF*-examinations was increasing until the middle of the 1980's, where the demographic development started to make itself felt. The annual output of students with these two examinations will however remain somewhat constant, i.e. 22 000 a year until the middle of the 1990's. The total number of qualifying examinations will be approximately 35 000 a year at the beginning of the 1990's.

There has been no direct relation between the number of qualifying examinations and the input to the courses. The capacity of the educational institutions is laid down by the Ministry of education, and the input is first and foremost an expression of the number of places established, as there have been more applicants than study places throughout the 1980's. The result of this development is that a growing number of applicants are being turned down. In 1990, 14 000 out of 49 000 applicants for higher education courses were turned down for capacity reasons.

In order to reduce the number of turned down applicants, the number of study places has been extended in recent years and further extensions of capacity are anticipated. The output of higher education graduates will therefore increase in the years to come, and despite the demographic development, no decrease in the output of graduates is likely to occur in the 1990's.

The "market-share" of higher education courses

An increasing percentage of the Danish population has completed some kind of higher education. In 1987, approximately 17 per cent of the adult Danish population had completed or were enrolled in a higher education course. The corresponding figure for 1980 was 15 per cent.

Table 6

Percentage of the Danish population between 15 and 60 who was enrolled in or had completed a higher education course in 1980 and 1987

	1980 Men	1980 Women	1987 Men	1987 Women
Enrolled, HE	3.7	3.5	4.1	4.0
Completed, KVU	3.4	6.1	3.7	7.4
Completed, MVU	4.2	3.4	5.0	4.2
Completed, LVU	3.6	1.1	4.3	1.7
Total	14.9	14.1	17.1	17.3

Source: (4)

The percentage of the population having completed some kind of higher education will continue to increase. In the middle of the 1980's, approximately 26 per cent of an elementary school age cohort (fictitious cohort, note by the Secretariat) completed a course of higher education. This rate has been relatively stable for some years, but it will grow in the years to come.

The figures in Table 7 are computed figures which show the percentage of an elementary school age cohort that will complete a higher education course, if all transfer rates between the different parts of the education system and between the education system and the surrounding world follow the same pattern as in the year under consideration.

Table 7

Percentage of an elementary school year group completing a higher education course (fictitions cohorts) (%)

	1983	1984	1985	1986
Short-cycle	12.9	11.2	10.7	10.4
Medium-cycle	7.9	8.4	8.2	8.6
Long-cycle	6.8	6.9	6.5	6.7
Total	26.6	26.5	25.4	25.7

Source: (3)

Figure 1 shows the flows of young people from an elementary school (fictitious) cohort through the education system if the 1986 transfer rates remain constant.

The transfers between short-cycle and long-cycle courses are not frequent. Only 2 per cent of a youth cohort with completed short-cycle education choose to pursue their studies at a long-cycle course of education.

Dropout rates

University courses have traditionally had a high dropout rate, whereas the long-cycle courses at university-level higher education institutions have had considerably higher completion rates than the universities. Courses within the humanities and natural sciences and to a certain extent within the social sciences account for the major part of dropout rates.

There does not seem to exist any clear connection between dropout rates and labour market prospects. The dropout rate is traditionally large for certain courses, particularly at the universities. There is a clear connection between the level of the dropout rate and the recruitment basis to the individual courses of education.

The dropping-out normally occurs at a very early stage -- often before the student has even sat for any examination. A great deal of the dropouts seem to be the consequences of a second choice rather than of educational failure. The majority of the students who dropout transfer immediately or after some years to another course, which they complete.

Some of those who give up a course spend one or several years in the labour market, before they start another course, but nothing indicates that the labour market has a very large permanent input of students who have dropped out from higher education.

Figure 1

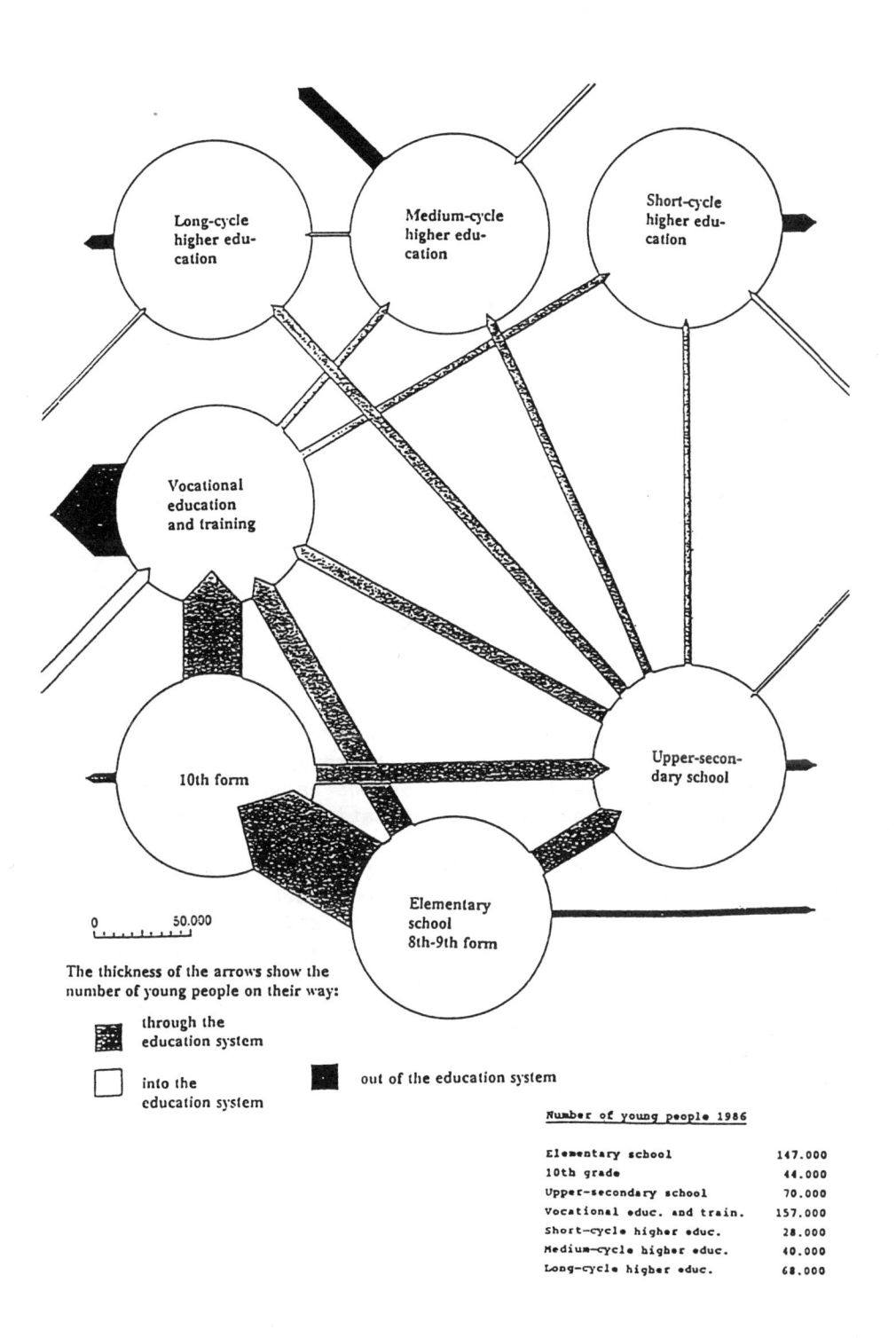

The thickness of the arrows show the number of young people on their way:

- through the education system
- into the education system
- out of the education system

Scale: 0 — 50.000

Number of young people 1986

Elementary school	147.000
10th grade	44.000
Upper-secondary school	70.000
Vocational educ. and train.	157.000
Short-cycle higher educ.	28.000
Medium-cycle higher educ.	40.000
Long-cycle higher educ.	68.000

Table 8 shows the percentage of students who actually complete a course among those who started it. The figures are computed on the basis of the total number of dropouts which was registered in these courses in a given year (fictitious cohorts). Students who break off a course in order to continue the same course at another institution are considered as dropouts. Therefore, the figures to some extent overestimate the real dropout rate.

Table 8

Completion rates in higher education by sex
(in %)

	Men	Women	Total
Short-cycle	73.7	79.3	75.9
Medium-cycle	59.3	62.3	61.0
Long-cycle	45.9	50.8	48.7

Source: (3)

III. THE STRUCTURE OF THE OUTFLOWS FROM HIGHER EDUCATION

The output of higher education graduates is controlled in that the Ministry of education lays down an annual maximum intake figure for each course. The intake figure is laid down on the basis of an evaluation of the employment prospects, the demand and the educational capacity.

It has been the policy of the Ministry to increase the number of study places in the courses which are directed towards the private sector, particularly the technical and certain social sciences courses and also in general to increase the number of study places at the medium-cycle and short-cycle higher education courses. At the same time, the number of study places at the courses in health science and the humanities as well as in teacher training has been reduced since regulation of admission to higher education (*numerus clausus*) was introduced in the middle of the 1970's. The results of this policy are shown in Table 9:

Table 9

Graduate numbers, by field of study

	1982	1985	1988
Social sciences			
Long-cycle	1 191	1 303	1 737
Medium-cycle	1 533	2 001	2 322
Short-cycle	20	60	329
Humanities			
Long-cycle	1 611	1 422	1 011
Medium-cycle	787	935	1 060
Short-cycle	1 082	1 245	420
Technical sciences			
Long-cycle	904	991	1 256
Medium-cycle	649	1 107	1 355
Short-cycle	1 180	1 057	1 577
Natural sciences			
Long-cycle	759	741	730
Health sciences			
Long-cycle	972	891	720
Medium-cycle	777	778	809
Short-cycle	2 268	2 384	2 444
Psychology/education			
Long-cycle	402	447	382
Medium-cycle	2 790	1 963	1 145
Short-cycle	2 785	2 989	2 429
Total	19 710	20 314	19 726

Source: (1)

Within the social sciences courses (see Table A2 in Annex), the increase has mainly occurred in business studies.

Within the humanities, there has been a drop in the output of graduates from the long-cycle courses in theology and languages. This is a result of the Ministry's admission regulation for these courses. At the same time, the medium-cycle language courses have been extended considerably.

The workforce of higher education graduates

The age distribution of higher education graduates in the labour market is such that the number of graduates retiring is in all education categories concerned much smaller than the number of new graduates. Therefore the workforce of higher education graduates is growing rather rapidly.

At the end of the 1980's, approximately 17 per cent of all the employed were higher education graduates. As it appears from table 10, the number of employed higher education graduates has increased throughout the 1980's both in absolute and in relative terms.

Table 10

The educational distribution of the employed population

Employed with the following qualifications	Men	Women	Total	% of the workforce
1983				
No voc. oriented qual.	572 251	545 575	1 117 826	41.83
Voc. sec. basic qual.	56 901	65 013	121 914	4.56
Completed voc. upp. sec. qual.	494 677	305 116	799 793	29.93
Short-cycle higher qual.	56 433	97 016	153 459	5.74
Medium-cycle higher qual.	74 698	58 784	133 482	5.00
Long-cycle higher qual.	68 227	22 517	90 744	3.40
Total	1 323 197	1 094 021	2 417 218	90.46
1985				
No-voc. oriented qual.	593 805	560 839	1 154 644	40.14
Voc. sec. basic qual.	72 879	76 277	149 156	4.38
Completed voc. upp. sec. qual.	537 851	336 273	874 124	28.72
Short-cycle higher qual.	56 626	104 821	161 447	5.51
Medium-cycle higher qual.	85 072	64 268	149 340	4.79
Long-cycle higher qual.	73 413	25 739	99 152	3.26
Total	1 419 646	1 168 217	2 587 863	86.80
1988				
No voc. oriented qual.	565 729	538 441	1 104 170	40.28
Voc. sec. basic qual.	76 296	82 349	158 645	5.20
Completed voc. upp. sec. qual.	547 697	372 321	920 018	30.49
Short-cycle higher qual.	61 314	113 903	175 217	5.63
Medium-cycle higher qual.	90 013	70 337	160 350	5.21
Long-cycle higher qual.	81 095	30 985	112 080	3.46
Total	1 422 144	1 208 336	2 630 480	90.28

Table 11

Unemployment rates in the active population, by level of qualifications (%)

Unemployed with the following qualifications:	1983	1985	1988
No voc. oriented qual.	11.97	9.43	10.77
Voc. sec. basic qual.	11.75	8.98	10.95
Completed voc. upp. sec. qual.	8.09	5.18	6.90
Short-cycle higher qual.	4.56	3.74	3.80
Medium-cycle higher qual.	3.29	2.44	2.57
Long-cycle higher qual.	4.60	4.23	3.39
Total	9.54	7.08	8.24

Table 12 shows how the numbers of active graduates will develop if admissions are maintained at the same level as in 1988. The table is drawn from a prognosis elaborated by the Economics and Statistical Division of the Ministry of Education, using the 1988 transfer rates within the education system and a population prognosis made by the Danish Bureau of Statistics.

The total workforce will decrease by approximately 4 per cent (after having increased up to 1995) over the whole period, but a considerable shift will occur in the educational composition of the workforce.

The number of short-cycle graduates in the workforce will increase from 1988 to 2010. The increase will occur within the technical sciences, health sciences, social sciences and psychology/education.

Although the entire medium-cycle category is more or less totally unchanged in numbers, the changes within the actual category are quite substantial. The social science, technical science and health science graduates will increase rapidly in number, whereas the number of psychology/education graduates will drop. In the latter area, it is only the number of priamry and lower secondary school teachers that will drop.

The very rapid growth in the number of graduates within the social sciences area (see table A3 in Annex) is a result of the very great increaase in the input to the social sciences courses in the 1970's and 1980's. Correspondingly, the effect of the admission regulations at the long-cycle humanities courses in the universities will be a drop in the number of vocationally active with such qualifications.

The rapid drop in the number of graduates with a medium-cycle pedagogical qualification is due to the primary and lower secondary school teachers. On the one hand, there has been a drastic reduction of the input to the teacher training courses in the 1980's, and on the other hand a growing number of teachers will reach pensioning age by the end of the 1990's. In the years to come, a diminishing need for teachers is expected as a consequence of the demographic development, but it will probably be necessary to increase the input to the teacher training courses in the 1990's in order to avoid teacher shortages after year 2000.

The workforce of long-cycle graduates amounted to approximately 105 000 in 1988 and will amount to approximately 140 000 in 2010. The number of economics graduates will triple, the number of engineering graduates will double, whereas the number of humanities and health sciences graduates will drop.

Table 12

Prognosis concerning the workforce of higher education graduates

	1988	2000	2010	% increase 1988-2010
Social sciences				
Long-cycle	20 630	32 426	39 950	94
Medium-cycle	27 266	37 496	41 366	52
Humanities				
Long-cycle	20 004	19 136	16 695	- 17
Medium-cycle	10 427	12 459	12 644	21
Short-cycle	18 814	18 261	16 435	- 13
Technical sciences				
Long-cycle	22 968	32 199	37 465	65
Medium-cycle	31 576	38 321	39 496	25
Short-cycle	38 207	46 294	47 433	24
Natural sciences				
Long-cycle	13 913	18 533	21 347	53
Health sciences				
Long-cycle	20 718	20 864	18 358	- 11
Medium-cycle	12 189	16 261	17 021	40
Short-cycle	50 657	59 275	61 636	22
Psychology/education				
Long-cycle	5 926	7 024	6 379	8
Medium-cycle	73 327	62 363	46 759	- 36
Short-cycle	49 848	62 259	62 848	26
Total	416 200	483 171	485 832	17

Source: (2)

IV. YOUNG WOMEN IN THE GENERAL STRUCTURE OF OUTFLOWS

Traditionally, women are over-represented in the shorter courses and under-represented in the longer courses. This pattern is about to change, as shown in table 13. As it appears from the table, the percentage of women is highest in the short-cycle courses, but women do to an increasing extent opt for long-cycle courses at the expense of the short ones.

Male and female students more or less have the same study behaviour and the same completion rate. Therefore, the sex distribution of the graduates will be the same as that of the applicants admitted to the courses.

Table 13

Percentage of women in higher education in 1980 and in 1987

	1980	1987
Enrolled, short-cycle	76.5	70.3
Enrolled, medium-cycle	43.1	42.7
Enrolled, long-cycle	38.1	43.0
Total	47.8	48.6
Completed, short-cycle	63.8	65.9
Completed, medium-cycle	44.8	45.2
Completed, long-cycle	22.2	27.5
Total	48.1	49.8

Source: (4)

A great part of the female students traditionally concentrate on certain courses, particularly within health sciences, education, languages and social work, whereas in the past there were very few female students in engineering, science and economics. Also this pattern is about to be breaking up.

In some cases, the shift has already taken place both in terms of enrolments and in employment. That for instance applies to psychologists, social workers and primary and lower secondary school teachers, where women are in the majority on the labour market. In other cases women are in the majority among the students and among the new graduates but not yet in employment. This for instance applies to dentists.

The majority of students now admitted to courses in medicine, theology, law and veterinary science are women, and this will soon make itself felt in the output of graduates. Only the engineering courses and the natural sciences courses still seem to remain male dominated.

The change in women's choices must be seen in relation to the fact that a great part of those courses which traditionally attracted many women in the 1970's and 1980's have either been subjected to very strict admission rules (many health education courses) or have had poor employment prospects (humanities courses). Another factor is that an ever increasing number of women have chosen the mathematics line of the upper secondary school, which has a tradition of leading to higher education courses in technology, natural sciences and economics. Changes in women's choice of higher education are thus partly a result of changes inprevious choices in education system. In all the other subjects there will be an equal sex distribution or an over-representation of women.

Women in technical courses

Traditionally, only very few women choose to enter courses in engineering or science. It has in recent years been the goal of both the Ministry of education and the educational institutions to increase the percentage of women enrolled in these courses. Table 14 shows that there has been a considerable growth in the input of women to the technical courses in the course of the 1980's. In certain engineering courses, women constitute a rather considerable percentage of the students today, in the chemical engineering courses for instan
ce, 50 per cent. But despite this development, only a very small percentage of engineers on the labour market will for many years to come be women.

Table 14

Percentage of women enrolled in technical higher education courses

	1980 %	Number	1987 %	Number
Short-cycle	9	189	15	494
Medium-cycle	3	83	13	848
Long-cycle	6	1 245	23	2 434

Source: (4)

V. CHANGES IN THE TRANSITION TO WORKING LIFE

The employment destinations of the newly graduated

Since 1984, the Danish Bureau of statistics has worked out the position of the newly graduated in the labour market two months after graduation. The latest figures available are from 1987.

Table 15 shows the large percentage of graduates that had found employment (further education excluded) two months after graduation. This percentage has increased from 1984 to 1987. This must be seen in connection with a general drop in the unemployment in the Danish labour market over the same period. Table 15 also shows the percentage of the new graduates who had found employment in the private sector.

Table 15

Percentages of new graduates employed 2 months after graduation (A)
and proportion of these graduates employed in the private sector (B)

	A 84	85	86	87	B 84	85	86	87
Short-cycle	80.2	84.2	87.0	86.6	29.1	27.3	26.3	29.0
Medium-cycle	81.2	84.5	86.6	86.1	34.3	42.5	48.8	50.2
Long-cycle	71.8	73.2	75.1	77.6	39.6	44.0	47.9	45.6

Source: (6)

Among short-cycle graduates, the percentage of those employed in the private sector has been relatively constant throughout the period (26-29 per cent). The relatively large percentage of graduates employed in the public sector is a consequence of the fact that the social and health sectors (social workers, preschool teachers, nurses, etc.) constitute a very large percentage of new graduates at this level.

Among the medium-cycle graduates, the percentage employed in the private sector increased from 34.3 per cent in 1984 to 50.2 per cent in 1987. This increase should be seen in the light of the fact that the number of graduates from the business schools (e.g. graduates with a bachelor's degree in commerce (*HD*) or a bachelor of science degree in business economics (*HA*) rose from 2 270 to 3 830 over the period). New graduates from these courses constitute approximately 90 per cent of those employed in the private sector.

Also from long-cycle courses, an ever increasing number of graduates find employment in the private sector. As it appears from table 4, there has been no growth during the 1980's in the total annual output of long-cycle university graduates. On the contrary, there has been a drop in the output from courses which traditionally aim at the public sector and a growth in the output from courses (business studies, engineering) which aim at the private sector, (see table 9). To an ever increasing extent the private sector employs graduates from courses which in the past were almost solely aimed at employment in the public sector.

Table 16 shows the distribution of recent graduates in 1981 and 1987 by employment areas. It can be seen that a relatively small but nonetheless increasing percentage of new graduates finds employment in the manufacturing industries. The service industry is the clearly dominant industry, and the private service sector has throughout the 1980's employed a rapidly growing percentage of the new medium-cycle or long-cycle graduates. The finance sector has in particular experienced a rapid growth in employment.

Table 16

Newly graduated in employment in 1981 and 1987 distributed on employment area

	Short-cycle 1981	Short-cycle 1987	Medium-cycle 1981	Medium-cycle 1987	Long-cycle 1981	Long-cycle 1987
Manufacturing industry	10.7	13.9	9.2	17.5	7.8	10.4
Private services	13.0	14.7	17.3	31.4	21.6	33.5
Public services	76.7	70.9	73.4	49.9	70.5	54.3
No information	0.0	0.5	0.1	1.2	0.1	1.8
Total	100.4	100.0	100.0	100.0	100.0	100.0

Source: (6)

Table 17 provides more detailed information for selected categories of new graduates. It shows the large differences in employment pattern for new graduates with different qualifications.

Table 17
Distribution of new graduates, by industry and field of study (1987)

	Agriculture	Manufacturing	Construction	Commerce, catering	Transport	Finance	Teaching	Social/health	Public services	Service	No answer
Nurse	-	3	2	8	1	2	96	1 575	2	2	-
Teacher	4	7	3	22	9	5	946	43	64	16	5
Journalist	-	77	-	2	2	14	3	1	2	26	3
B.sc. (eng)	1	339	88	75	16	207	11	11	49	7	15
Humanities graduate	1	13	2	10	2	16	94	20	37	49	8
Social sciences	4	22	5	20	7	235	34	14	298	32	13
Natural sciences	2	25	1	6	-	48	126	15	55	6	8
Medicine	1	1	1	2	1	2	13	438	38	1	-
M. sc. (eng.)	2	153	26	47	15	176	89	6	48	4	9

Source: (6)

VI. THE LABOUR MARKET SITUATION OF NEW GRADUATES

Unemployment

According to Danish legislation, all newly graduated who have completed a course of education of at least 18 months' duration are entitled to receive unemployment benefits. Higher education graduates therefore receive unemployment benefits if they do not find employment immediately after graduation. If the newly graduated can only find part-time employment, they can receive benefits corresponding to that part of a normal working week where they have not been employed.

The unemployment of higher education graduates is lower than the average unemployment in Denmark. The unemployment is higher for women than for men and lowest for medium-cycle graduates. Female long-cycle graduates are particularly affected by unemployment. Part of the explanation to this is that those university level courses which are affected by a high rate of unemployment are the courses where women constitute a great percentage of the students. This is particularly the case of courses within the humanities, psychology and social sciences.

Table 18

Unemployment rates, 1988

	Total	Women	Men
No completed vocational educ.	10.5	12.0	9.0
Basic voc. upper sec. educ.	10.2	12.8	7.6
Voc. upper secondary educ.	6.4	7.5	5.7
Short-cycle higher educ.	4.5	4.8	3.8
Medium-cycle higheer educ.	2.9	3.4	2.5
Long-cycle higher educ.	4.6	7.2	3.5
Total workforce	8.0	9.5	6.7

Source: (5)

Around 20 per cent of the new graduates are generally registered as unemployed during the first months after graduation, (cf. table 15). After a few months, unemployment rates drop. For some categories of new graduates however, *part-time employment* is very common. This is particularly the case with teachers, humanities graduates, preschool teachers and social workers.

There are actually very large differences in the level of unemployment of the various categories of graduates. As far as the long and the medium-cycle courses are concerned, the Ministry of Education elaborates on a yearly basis a very detailed account of the level of unemployment in the different education categories.

Some key figures are shown in Table 18. More detailed unemployment figures by field of study are shown in the Annex. For comparison average unemployment rates for the total workforce are given.

Table 18 shows that unemployment is highest for university graduates in subjects such as the humanities and psychology. Unemployment has been increasing up to the middle of the 1980's and subsequently has in general been decreasing. There has in particular been a huge drop in the unemployment of humanities graduates.

The development of unemployment must be seen in the light of the fact that there has been for all education categories a considerable increase in the number of new graduates in the workforce (see table 10).

Table 19

Unemployment rates, by main field of study

	1982	1985	1987	1989
Social sciences				
Long-cycle	3.6	4.1	2.7	4.0
Medium-cycle	4.1	3.8	2.9	3.5
Humanities				
Long-cycle	15.3	22.1	15.5	13.1
Medium-cycle	10.0	9.7	8.7	7.7
Engineering				
Long-cycle	2.9	2.0	2.7	5.8
Medium-cycle	3.6	2.0	2.9	4.0
Natural sciences				
Long-cycle	5.1	6.2	4.8	4.9
Health science				
Long-cycle	2.1	3.5	3.5	2.8
Short-cycle	0.2	0.6	0.8	1.3
Education and psychology				
Long-cycle	14.9	18.5	15.6	14.3
Short-cycle	4.7	6.6	5.5	5.5
Graduates, total				
Long-cycle	5.4	7.9	6.1	6.1
Short and medium-cycle	3.2	4.7	4.1	4.3
Total workforce	10.0	9.1	7.9	9.4

Source: (7)

The fact that the natural departure from most categories is very small means that each year a great number of new jobs must be created in order to avoid a growing unemployment rate. The growing unemployment up to 1985 can be seen as an expression of the fact that the Danish labour market had not yet adjusted to the huge growth in the number of new higher education graduates.

The drop in the unemployment rate after 1985 can be explained in that the unemployment rate of the **entire** Danish labour market was dropping between 1985 and 1987. But it is striking that the unemployment rate for most higher education categories has continued to drop also after 1987, where the general unemployment started to increase again.

The most evident explanation is that the labour market is now about to adjust to a relatively large input of highly qualified people. New graduates have become more flexible in their choices of employment and employers have become more open to employing certain groups of long-cycle graduates than they were in the past.

The Danish labour market has generally been able to take on a considerably greater number of higher education graduates than forecasted in the prognoses which were based on the traditional employment pattern. In other words, there exists an adaptation mechanism in the labour market in the form of substitution effects, etc. which appear to be relatively effective for graduates with long-cycle higher education qualifications. In recent years, it has been attempted to include these adaptation mechanisms in Danish prognoses for the labour market of graduates with long-cycle higher education qualifications (see References, n°. 2 and 9).

One may say that the supply of higher education creates its own demand. The effect is most pronounced for the humanities courses at the universities, where new graduates, who ten years ago were almost solely employed in the education system, are to an ever increasing extent being employed in private businesses. A corresponding development may, although not quite as pronounced, be seen within most other areas of education.

Some education categories have however experienced a growing unemployment at the end of the 1980's. This is particularly the case of a number of social sciences and engineering graduates. Recent years have seen staff reductions in the public administration which have meant that very few new graduates were taken on in 1989-90. This had led to growing unemployment among young law and public administration graduates.

During the 1980's, the unemployment rate has been low among graduates with higher education qualifications in the areas of health and agriculture (two areas in which the intake has been strictly regulated), in mathematics, physics and chemistry (areas in which the intake has been rather small) as well as in business economics and engineering (areas in which the intake has been rapidly increasing).

As far as the engineering graduates are concerned, a shortage of engineers in the middle of the 1980's has been replaced by a situation where it is difficult for new graduates to find a job. Some of the reasons for this can be ascribed to the general business situation. But another contributing factor is that the yearly output of new engineering graduates has increased due to an increased input to the courses in the first half of the 1980's. At that time, there was a shortage of engineers, and the salaries were skyrocketing. The salary level has not yet adjusted to the new labour market situation for engineers.

Salary conditions

New graduates who are employed in the public sector are paid according to an agreement between the Government and their trade union. The agreements provide for more or less homogenous salaries for all new university graduates. The main principle is that the salaries tend to follow the **level** of the course rather than its nature, although the public sector has in recent years taken initiatives for a more individual fixing of salaries.

There are no available information on the salary of new graduates in the **private sector**. The Confederation of Danish employers, which represents the majority of the major Danish businesses, elaborates salary statistics which indicate the salary of various education categories. The salaries of the 25-29-year-olds, the typical age of the new graduates from Danish universities, may give a picture of the salaries which the young graduates will typically receive in the private sector:

Table 20

Average salary of 25-29-year-old employees in the private sector in 1989 (DKK per month)

Long-cycle	
Law graduates	18 206
Economic graduates	20 500
Humanities graduates	16 500
Natural sciences graduates	20 000
M.sc. (engineering) graduates	21 888
M.sc. (business economics) graduates	18 660
Medium-cycle	
Academy engineers (B.sc.)	20 778
Teknikum engineers (B.sc.)	20 683
Bachelor of commerce graduates	20 168
B.sc. (business economics) graduates	17 550
Teachers trained at training colleges	14 922

Source: (8)

It is striking that areas of education seem to be of greater importance than **level** of education. As an example can be mentioned that engineers with medium-cycle qualifications received higher salaries than many university graduates and economics graduates with a 5-year university course behind them, and graduates from the 4-year part-time courses at the business schools are paid at the same level.

VII. CONCLUSIONS

At the end of the 1980's, approximately 13 per cent of the population in the vocationally active age were higher education graduates. The percentage will increase in the years to come. In the 1980's, approximately 1/4 of a youth cohort had completed a course of higher education, and this proportion will increase in the years to come. The number of higher education graduates in the workforce is expected to grow by 17 per cent from 1988 to 2010.

The dropout rate from higher education courses is relatively high, particularly in the longest courses, where the dropout rate is more than 50 per cent. Most of those students who dropout will later on complete another course of education.

Considerable changes have taken place in the structure of the output from higher education. The reason for this has on the one hand been the Ministry of education's administration of the input to the courses and on the other hand changes in the educational choices of the students. These changes will continue in the years to come. There has in particular been a considerable increase in the output from the technical sciences and some social sciences courses and a decrease in the output from in particular the teacher training courses and the long-cycle humanities courses.

In total, a more or less equal number of men and women are trained, but women clearly outnumber men in short-cycle courses, whereas the opposite is the case in the medium-cycle and long-cycle courses. Women constitute a growing percentage of the higher education graduates. This development is particularly pronounced in the long-cycle university courses. In the case of university courses in medicine, psychology, veterinary science, law and theology, women will in a few years' time constitute more than half of the new graduates. In the technical courses, the percentage of women has been clearly growing throughout the 1980's, but the female students will continue to constitute a minority of the students.

The average unemployment of higher education graduates is lower than that of the workforce as a whole. Among the graduates, the unemployment is higher among women than among men. A relatively high unemployment rate for new higher education graduates in the middle of the 1980's has been replaced by a decreasing unemployment for almost all education categories. There are however still categories of newly graduated who are affected by a high unemployment rate, i.e. due to a great extent to part-time employment which according to Danish legislation entitles them to unemployment benefits.

Traditionally, most long-cycle and medium-cycle higher education courses aim at employment within the public sector. In the course of the 1980's, an ever increasing percentage of the newly graduated became employed within the private sector. There is an obvious connection between education and start salary in the private sector. The salary seems to depend more on the **area** than on the **level** of education.

ANNEX

Table A.1

**The unemployment rate for higher education graduates.
Total number of graduates receiving unemployment benefit
in per cent of total number of graduates potentially in the workforce.**

	1981	1982	1983	1984	1985	1986	1987	1988	1989
Agricultural science	1.2	2.0	2.3	2.0	2.0	2.3	2.7	2.9	4.0
Architecture	18.2	18.0	20.4	17.0	13.9	11.5	10.7	11.3	13.2
Librarianship	15.5	16.0	17.7	17.9	17.1	16.0	14.2	14.1	13.5
Preschool & Recreation centre teachers	6.7	9.0	12.0	12.6	12.7	11.3	10.0	9.5	7.8
Veterinary surgeons	1.8	2.0	1.6	1.6	3.0	3.6	3.5	2.7	3.1
Occupational & physiotherapy	1.0	1.0	2.3	3.1	–	–	–	–	–
Occup. therapy	–	–	–	–	5.7	5.0	5.3	5.8	7.2
Physiotherapy	–	–	–	–	2.2	2.1	2.6	3.4	4.4
Bilingual etc. secretaries	6.3	6.0	8.2	8.3	8.3	5.3	4.2	4.4	4.8
Business languages	16.0	21.0	24.9	19.5	18.6	14.9	15.0	8.2	7.0
Business economics	1.6	2.0	2.4	4.1	2.8	3.1	2.5	3.1	4.6
Pharmacy	2.9	3.0	3.5	3.5	3.7	3.4	3.3	4.2	4.7
Folkeskole teacher	2.6	3.0	4.6	4.4	3.2	2.5	1.8	2.2	3.0
Forestry	3.8	2.0	2.5	2.0	2.0	2.4	2.1	2.3	3.1
Horticulture	5.2	7.0	7.5	7.2	6.4	6.0	5.0	6.3	7.1
Humanities	18.2	17.0	19.5	23.8	24.1	18.5	16.3	16.5	14.9
Engineering	3.5	3.0	2.7	2.4	2.0	2.2	2.9	–	–
Midwifery	–	2.0	2.8	3.1	2.6	2.9	2.7	3.3	2.4
Journalism	6.5	12.0	11.3	8.1	5.8	5.5	6.5	6.9	7.4
Law	2.7	3.0	3.1	3.3	3.2	2.5	2.3	2.6	3.3
Land surveying	8.0	8.0	6.1	5.6	4.0	2.9	2.7	4.3	5.3
Food science	22.1	20.0	18.9	12.2	16.7	13.5	9.1	4.7	8.4
Medicine	3.7	1.0	2.1	2.9	2.7	2.5	2.5	2.7	1.2
Dairy science	3.5	3.0	1.7	3.0	1.6	3.2	3.1	3.2	2.8
Biology	15.4	16.0	13.5	15.4	15.5	12.9	10.0	9.1	8.4
Computer science	1.5	1.0	0.0	0.0	0.9	0.8	2.7	2.7	3.5
Geography	9.7	10.0	12.1	16.2	15.4	10.3	10.0	8.8	10.5
Geology	4.0	6.0	8.3	8.9	7.2	6.3	5.6	7.0	8.0
Math, Physics, Chemistry	3.0	2.0	2.5	2.5	2.3	1.7	1.9	–	–
Physical education	12.4	13.0	13.6	19.1	18.0	16.2	12.1	7.3	4.5
Statistics	1.1	1.0	0.0	0.5	1.6	0.6	0.0	0.0	0.0
Psychology	14.0	14.0	18.9	20.2	18.6	17.2	15.6	15.2	14.3
Social science	16.7	13.0	14.8	18.0	15.5	13.2	10.6	9.4	7.0
Social work	10.1	10.0	12.5	12.6	10.3	8.9	7.0	7.1	8.0
Sociology etc.	23.8	25.0	32.9	22.3	22.5	17.5	13.7	12.8	12.8
Political science	6.3	8.0	11.0	9.4	8.0	5.3	3.1	5.0	7.9
Nursing	–	0.0	0.1	0.4	0.2	0.3	0.4	0.6	0.7
Dentistry	3.9	5.0	7.4	8.9	6.1	7.0	6.8	6.6	6.0
Theology	3.0	4.0	5.4	6.2	5.2	5.8	6.0	5.7	6.0

Table A.2

Numbers of graduates by field of study
Disaggregated data for the group social sciences and humanities

	1982	1985	1988
Social Sciences			
Long-cycle courses:	1,190	1,303	1,737
Law	441	446	537
Social Studies	355	310	374
Economics/Political Economics	159	172	187
Business Economics	207	345	600
Other	28	30	39
Medium-cycle courses:	1,533	2,001	2,322
Social work	387	412	278
Bachelor of Commerce (HD)	593	709	1,045
BSc (Business Economics)	553	880	999
Short-cycle courses:		60	329
Assistant/policeman/transport	17	53	62
Business analyst/acad.econ.	3	7	190
Computer specialist/ micro instructor	0	0	77
Humanities			
Long-cycle courses:	1,611	1,422	1,011
Humanities/History	276	254	265
Theology/Religious Studies	117	119	86
Languages	978	800	406
Art/Aesthetic courses	240	249	254
Medium-cycle courses:	787	935	1,060
ED (Business language course)	204	184	85
Business Economics/languages		11	38
Bi/trilingual secretary		183	567
Journalist	157	161	179
Librarian	261	228	120
Art/Aesthetic courses	165	168	71
Short-cycle courses:	1,082	1,245	420
Business language courses	855	1,047	184
Art/Aesthetic courses	201	196	192
Other	26	2	44
Psycology-Educational Studies/ Psychology	177	189	175

Table A3

Prognosis of the workforce of higher education graduates
Disaggregated data for the groups social sciences and humanities

	1988	2000	2010	Increase in %
Social Sciences				
Long-cycle courses:	20,630	32,426	39,950	93.65
Law	9,655	12,023	12,644	30.8581
Social science course	2,105	3,074	3,620	71.9715
Political science	1,892	2,509	2,808	48.4144
Economics (cand.pol., cand.oecon., cand.merc.)	6,978	14,820	20,878	199.197
Medium-cycle courses:	27,266	37,496	41,366	51.7128
BCom, BSc (Business Econ.)	20,179	29,215	33,518	66,1034
Social work	7,087	8,281	7,848	10.738
Humanities				
Long-cycle courses:	20,004	19,136	16,695	-16.542
Cand.mag., cand.theol. etc.	17,041	15,665	13,354	-21.636
Music, art and theatre	2,963	3,471	3,341	12.7573
Medium-cycle courses:	10,427	12,459	12,644	21.2621
Business languages	1,673	3,766	4,904	193.126
Journalist	3,187	3,788	3,765	18.1362
Librarian	4,567	4,325	3,630	-20.517
Art-Aesthetic course	1,000	580	345	-65.5
Short-cycle courses:	18,814	18,261	16,435	-12.645
Business languages/ Economics ("sprøk")	15,018	13,884	12,119	-19.304
Art-Aesthetic course	3,796	4,377	4,316	13.6986

REFERENCES

1) *Statistisk Arbog 1982-1990* (Statistical Yearbook 1982-1990)

2) *Uddannelsesbetingede tilpasningsbehov pa arbejdsmarkedet.* Undervisningsministeriet, (Need for educational adjustment in the labour market, Ministry of Education, May 1990)

3) *Bevaegelser inden for uddannelsessystemet i perioden 1981-1986.* Undervisningsministeriet (Flows within the education system over the period 1981-1986. Ministry of Education)

4) *Danmarks Statistik, Statistiske Efterretninger, uddannelse og kultur,1990:3* (Danish Bureau of statistics, statistical forecasts, education and culture, 1990:3)

5) *Danmarks statistik, statistiske Efterretninger, Arbejdsmarked 1990:1* (Danish Bureau of statistics, statistical forecasts, labour market 1990:1)

6) *De nyuddannedes indplacering pa arbejdsmarkedet 1984-87.* Undervisningsministeriet, Okonomisk statistisk kontor (The position of new graduates on the labour market 1984-87. Ministry of Education, Economics and Statistics Division)

7) Ministry of Education, Economics and Statistics Division

8) Salary statistics of the Confederation of Danish employers

9) N. Groes: *Fleksibilitet pa arbejdsmarkedet - oplaeg til nye undersogelser af arbejdskraftens fleksibilitet.* Notater nr. 12, Institut for Graenseregionsforskning, 1984. (N. Groes: Flexibility in the labour market - proposals for new studies of the flexibility of the workforce. Notes n° 12, Institute of regional studies, the Danish border region, 1984).

ESPAGNE

SPAIN

Antonio Casanueva de Luis

Secreteria General, Consejo de Universidades

Contents

I.	The Spanish educational system	89
II.	The outflow from the educational system Non university education	91
III.	Trends in numbers of university students and numbers leaving higher education	96
IV.	Recent developments in graduate employment	105
V.	Destination of graduates	116
VI.	Policy for matching graduate supply and demand	123
Annex		127

I. THE SPANISH EDUCATIONAL SYSTEM

The structure of the Spanish educational system was established by the 1970 General Education Act and modified by later changes in the University Reform Act (1983) and the Right to Education Act (1985) both of which followed the new Constitution introduced at the end of 1978 (1). The Spanish system has the characteristic features of democratic educational systems in the West: the right to education as a fundamental right that must be guaranteed by the state; free provision of compulsory basic education; democratic participation and control in the management of public schools; academic freedom, etc. There are in addition certain features which are distinct to the Spanish educational system, such as its unified primary and lower secondary education, its flexibility in allowing ready transfer across courses at the higher levels and university autonomy.

The General Education Act established four educational levels:

- Pre-school, General Basic Education (E.G.B.)
- Unified and Comprehensive Baccalaureate (B.U.P.)
- University Preparation Course (C.O.U.)
- University Education

Vocational training was originally devised for those entering the labour market following the E.G.B. and B.U.P. rather than as an education level in itself. However today it is a key part of the secondary education system, together with B.U.P. Finally, the united system established by the General Education Act in 1970 also covers Continuing Adult Education, Special Education, Specialized Studies (2) and Distance Education.

Only the E.G.B. is compulsory; it is the corner stone of the system and is intended to provide a basic level of socialisation for all pupils. B.U.P. educates young people for entry to university training and also for the labour market. Pupils wishing to enter university must first go through secondary education, followed by C.O.U. and then pass the university entrance examination. There is in addition a 'special route' open to those aged over 25 who have no secondary education. They can qualify for university if they can show in the entrance evaluation tests that they have the same academic ability as those who have gone through secondary education.

Universities award qualifications at three levels. First is the Bachelor degree (*diplomado*) or an equivalent title, such as Technical Architect or Technical Engineer. The next level up is the Master's degree (*licenciado*) with equivalent titles, such as Architect or Engineer. Finally the highest level is the Doctorate (*doctor*).

The current basic structure of the Spanish educational system will shortly disappear with the passing, first of the General Planning of the Educational System Act -- already brought before the Congress of Deputies -- and also with the reform of university certificates provided in the 1983 University Reform Act. This latter reform is currently under way and will mean a fundamental change in the training to be given to Spanish university students in the future -- making this more like the European education and better adapted to the demands of the economy.

Notes

1) At the end of this report, two diagrams of the Spanish educational system are given, one produced by the *Instituto Nacional de Estadistica de España (INE)* in its publications on "Statistics of Higher Education in Spain", similar to that in the annual OECD statistical publication, the other drawn from *"Estudios en España. II. Nivel universitario"*, published by the *Secretaria General Técnica* of the Ministry of Education and Science. Both could be improved. Perhaps they complement one another. (Figures 1a and 1b).

2) The General Education Law defines as "specialised studies" (*Enseñanzas Especializadas*) those courses which, because of their distinct nature, are not part of the levels, courses or sectors of the main higher education system. In fact, this category and the equally obscure "other studies" (see Figure 1a) covers a very diverse range of subjects: ceramics, criminology, languages, restoration of art works. Given that, in general, the BUP is needed for entry to these courses, they can be regarded as 'post-secondary education'.

Although data exist on enrolments in these courses, we chose not to quote them in order to keep to our primary concern, higher university education and, in addition, because we think these 'post-secondary' courses are complementary in nature, being followed in parallel to, or after, other courses. In 1986-87, enrolments were 487 000 (453 000 in public, 34 000 in private institutions).

II. THE OUTFLOW FROM THE EDUCATIONAL SYSTEM
NON-UNIVERSITY EDUCATION (1976 to 1986)

General Basic Education (E.G.B.)

Over five and a half million children, 15% of the Spanish population were enrolled in General Basic Education (*Enseñanza general basica*, E.G.B.) in the school year 1986-87. This percentage has remained unchanged throughout the 80's due to compulsory school attendance. However it is about to fall because of the gradual lowering of the country's birth rate.

The students who finish their studies at this level of education are about one in eight of those enrolled in each school year (just under seven hundred thousands) which therefore shows the even spread of students in each year and the insignificant dropout (Table 1).

Table 1
Pupils enrolled in E.G.B. studies and pupils who completed them

	Enrolled	Completed
1980-81	5 605 452	648 864
1984-85	5 640 938	668 715
1985-86	5 594 285	679 574
1986-87	5 575 519	673 280

Source: Estadística de la enseñanza superior en España. Niveles de Preescolar, General Básica y Enseñanzas Medias. 1986/87. Ministry of Education and Science.

Unified and Comprehensive Baccalaureate (B.U.P.), University Preparation Course (C.O.U.) and Vocational Training (F.P.)

The number of students enrolled in B.U.P.(*Bachillerato unificado polivalente*), C.O.U.(*Curso de Orientacion universitaria*) and Vocational Training (*Formacion profesional*) steadily increased between 1975-76 and 1986-87 (Table 2), although annual growth is now stabilising at the lower end of the range seen over the period. Vocational Training has also firmly established itself as a distinct educational level with a rise in enrolments as a proportion of those in B.U.P. and C.O.U. from 33.86% to 36.70%.

The increase in the number of pupils who finished the C.O.U. and Vocational Training between school years 1980-81 and 1986-87 (Table 3) was less than the growth in the total number of pupils enrolled over the same period (19.85% as compared to 21.21%). This is because of "pupil failure" or dropout on C.O.U. and Vocational Training. Nevertheless, in recent years, almost a third of a million pupils completed C.O.U. and Vocational Training courses (1).

Table 2
Pupils enrolled in B.U.P.-C.O.U. and Vocational Training

	BUP/COU	Voc. train.	Total
1980-81	1 091 197	558 808	1 650 005
1984-85	1 182 154	726 000	1 908 154
1985-86	1 230 029	726 249	1 956 278
1986-87	1 265 894	734 186	2 000 080

Source: Estadística de la enseñanza superior en España. Niveles de Preescolar, General Básica y Enseñanzas Medias. 1986/87 Ministry of Education and Science.

Table 3
Pupils who completed C.O.U. and Vocational Training

	C.O.U.	Voc. train.	Total
1980-81	153 200	116 371	269 571
1981-82	155 804	126 304	282 108
1982-83	160 096	141 150	301 246
1983-84	167 688	150 754	318 442
1984-85	170 929	168 167	339 096
1985-86 (1)	161 057	156 037	317 094
1986-87 (2)	167 463	155 581	323 044

(1) Andalusia, data on the academic year 1984-85.
(2) Andalusia, Canarias and Cataluña, provisional data.

Source: Estadística de la enseñanza en España. Niveles de preescolar, general básica y enseñanzas medias. 1986-87.

Tables 2 and 3 can be understood more easily by noting that there were 389 016 and 142 483 pupils enrolled respectively in the first year of B.U.P. and in the first year of Vocational Training. This shows that the main exit from the education system is not straight after pupils finish the upper E.G.B, but rather throughout B.U.P. and Vocational Training and, more significantly, when they finish C.O.U.

University Preparation Course (C.O.U.)

C.O.U. was introduced in 1971 as a result of the General Education Act, and it is intended to be a transition or "bridge" year, prior to entering university. It has two aims: to provide academic training and to prepare pupils for the structure and content of university studies.

C.O.U. marks "a clear division for each yeargroup of young people between those who go on to one or more years in C.O.U. and pass the university entrance examination and their contemporaries who drop out at this final rung on the Spanish educational ladder" (2). The great majority of pupils who finish B.U.P. enrol in the University Preparation Course. This is clear from the number of pupils enrolled in relation to those attending the last year of B.U.P. In 1986-87, there were 275 000 pupils in third year B.U.P. and about 266 000 in C.O.U., which shows that C.O.U. is a mere prolongation of secondary studies.

The figures for pupils enrolled and passing the C.O.U. (Table 4) suggest that this last stage in the educational system, prior to university, is a significant obstacle which limits access to higher education. It divides those who will study at university from the rest who will enter the labour market. Over 167 000 pupils passed the C.O.U. - almost 63% of those who enrolled.

Table 4
Pupils enrolled in C.O.U. and pupils who passed (1986-87)

	Male	Female	Total
Enrolled	123 344	142 984	266 328
Passed	76 426	91 037	167 463
Pass rates (%)	61.96	63.67	62.88

Source: Estadística de la enseñanza en España. Niveles de preescolar, general básica y enseñanzas medias 1986-87.

For all its distinct role as the main route for pupils wishing to go to university it has become just another school year added to B.U.P.. However those in charge of secondary education tend to see it as part of the university, while higher education institutions complain that they control neither its structure nor its content. The great contradiction of C.O.U., stressed in the 1975 FOESSA report, is that: "a pupil who has undergone preparation for entering University for a year can then be denied this very entry -- by not passing the entrance tests --, which leaves him with no alternative but second cycle Vocational Training, for which a year's C.O.U. is not required". The report also noted that ex-C.O.U. pupils seeking training would thereby lack "adequate information about the labour market and career implications of different types of education and training for the various courses and subjects on offer" (3).

It is not surprising therefore, that the future of the C.O.U. is bleak and it is condemned to disappear in a coming reform of the educational system. The "White Book for the Reform of the Educational System," which includes B.U.P. and C.O.U. in the "Secondary Education", points out that the new B.U.P.-C.O.U. introduced after the General Education Act "has never succeeded in obtaining a satisfactory balance between its role as preparation for higher education and its need to be a useful qualification in its own right" (4).

Entrance examinations and limits on access to university

The entrance examinations were introduced because the secondary education courses were insufficiently selective and could not identify whether students had the ability to undertake university education. The entrance examinations have gradually become the main barrier to be overcome by pupils of B.U.P. and C.O.U. wishing to enter University. Selection for university is based on an average mark taken from the entrance examination and the achievements in B.U.P. and C.O.U. This average mark has to be higher than that required by the higher education institutions. This reveals a number of contradictions in the educational system: relative position of state-run and private schools; lack of coordination between the different educational levels; different entry requirements among the various institutions. This sometimes forces students to choose courses for which they have no particular vocation (5). Almost a quarter of those who take the entrance exam fail (Table 5) and therefore do not go to university.

Table 5
Pupils sitting university entrance examinations and pupils who passed (1986-87)

	Male	Female	Total
Enrolled	93 937	112 488	206 425
Passed	71 651	87 431	159 082
Pass rates (%)	76.27	77.72	77.06

Source: Estadística de la enseñanza en España. Nivel superior. Curso 1986-87. I.N.E., Madrid, 1989.

The University Reform Act introduced a new feature into the selection system by allowing individual universities to set limits on the numbers of students they accepted. This meant that students who failed to qualify for one faculty might be eligible for another with a lower entry standard, on the basis of an evaluation which has no legal value, but which is recognized by academic authorities. These authorities establish the maximum limit for the admission of students at the Academic Committee of the Universities Council, at which all the public universities are represented.

The maximum entry agreed for the academic year 1990-91 allows for a significant increase in the number of places available at faculties which restrict entry compared with the previous year. The total number of places available for new students rose from, 149 981 to 163 844, a 9.24 per cent increase. These figures have to be seen in the light of the number of institutions which do restrict the entry of new students and of those which do not. The number with limited access has increased, as another 43 centres (a little over 5%) have set new restrictions. Most of these are recently established courses with limited capacity and resources, such as the Universities of La Coruña, Vigo and Carlos III in Madrid, which was established in 1989.

The supply of first year places in Spanish public universities is not restricted, however, to those in faculties with limited access. In addition to those faculties which do not limit entry there are also an additional, unquantified, number of places at the newly established centres, not included in the regulations on limited entrance published in the Official Gazette, that will start their teaching activities in the forthcoming academic year. Numbers to be admitted will be set by the university responsible, on the basis of initial planning. Finally, the National Distance University has set no limits on the number of students it will take and in the light of this, in overall numerical terms, the supply and demand for first year places are in balance. In qualitative terms however this is not so and there is excess demand for places.

Notes

1) The output from vocational education (155 581 in 1986-87) corresponds to the total output of FP. Students completing FP1 in that year numbered 97 597 of whom 50 000 were women. Students completing FP2 in that year numbered 57 984 of whom 5 394 were from the ordinary system (4 490 were women) and 52 590 were from *Enseñanzas Especializadas* (24 186 women).

   We are not aware of data on the flows of students having completed secondary education entering FP2 or 'other non-university courses'. There are 'bridges' available between BUP and FP but our impression is that these are seldom used. However the INE publishes data on non-university higher education (tourism, physical education, military academies etc): enrolments in 1986-87 were about 52 000 (of which over half were from the *Escuelas de Graduados Sociales*, now integrated into the university) and graduates were about 6 500.

2) Moncada, A.: "*Educación y empleo*", p. 46.

3) FOESSA, 1975: "*Estudios sociológicos sobre la situación social de España. 1975*". Ed. Euramérica, Madrid, 1976, pp. 260-261.

4) Ministry of Education and Science: "*Libro Blanco para la Reforma del Sistema Educativo*". Madrid, 1989, p. 17.

5) "In the academic year 1984-85, the average mark required for studying Medicine was 7.2. Students who did not attain this minimum as an average in the university entrance tests, B.U.P. and C.O.U., were obliged to take other courses. The most frequent second choice subjects were Biology and Psychology, particularly the former, as these studies are similar (at least the first year) to those of Medicine. However, only a small group of students were allowed to study Biology and Psychology. This problem was just as severe with Veterinary studies. Consequently, students who wanted to study Medicine or Veterinary studies had to choose between Physics, Chemistry or Mathematics. Most of them ended up studying Chemistry". (Latiesa, M.: "*Demanda de educación superior: evaluaciones y condicionamientos de los estudiantes en la elección de carrera*", in *Revista Española de Investigaciones Sociológicas*, 45/89, p.109).

III. TRENDS IN NUMBERS OF UNIVERSITY STUDENTS AND NUMBERS LEAVING HIGHER EDUCATION

Trends in university student numbers

In the academic year 1986-87, 167 463 B.U.P.-C.O.U. pupils finished their courses as did 155 581 Vocational Training pupils. First-year university entrants in the following academic year (1987-88) rose to 201 794 applications. This includes students repeating their first year, mature students and foreign students registered in Spanish universities (1).

The internal distribution of first year students across the sectors of higher education in 1987-88 repeats the imbalanced pattern of previous years. Some 80 615 students entered University Schools (*Escuelas Universitarias*) and another 121 179 registered in the Faculties (*Facultades*) and Higher Technical Schools (*Escuelas Técnicas Superiores*).

The expansion of university student numbers in Spain over the last twenty years has been continuous and remarkable (Table 6). In nineteen years Spanish university institutions have trebled their 1970-71 student numbers to reach over a million students in 1988-89. The number of students enrolled in the 18-24 age group rose from 9.81% in 1970-71 to 15.50% in 1979-80 and 23.11% in 1987-88, which is very close to what can be considered the optimum level (between 25% and 30%).

Table 6
Population aged 18-24 (A), higher education students (B) (thousands) and higher education participation rates (%)

	A	increase	B	increase	B/A
1970-71	3 614.6	100	354.9	100	9.81
1975-76	3 810.4	105.4	557.4	157	14.62
1980-81	4 199.4	116.1	651.1	183	15.50
1985-86	4 537.7	125.5	854.1	240	18.82
1987-88	4 621.9 *	127.8	960.9	270	20.79
1988-89	4 619.0 *	127.7	1 067.8 **	300.8	23.11

(*) INE evaluation on 1.7.88 and on 1.7.89, in "Proyección de la población española para el período 1980-2010".
(**) Provisional data.

Source : Calculations based on the 1970 and 1981 population censuses, the municipal censuses and the statistics of the university population.

The growing university enrolment rate contrasts with the falling numbers in the population aged 18-24 at the end of the 80's. Between 1987-88 and 1988-89 the 18-24 year population fell again while the number of higher education students rose by 11.13%. The number of university students might therefore tend to stabilise or fall in the medium term but this will be offset by factors working in the opposite direction. Examples are greater social equality of access to education, re-entrance of former university students, the greater popularity of university degrees after their reform, and growth in the general cultural level of society.

The distribution of students amongst the Faculties, the *Escuelas técnicas superiores* and *Escuelas universitarias* is very unequal (Table 7). The Faculties accounted for over 66% of the university students in 1987-88, while the students at *Escuelas técnicas superiores* were just 6% of the total and the *Escuelas universitarias* made up the other 27.50%. Some 70% of students in this latter group were enrolled in the non-technical *Escuelas universitarias*, reflecting a similar imbalance.

Table 7
Students enrolled, by type of institution (Absolute values)

	1982	1983	1984	1985	1986	1987
Total	691.152	744.115	788.168	854.104	902 284	960.936
Faculties	464.105	506.398	537.725	576.896	605 543	638.132
E.T.S.	46.278	48.700	50 991	53.701	55 967	58.541
Techn. U. Schools	53.676	54.898	57.564	64.054	69.952	78.690
Non-techn. U. S.	128.093	134.119	141.886	159.453	170.822	185.573

Source: Universities Council. Anuario de estadística universitaria. 1989.

Table 8
Students enrolled, by type of institution (Index numbers)

	1982	1983	1984	1985	1986	1987
Total	100	107.5	113.9	123.4	130.4	138.8
Faculties	100	109.1	115.9	124.3	130.5	137.5
E.T.S.	100	105.2	110.2	116.0	120.9	126.5
Techn. U. Schools	100	102.3	107.2	119.3	130.3	146.6
Non-techn. U. S.	100	104.7	110.8	124.5	133.4	144.9

Source: Universities Council. Anuario de estadística universitaria. 1989.

Trends in student numbers, taking 1982 as the base (Table 8), show the greater popularity of the *Escuelas universitarias* in 1986-87 and 1987-88 compared to the Faculties and particularly relative to the *Escuelas técnicas superiores* where the number of students rose by just an annual 5% since 1982.

The net outflow (totals)

Table 9 shows the numbers of students who completed their studies between 1982-83 and 1986-87. The Table shows that, of every hundred students who finish their studies in Spain, sixty have taken graduate studies in a Faculty; about thirty one completed undergraduate studies in a non-technical *Escuela universitaria* six took undergraduate studies in a technical *Escuela universitaria* and only three obtained a degree in an *Escuela técnica superior*.

Table 9
Students who completed higher education courses (absolute values)

	1983	1984	1985	1986	1987
Total	76.814	81.046	85.087	90.873	98.820
Faculties	37.835	43.456	47.538	52.343	58.979
E.T.S.	3.156	2.823	3.017	3.031	3.308
Techn. U. Schools	4.918	5.137	5.415	5.516	5.967
Non-techn. U. S.	30.905	29 630	29.117	29.983	30 566

Source: Universities Council. Anuario de estadística universitaria. 1989.

Table 10 shows the trend between 1983 and 1987 in the number of students graduating by sector (indices). The Table shows that the numbers graduating with a Masters degree from the Faculties rose much faster that the overall graduate total. On the other hand, the numbers with degrees from non-technical *Escuelas universitarias* fell over the period to below the 1983 level.

Table 10
Students who completed higher education courses (index numbers)

	1983	1984	1985	1986	1987
Total	100	105.5	110.8	118.3	128.6
Faculties	100	114.9	125.6	138.3	155.9
E.T.S.	100	89.4	95.6	96.0	104.0
Techn. U. Schools	100	104.5	110.1	112.2	121.3
Non-techn. U. Schools	100	95.9	94.2	97.0	98.9

Source: Universities Council. Anuario de estadística universitaria. 1989.

The figures in Table 10 can be linked to the growth in the numbers of students in the Faculties and non-technical *Escuelas universitarias* over the same period (Tables 8 and 9). This shows that the fall in the number of students with a degree from the non-technical *Escuelas universitarias* is not because of a transfer from first to higher degree study. The relative increase of students at non-technical *Escuelas universitarias* was greater than that at the Faculties. There must be other reasons such as the higher standard demanded at the former and the greater drop-out rate due to favourable economic circumstances or to students' disillusionment with university life.

The number of graduates from *Escuelas técnicas superiores* or technical *Escuelas universitarias* has grown fairly slowly. The increase has been steadier at the undergraduate level (up about 5% between 1983 and 1987) than for the graduate institutions where numbers fell below their 1983 levels before recovering and increasing slightly in 1987.

The net outflow (by field of study)

Looking at the figures in more detail, by subject and sector of higher education (Table 11), the University graduate subject distribution has been fairly steady between 1983 and 1989. However the impact of new subjects (Computer science, Library Science, Physiotherapy, Social work) can be seen as the effects of the entrance restrictions for Medicine and E.G.B. Teaching. Perhaps the most significant change is that the imbalance between graduates from Faculties and *Escuelas técnicas superiores* and those from *Escuelas universitarias* is gradually becoming more pronounced. In 1983, the latter accounted for 47% of the total number of graduates but in 1987 they only accounted for 37%. This shows that graduate studies have risen at the expense of undergraduate studies so that, at the end of 1986-67, two out of every three graduates were Masters (*licenciados*) and only one out of three had a Bachelor degree (*diplomados*).

Figures on University enrolments in 1987-88, as noted earlier, show that the proportion of all degrees awarded by *Escuelas universitarias* will continue to fall.

Some 77.01% of those graduating in 1983 came from just seven university courses (Sciences, Economics and Business Studies, Law, Arts and Humanities, Medicine, Nursing and E.G.B. Teaching). In 1988 these seven subjects accounted for a slightly lower proportion of the total at 73.3%.

It is also notable that in 1987 just over 3 300 engineers obtained a Master's degree and 5 900 a Bachelor's degree. Such low figures hardly suggest any "boom" in higher technological training. Indeed a well-known work, published in 1979, on the Spanish university system pointed out that 2 370 engineers graduated in 1976, "a figure which has remained almost the same since 1969, when educational reform began to be talked about and the demand for higher education rose sharply" (2).

As various authors have indicated, "Spanish engineers have been closely bound up with capital and management in large and middle-sized factories. Given the technological choices of the country, which depends on foreign patents and licences, and the comprehensive nature of their studies, they have

Table 11
Students who completed higher education courses, by type of institution and field of study (absolute numbers)

	1983	1987
Faculties	37 835	58 979
- Fine arts	379	1 603
- Sciences (*)	3 894	6 973
- Economics and Business Studies (*)	3 061	6 343
- Media and Communication Sciences	873	2 028
- Marine Sciences		44
- Political and Social Sciences	300	523
- Law (*)	4 977	10 681
- Canon Law	34	29
- Pharmacy	1 533	2 240
- Humanities (*)	8 901	17 349
- Computer Science	221	625
- Medicine (*)	10 355	6 703
- Psychology	2 737	2 994
- Theology	114	81
- Veterinary	456	1 303
Higher Technical Schools	3 156	3 308
- Architecture	926	969
- Public Works Engineering	330	346
- Industrial Engineering	1 101	1 031
- Telecommunications Engineering	288	275
- Other types of engineering	511	687
Technical University Schools	4 918	5 967
- Technical Architecture	988	1 133
- Technical Agricultural Engineering	774	1 115
- Technical Industrial Engineering	2 333	2 606
- Technical Public Works Engineering	164	168
- Technical Telecommunications Engineering	224	319
- Technical Topographical Engineering	22	103
- Other types of Technical Engineering	413	523
Non-Technical University Schools	30 905	30 566
- Library and Documentation Science	14	156
- Nursing (*)	4 662	5 257
- Statistics	10	41
- Business Studies	2 630	3 698
- Physiotherapy		65
- Computer Sciences	12	249
- Optics	163	230
- E.G.B. Teaching (*)	23 307	19 141
- Social Work		1 578
Total	76 814	98 820

Source: Universities Council. Anuario de estadística universitaria. 1989.

tended to avoid the presence of colleagues from their own field, with a certain degree of training, and to make do with technicians from amongst the specialized workmen or from vocational training who sufficed for productive ends from both the scientific and capitalist points of view (...). This matter has been echoed in the disputes between the different Professional Societies over settling remuneration and job levels..." (3). Also, "the lack of a real attachment of the *Escuelas universitarias* to the Spanish university, in spite of their formal integration after 1970; the scant appreciation, even knowledge, of this type of training in Spanish society; the traditional prevalence of a humanistic and literary type of culture and the fact that scientific thought, practice and research have no firm roots in Spain; differences between the social classes in their subject choices with a clear bias in the upper classes towards technical education and in the lower classes towards arts-based education, leading to teacher training, because this is the only readily observable professional role model (together with that of the medical doctor), the malthusianism of the engineering Schools (fearing that more engineers will depress pay and job prospects); and above all the university expansion policy of the 70's, whose only aim was to create cheap higher education places, ignoring any type of planning": all these are factors that have influenced the profound bias of the university courses towards arts and social sciences.

Academic failure. Dropouts and successes in higher education

The percentage of students completing university studies relative to entrants 3, 5 or 6 years earlier has fallen slowly between 1984 and 1987. This percentage varies markedly by subject and between the non-technical *Escuelas universitarias* (54%) and the other sectors: Faculties (22.9%), *Escuelas técnicas superiores* (22.9%), and technical *Escuelas universitarias* (21.4%). Clearly it is the non-technical *Escuelas universitarias* which raise the overall average.

Table 12
*Students completing higher education courses,
as a % of those entering 3, 5 or 6 years earlier*

	1984	1985	1986	1987
Total	44.9	44.4	43.0	42.6
Faculties	43.7	44.2	43.7	44.2
E.T.S.	29.7	24.0	21.7	22.9
Technical University Schools	19.2	21.2	20.9	21.4
Non-technical University Schools	66.0	63.4	58.6	54.0

Source: Universities Council. Anuario de estadística universitaria. 1989.

Another factor to be considered is the large minority of students -- about four out of ten -- who are repeating an academic year. Here too there are significant differences between sectors. While about 38% of students in Faculties and non-technical *Escuelas universitarias* repeat academic years, over 55% of the students at *Escuelas técnicas superiores* and almost 50% of the students at technical *Escuelas universitarias* have to repeat some year of their course.

A further way of measuring failure is to compare the average age of students in each year of their course with the age that would be predicted from the entrants. For the faculties the actual age is four years more than predicted. However these figures include mature students from the Distance University and this will distort the comparison. The actual/predicted difference for the *Escuelas técnicas superiores* is a little over three years.

Dropping out and repeat years are clearly two aspects of the same problem although each has distinct features and both will reflect not just purely academic circumstances (quality of education), but economic and social factors.

Women graduates in Spain. Recent trends

In the 80's women became the majority at Spanish universities. In 1982-83 men were slightly in the majority but by 1986-87, this majority had disappeared as the proportion of women enrolling had increased since the beginning of the decade. This is apparent from Table 13, which also shows that the proportion of women students at non-technical *Escuelas universitarias* has been almost constant over the last five years. Most of these students were studying Education, Nursing, and to a lesser extent, Social Work.

Annual figures for the number of university students and graduates suggest that technical education in Spain is mainly a male preserve. The percentage of women at *Escuelas técnicas superiores* and at technical *Escuelas universitarias* was under 15% in each case.

Table 13
Female shares of higher education enrolments, by type of institution

	1982	1983	1984	1985	1986
Total	46.8	48.1	48.4	49.5	50.1
Faculties	49.5	51.0	51.5	52.8	53.7
E.T.S.	11.0	12.2	13.1	14.1	14.8
Techn. U. Schools	10.5	11.1	11.4	11.9	12.6
Non-techn. U. Schools	65.2	65.3	64.5	64.2	64.3

Source: Universities Council. Anuario de estadística universitaria. 1989.

However, there is beginning to be a change in the subjects chosen by women, who have discovered, somewhat late in the day, the better job opportunities in the technical fields. Nevertheless, there is no prospect yet that the distribution of women across the four sectors of higher education will be comparable to that of men (Table 13).

The most popular subjects for women have been the Humanities, Social Sciences, and the Health Sciences. However the greatest growth in subject demand in recent years has been for the Humanities and Social Sciences and for Engineering and Technology (Table 14).

Table 14
Female higher education enrolments, by field of study (index numbers)

	1982	1983	1984	1985	1986
Fields of study	100	110.5	117.9	130.4	139.7
Humanities and Social Sciences	100	112.9	121.9	137.2	147.7
Exact and Natural Sciences	100	111.7	117.3	128.2	136.5
Health Sciences	100	100.2	101.4	103.0	106.1
Engineering and Technology	100	111.9	123.9	142.3	160.1

Source: Universities Council. "Anuario de estadística universitaria. 1989".

In 1986-87 women were 56 152 out of a total of 98 820 university graduates. But the most significant factor in these figures is not the total numbers and their growth from year to year (Table 15), but rather the very small number of women, less than 1 200, amongst graduates of *Escuelas técnicas superiores* and of technical *Escuelas universitarias*.

Table 15
Female graduates, by type of institution (absolute numbers)

	1983	1984	1985	1986	1987
Total	41 274	43 607	44 861	49 585	56 152
Faculties	18 440	21 977	23 550	26 974	32 460
E.T.S.	257	234	267	330	421
Techn. U. Schools	432	495	599	669	760
Non-techn. U. Schools	22 145	20 901	20 445	21 612	22 511

Source: Universities Council. "Anuario de estadística universitaria. 1989".

Women made up the majority of non-technical *Escuelas universitarias* graduates (73.64%) and they were also over half of the graduates in Faculties (56.82%) but they were just 13% of the output from *Escuelas técnicas superiores* and *Escuelas universitarias* (Table 16).

Table 16
Female shares of higher education graduates, by type of institution

	1982	1983	1984	1985	1986
Total	53.73	53.80	52.72	54.56	56.82
Faculties	48.73	50.57	49.53	51.53	55.03
E.T.S.	8.14	8.28	8.84	10.88	12.76
Techn. U. Schools	8.78	9.63	11.06	12.12	12.73
Non-techn. U. Schools	71.65	70.53	70.21	72.08	73.64

Source: Universities Council. "Anuario de estadística universitaria. 1989".

In contrast with the steady growth of women graduates from the technical *Escuelas universitarias*, in the non-technical *Escuelas universitarias* the number of women graduates fell between 1982 and 1984. Numbers subsequently recovered but this seems to have been because of the fall in the number of female students in E.G.B. teacher training who later transferred to Nursing Schools.

The only available measure of academic failure amongst women university students is by comparison of numbers graduating with numbers of entrants three, five or six years earlier. Non-completion for women is lower than for men. The higher success rate for women is also evident in the University Preparation Course studies and in the university entrance exams in 1986-87 (Tables 4 and 5).

However, any comparison between the sexes should take account of their differing social circumstances. Men have a privileged position in the labour market, which is still male-dominated, and so can afford to give less importance than women to university studies.

Notes

1) The authors of the report consider the transfer rate from C.O.U. to university year to be around 80.85%; see Fig. 2 at the end of this report (Note by the Secretariat).

2) Martin Moreno, J. and de Miguel, A.: *"Universidad: fabrica de parados"*. Editorial Vicens Vives, Barcelona, 1979, p. 130.

3) Moncada, A.: op. cit, p. 49.

4) Lamo, E.: *"Universidad y mercado de trabajo"*, in *"Planificacion de la educacion y mercado de trabajo"*, VV.AA (coord. Julio Grao). Ed. Narcea. Madrid, 1988, p 160.

IV. RECENT DEVELOPMENTS IN GRADUATE EMPLOYMENT (1987-1990)

The "stock" of graduates

The number of graduates in Spain is over two million two hundred thousand persons; the number who are economically active amount to less than one million seven hundred thousand. The growth of the university system between 1981 and 1989, when student demand for higher education was at its height, has meant that the number of persons with a university qualification has risen by more than seven hundred thousand (Table 17). The decrease in the labour force participation rates which took place in the middle of the decade might be because of the legal measures and the agreements between unions and employers which imposed retirement at sixty five years of age (Reform of the Public Administration Act and Framework Agreement for Workers). The subsequent recovery of this participation has been because graduates have been in a better position to continue working in the private sector once their employment in the public sector has ended (1).

Table 17
Total and active graduate population (thousands) and labour force rates (%) Higher and first degrees

	higher degree	first degree	Total
1981			
Total	678.2	834.3	1 512.5
Active	529.3	643.8	1 173.1
Participation rate	78.04	77.16	77.56
1986			
Total	902.4	1 031.1	1 933.5
Active	634.6	707.3	1 341.9
Participation rate	70.32	68.59	69.40
1989			
Total	1 005.8	1 283.8	2 289.6
Active	824.7	873.1	1 697.8
Participation rate	81.99	68.00	74.15

Source: 1981 Census, Labour Force Survey III-1986 and Labour Force Survey IV-1989.

On the other hand, the average age of university graduates has decreased slightly between 1981 and 1989, since graduates less than 35 years old have increased their proportion from 45.09% to 50.88% (Table 18).

Table 18
Distribution of graduates by age group (thousands)

	1981	1989
Under 20	1.5	1.0
from 20 to 24	167.7	348.5
from 25 to 34	512.9	815.5
from 35 to 44	311.0	499.5
from 45 to 54	220.7	261.5
from 55 to 64	143.6	202.2
65 and over	155.0	161.5

Source: 1981 Census and Labour Force Survey IV-1989

It is important to consider here whether there is an over-supply of graduates and should their number be reduced or, on the contrary, are there too few graduates and their numbers should be increased. Clearly the number of Spanish university students cannot be considered to be excessive in relation to the country's level of development and to the ratio of the number of university students per 100 000 inhabitants. Neither should the number of graduates be considered as disproportionate, since the size of the stock follows from the flow of newly qualified. Any assessmenmt of the extent of over -- or under -- supply should look both at the output of the university system, noting particularly its concentration on the humanities - but also the labour market for different occupations (2).

Employment of graduates (aggregated data)

In Spain, the National Statistics Institute operates a "Labour Force Survey" on a quarterly basis which monitors changes in the economy and the labour market. The survey gives details of the total, economically active, employed population, the unemployed, those not in the labour force, as well as of those in full-time education, type of work contract, under employment, 'discouraged workers', etc. However, beginning in the second quarter of 1987, the survey underwent major changes, the design and contents of the questionnaire and the definitions used for estimating the basic labour market variables, including economic activity, occupation and unemployment. This means that it is only possible to make reliable comparisons over time from 1987 quarter two.

The boom in the Spanish economy at the end of the 1980's meant that the increase in the working population resulting from demographic factors did not lead to higher unemployment. Indeed unemployment fell for all educational levels but particularly for those with secondary education (*Bachillerato* and Vocational Training).

The Labour Force Survey for the fourth quarter of 1989 shows that there were a little over two hundred and twenty thousand university graduates unemployed (Table 19). The unemployment rate for persons with university education was 13%, lower than the overall unemployment rate (on the new, post-1987 Q2 definition) of 16.89%. Paradoxically, the unemployment rate of those who had been educated only to primary level was the same as for higher degree graduates.

Growth in graduate employment has been satisfactory, but it has not been sufficient to absorb the growing flows of new graduates and the already existing "stock" of unemployed graduates. The active population educated at first degree increased by almost 120 000 and the active population of those with higher degrees rose by a little over 150 000. However the numbers employed at both of these levels grew by approximately 140 000. Overall, graduate unemployment was reduced by some 7 000, thanks to the better performance in employment of first degree graduates. For those with higher degrees the numbers unemployed rose from 100 200 to 113 600 persons (3).

Some graduates -- approximately five thousand according to the latest Labour Force Survey for the last quarter of 1989 -- are regarded as in 'underemployment'. This is defined as 'employment which is below the level that a person with a particular qualification would be expected to occupy' (4). Underemployed graduates represented 12.46% of the total number of unemployed graduates and just 0.33% of all persons in professional employment. So underemployment is not so far specially significant in the official statistics. However it is potentially important because "one of the difficulties in assessing the level of underemployment is the changing nature of the link between education and employment' (5).

Employment of graduates (disaggregated data)

Graduates enter the labour market at a relatively young age, having just finished their studies and with little information on the requirements and the recruitment methods of companies. This might explain why they tend to take some time to decide a first career. The biggest problem when they have decided, is to find their first job because once in employment very few become unemployed again. Thus the unemployment rate of graduates aged 30 and over is much lower than that for new graduates.

Age and sex

Women graduates have higher unemployment than men and unemployment is highest for women under 40 years of age and for those who have taken a higher degree. The unemployment rate of women with higher degrees aged under thirty was 50%. The unemployment rate for men graduates under thirty is also high: one in three was unemployed. Men under 24, who have just finished their studies, had very high unemployment rates (Table 20).

There are more women than men graduates entering the labour force each year and they are younger on average (women first degree graduates are on average under 30 and higher degree graduates are under 35). However women graduates' labour force participation rate decreases considerably for older age-groups (Table 21).

Table 19

Numbers active, employed and unemployed (thousands)
and unemployment rates (%) by level of education

	Active	Employed	Unemployed	Unemployment rate
1980				
No education	1 971.3	1 764.0	207.3	10.52
Primary education	7 810.1	7 077.1	733.0	9.39
Secondary education	2 421.4	1 972.2	449.2	18.55
First degree level	506.0	459.3	46.7	9.22
Higher degree level	408.3	373.7	34.6	8.49
Total	13 117.1	11 646.3	1 470.9	11.21
1987				
No education	1 659.6	1 326.1	333.5	20.09
Primary education	6 376.7	5 349.1	1 027.6	16.11
Secondary education	4 804.1	3 456.1	1 348.0	28.06
First degree level	754.7	627.5	127.2	16.85
Higher degree level	671.0	570.8	100.2	14.94
Total	14 266.0	11 329.6	2 936.5	20.58
1989				
No education	1 721.9	1 439.1	282.8	16.42
Primary education	5 726.4	4 938.8	787.6	13.75
Secondary education	5 783.8	4 553.2	1 230.6	21.28
First degree level	873.1	765.9	197.2	12.28
Higher degree level	824.7	711.2	113.6	13.77
Total	14 929.9	12 408.2	2 521.8	16.89

Source: National Statistics Institute (Labour Force Survey II-87 and IV-89).

A recent study of women's economic activity has emphasized the point that women have higher unemployment than men at all levels of education (6). The Labour Force Survey for the last quarter of 1989 shows this, but the unemployment differential is particularly marked for higher degrees. Nearly one in four women higher degree graduates was unemployed, compared with just one in twelve men. For first degrees one woman in six but just one man in fourteen was unemployed (Table 22).

Table 20
*Unemployment, by level of education, age group and sex
numbers active and unemployed (thousands) and unemployment rates (%)*

	First degrees			Higher degrees		
	Active	Unemployed	%	Active	Unemployed	%
Both sexes						
Total	873.1	107.2	12.28	824.7	113.6	13.77
from 16 to 19	1.0	.5	54.32	-	-	
from 20 to 24	92.3	35.9	38.94	44.9	23.8	53.02
from 25 to 29	170.6	36.0	21.09	191.4	58.9	30.77
from 30 to 44	402.0	28.9	7.20	385.1	26.3	6.82
from 45 to 54	131.7	4.2	3.16	107.0	2.9	2.68
55 and over	75.6	1.7	2.21	96.3	1.7	1.80
Men						
Total	401.5	28.6	7.12	519.9	39.4	7.57
from 16 to 19	.7	.5	77.76	- -	- -	- -
from 20 to 24	21.6	7.1	32.78	18.0	7.6	42.08
from 25 to 29	64.3	9.4	14.62	85.3	18.1	21.22
from 30 to 44	192.6	8.1	4.20	245.7	10.7	4.36
from 45 to 54	77.0	2.8	3.62	86.2	1.9	2.18
55 and over	45.4	.7	1.62	84.8	1.1	1.34
Women						
Total	471.6	78.6	16.66	304.8	74.2	24.34
from 16 to 19	.3	.0	.00	- -	- -	- -
from 20 to 24	70.7	28.9	40.82	26.9	16.2	60.31
from 25 to 29	106.3	26.6	25.00	106.1	40.8	38.45
from 30 to 44	209.4	20.8	9.95	139.4	15.6	11.16
from 45 to 54	54.7	1.4	2.52	20.8	1.0	4.76
55 and over	30.2	.9	3.09	11.6	.6	5.17

Source: National Statistics Institute (Labour Force Survey IV-89).

Time spent looking for work

Table 23 shows that 40% of unemployed graduates (89 500) had been seeking work for two years or more. The majority of that 40% (some 70%) was women, consisting of equal numbers of university graduates and higher degree graduates. For men graduates, less than 12% of all those unemployed (26 000) had ben looking for a job for two years or more.

Table 21

Labour force participation, by level of education, age group and sex; total and active population (thousands) and labour force participation rates (%)

	First degrees			Higher degrees		
	Total	Active	%	Total	Active	%
Men						
Total	576.6	401.5	69.76	625.7	519.9	83.10
from 16 to 19	.7	.7	100	-	-	-
from 20 to 24	105.1	21.6	20.50	37.5	18.0	47.87
from 25 to 29	97.0	64.3	66.27	107.4	85.3	79.41
from 30 to 34	76.3	74.1	97.13	96.0	93.1	96.90
from 35 to 39	64.3	62.9	97.94	81.4	80.3	98.74
from 40 to 44	56.0	55.6	99.23	73.1	72.3	98.94
from 45 to 49	45.8	45.8	100	51.2	51.1	99.53
50 and over	130.4	76.6	58.74	179.0	119.9	66.98
Women						
Total	708.3	471.6	66.58	380.1	304.8	80.19
from 16 to 19	.4	.3	74.46	-	-	-
from 20 to 24	166.7	70.7	42.40	39.1	26.9	68.90
from 25 to 29	129.5	106.3	82.09	124.0	106.1	85.56
from 30 to 34	105.9	88.5	83.53	79.3	67.4	84.94
from 35 to 39	74.3	65.3	87.95	52.2	45.3	86.72
from 40 to 44	67.4	55.6	82.53	31.0	26.8	86.24
from 45 to 49	38.8	30.9	79.67	19.4	14.9	76.84
50 and over	125.2	54.1	43.21	35.0	17.5	50.00
Both sexes						
Total	1 283.8	873.1	68.01	1 005.8	824.7	82.00
from 16 to 19	1.0	1.0	90.64	-	-	-
from 20 to 24	271.9	92.3	33.93	76.6	44.9	58.60
from 25 to 29	226.5	170.6	75.31	231.4	191.4	82.70
from 30 to 34	182.2	162.6	89.22	175.4	160.4	
from 35 to 39	138.5	128.3	92.59	133.6	125.6	94.04
from 40 to 44	123.3	111.1	90.11	104.1	99.1	95.16
from 45 to 49	84.6	76.7	90.68	70.6	66.1	93.56
50 and over	255.8	130.7	51.09	214.2	137.3	64.09

Source: National Statistics Institute (Labour Force Survey IV-89).

Table 22
*Numbers active, employed, unemployed (thousands)
and labour force participation and unemployment rates (%),
by sex and level of education*

	Men	Women	Total
1987			
Total active population	9 573.9	4 692.1	14 266.0
Employed	7 947.2	3 382.3	11 329.6
Unemployed	1 626.7	1 309.8	2 936.5
L.F.P. rate	83.00	72.08	79.41
Unemployment rate	16.99	27.91	20.58
Active population with first degrees	375.3	379.4	754.7
Employed	334.7	292.9	627.5
Unemployed	40.6	86.6	127.2
L.F.P. rate	89.18	77.20	83.14
Unemployment rate	10.82	22.81	16.85
Active population with higher degrees	445.5	225.5	671.0
Employed	400.6	170.1	570.8
Unemployed	44.9	55.3	100.2
L.F.P. rate	89.92	75.43	85.06
Unemployment rate	10.07	24.54	14.94
1989			
Total active population	9 759.7	5 170.3	14 929.9
Employed	8 520.1	3 888.1	12 408.2
Unemployed	1 239.6	1 282.2	2 521.8
L.F.P. rate	87.20	75.20	83.10
Unemployment rate	12.70	32.97	20.32
Active population with first degrees	401.5	471.6	873.1
Employed	372.9	393.0	765.9
Unemployed	28.6	78.6	107.2
L.F.P. rate	92.80	83.30	87.70
Unemployment rate	7.12	16.66	12.88
Active population with higher degrees	519.9	304.8	824.7
Employed	480.5	230.6	711.2
Unemployed	39.4	74.2	113.6
L.F.P. rate	92.40	75.60	86.20
Unemployment rate	7.57	24.34	13.77

Source: National Statistics Institute (Labour Force Survey II-87 and IV-89).

Table 23

Numbers unemployed, by duration of job search, level of education and sex
(thousands)

	All levels	Illierates	No educ.	Primary educ.	Second. educ.	Vocat. train.	First degree	Higher degree
Both sexes								
Total	2 521.8	52.1	30.7	787.6	981.7	248.9	107.2	113.6
Less than 1 month	51.3	1.5	7.7	16.4	15.2	7.6	1.5	1.4
From 1 to 2 months	423.6	9.8	47.4	135.3	161.7	41.3	13.1	15.0
From 3 to 5 months	314.0	8.8	27.0	104.7	118.9	28.7	13.8	12.0
From 6 to 11 months	321.7	8.3	36.4	103.3	121.0	28.4	13.1	11.2
From 1 to 2 years	433.3	9.3	34.5	132.3	171.0	42.0	20.6	23.4
More than 2 years	945.2	14.4	74.6	287.6	382.4	96.8	42.0	47.5
Not classifiable	32.7	.2	3.0	8.0	11.4	4.0	2.9	3.1
Men								
Total	1 239.6	34.2	163.1	443.8	428.2	102.3	28.6	39.4
Less than 1 month	32.5	1.4	6.4	10.5	9.0	4.2	.3	.7
From 1 to 2 months	259.5	6.6	36.0	91.0	95.8	22.9	3.3	4.0
From 3 to 5 months	179.9	6.0	20.5	68.3	62.5	13.7	3.7	5.2
From 6 to 11 months	173.9	5.7	25.0	59.6	60.0	14.8	4.4	4.4
From 1 to 2 years	205.0	6.0	24.1	74.1	71.8	16.1	6.2	6.7
More than 2 years	370.4	8.6	49.1	133.8	124.7	28.1	9.8	16.2
Not classifiable	18.4		2.0	6.4	4.3	2.5	.9	2.2
Women								
Total	1 282.2	18.0	67.5	343.9	553.5	146.6	78.6	74.2
Less than 1 month	18.7	.1	1.3	5.8	6.2	3.4	1.2	.7
From 1 to 2 months	164.1	3.2	11.4	44.3	65.9	18.5	9.8	11.0
From 3 to 5 months	134.1	2.8	6.6	36.4	56.4	15.0	10.1	6.8
From 6 to 11 months	147.8	2.6	11.4	43.8	61.0	13.6	8.7	6.9
From 1 to 2 years	228.3	3.3	10.4	58.2	99.2	25.9	14.6	16.7
More than 2 years	574.8	5.8	25.5	153.7	257.7	68.7	32.2	31.3
Not classifiable	14.3	.2	1.0	1.6	7.1	1.6	2.0	.8

Source: National Statistics Institute (Labour Force Survey IV-89).

Table 24

Unemployed according to whether they have worked before or not, by level of education * and sex (thousands)

	Total unemployed			Had worked before			First-job seekers		
	both sexes	men	women	both sexes	men	women	both sexes	men	women
All levels	2 521.8	1 239.6	1 282.2	1 765.4	975.6	789.8	756.4	264.0	492.3
0. Illiterates	52.1	34.2	18.0	49.5	33.2	16.3	2.6	1.0	1.7
1. No education	230.7	163.1	67.5	214.6	155.6	59.0	16.1	7.6	8.5
2. Primary educ.	787.6	443.8	343.9	665.9	396.1	269.8	121.7	47.7	74.0
3. Secondary educ. **	981.7	428.2	553.5	598.3	290.4	307.9	383.4	137.8	245.6
4. Voc. training	248.9	102.3	146.6	134.7	61.6	73.1	114.3	40.7	73.5
5. First degree	107.2	28.6	78.6	55.0	18.8	36.2	52.2	9.9	42.3
6. Higher degree	113.6	39.4	74.2	47.5	20.	27.1	66.1	19.4	46.7

* These code numbers for educational level will be used in Tables 27 and 28.
** Vocational training excluded.

Source: National Statistics Institute (Labour Force Survey IV-89).

Unemployed women first and higher degree graduates looking for their first job (87 000) were 73% of the total new graduate unemployed and were almost 40% of all unemployed graduates (Table 24).

Table 25
Degree courses with the highest absolute levels of unemployment (1987)
Percentage

1.	E.G.B. Teaching	29.3
2.	Humanities	16.4
3.	Medicine	13.5
4.	Law	4.6
5.	Biology	4.4
6.	Social Workers, Tourism	3.5
7.	Nurses	2.9
8.	Business Studies	2.5
9.	Economics and Business Sciences	2.5
10.	Industrial Technical Engineering	2.3
11.	Chemistry	2.3
12.	Pharmacy	1.6
13.	Information Sciences	1.2
14.	Other University Schools	1.2

Level of degree

The position of the graduates from the *Escuelas universitarias* has been improving between 1987 and 1989; this led to a substantial decrease in long term unemployment (more than 2 years), particularly for women (Table 25).

Over the same period, unemployment among male higher level graduates has been decreasing (by 5 600). There has been however a significant increase of unemployment among female higher level graduates (up by 18 900), particularly short term unemployment (less than one year).

In percentage terms, between the second quarter of 1987 and the fourth quarter of 1989, the only increase in unemployment was for women higher degree graduates, up 34%. For first degrees the numbers unemployed fell by 29.55% for men and by 9.23% for women. For men higher degree graduates unemployment fell by 12.44%.

In the light of the figures quoted so far and noting also that some 29% of all unemployed graduates were women who had previously been in employment (63 700), graduate unemployment in Spain basically reflects the labour market for women and for the newly qualified. Furthermore for both groups their situation is getting worse.

Field of study

In 1987 fourteen university degree subjects accounted for 85% of all unemployed graduates and, of these, the five subjects with the highest unemployment provided 68.2% of the total unemployed (7). Two of the five are large subjects (E.G.B. Teaching and Humanities). A further two are the classic university subjects Medicine and Law which, until a few years ago had good employment prospects but currently have fewer job openings. Finally, for Biology, there has never been a significant employer demand either from companies or from government (Table 26).

Table 26
Numbers of unemployed university graduates, by sex and duration of job search (thousands).

	II-87 Men	II-87 Women	IV-89 Men	IV-89 Women	Change Men	Change Women	% Men	% Women
Level below higher	40.6	86.6	28.6	78.6	-12.0	-8.0	-29.55	-9.23
Short duration	13.1	21.1	11.7	29.8	-1.4	8.7		
Long duration	7.5	13.1	6.2	14.6	-1.3	1.5		
Very long duration	19.7	52.2	9.8	32.2	-9.9	-20.0		
Not classifiable	0.2	0.3	0.9	2.0	0.7	1.7		
Higher	45.0	55.3	39.4	74.2	-5.6	18.9	-12.44	34.17
Short duration	11.4	15.9	14.3	25.4	2.9	9.5		
Long duration	11.0	9.4	6.7	16.7	-4.3	7.3		
Very long duration	21.7	29.7	16.2	31.3	-13.5	1.6		
Not classifiable	0.9	0.3	2.2	0.8	2.1	0.5		

Note: Short duration: less than one year seeking job; Long duration: one year or more seeking job; Very long duration: two years or more seeking job.
Source: National Statistics Institute (Labour Force Survey II-87 and IV-89).

The growing proportion of students in subjects with poorer prospects of employment will undoubtedly contribute to increasing graduate unemployment in the future. This process has become worse in Humanities, but fortunately the trend has reversed in Medicine and E.G.B. Teaching, as can be seen in Table 11. It would not therefore be surprising if, in the future, unemployment rates amongst doctors and teachers hold steady or increase slightly while unemployment rates for Humanities graduates increase considerably. This will be all the more so because of the reduction in the number of E.G.B. and B.U.P. pupils which almost necessarily means that the number of teachers will remain constant.

Unemployment or underemployment amongst law graduates will become more evident over the next few years, in spite of the diverse nature of the course. It is likely that neither government nor companies can absorb the large number of graduates in this subject leaving university each year, unless the present period of economic growth continues for a long time unless these graduates improve their position at the expense of those with other degree subjects.

V. DESTINATION OF GRADUATES

With respect to the destination of graduates by sector (public/ private, primary/secondary/tertiary), by occupation (teaching, banking, insurance, etc.) two tables from the INE which although not directly usable without accompanying explanation, are quite informative (Tables 27 and 28). From these tables, as well as Table 19, the following conclusions can be reached.

Employment growth

The total number of graduates (first and higher degrees) who were economically active increased by 272 000 between 1987 and 1989, (i.e. from 10 per cent to 11.4 per cent of the total economically active population).

The number of employed graduates also increased between 1987 and 1989, from 1 198 300 to 1 477 700 which represents an increase of their proportion in the employed population from 10.57 to 11.90 per cent.

It follows therefore that the number of unemployed graduates fell between 1987 and 1989, from 227 000 to 220 000. In other words, this suggests that the labour market readily absorbed the flow of new graduates each year from 1986 to 1989 with, in addition, a slight decrease in the pre-existing stock of unemployed graduates (by nearly 7 000).

Distribution by sector

The number of graduates employed in the primary sector did not fall but their proportion decreased. This sector gained 100 graduates (from 19 000 to 19 100) between 1987 and 1989, but their percentage of the total number of employed decreased from 1.58 to 1.2 per cent.

Industry recruited about 56 500 graduates between 1987 and 1989, the number of graduates employed increasing from 307 700 to 364 200 (18.4 per cent). As with the primary sector, the secondary sector saw a fall in its share of graduates, down from 25.6 to 24.6 per cent.

Employment in the service sector increased both in absolute and relative terms. Graduate numbers in this sector increased by 222 100, (ie 25 per cent, so that their proportion in total (graduate) employment increased from 72.76 to 74.06 per cent). These data indicate that, over the period 1987-1989, the tertiarisation of graduate employment increased.

Table 27
*Employed population, by branch of economic activity and level of education
(thousands and percentages to the total in each branch) 1987*

Levels of education *		0	1	2	3	4	5	6
Total	11 329.6	1.8	9.9	47.2	25.5	5.0	5.5	5.0
Agriculture	1 619.7	5.4	23.9	56.5	11.9	1.1	.6	.5
Fisheries	102.8	3.5	11.1	65.1	12.6	6.5	.4	.8
Fuel extraction	58.4	.9	3.3	61.2	22.6	5.2	3.9	2.9
Electricity & Gas	80.5	1.0	6.5	45.7	22.5	10.3	7.9	6.1
Mining	256.1	1.8	10.6	58.3	19.5	4.8	3.0	1.9
Chemical industries	138.0	.3	6.6	44.5	27.3	6.2	8.4	6.6
Metallurgy, Machines	568.5	.3	6.7	52.0	23.6	11.6	2.9	2.8
Transport equipment	266.7	1.1	5.1	60.5	16.4	11.3	3.4	2.2
Food industries	390.5	1.2	10.4	54.8	25.7	4.6	1.6	1.8
Textile & Leather	485.7	1.1	7.9	50.5	34.9	3.2	1.2	1.1
Wood industries	221.6	.2	7.1	59.8	27.1	4.4	1.0	.4
Paper & Printing	147.0	.1	3.1	46.4	34.1	7.5	3.4	5.3
Rubber & Plastics	142.7	.7	7.8	52.5	26.4	9.7	1.7	1.2
Building	914.3	1.7	12.8	59.7	18.2	4.8	2.0	.8
Commerce & Repairs	1 884.6	1.0	7.5	47.7	34.2	5.1	2.4	2.1
Catering	587.0	1.7	9.1	55.4	28.3	3.6	1.4	.6
Transports	518.8	.2	7.6	58.5	23.0	5.1	2.9	2.7
Communications	110.6	-	3.1	40.9	36.7	6.0	8.2	5.1
Finance, Insurance	293.8	.4	1.7	18.5	54.3	3.2	11.1	10.7
Services to enterprises	234.4	.1	1.1	11.5	37.0	12.2	12.2	25.9
Education, Health	1 094.1	1.4	4.7	20.6	18.2	4.8	28.9	21.4
Other services	1 213.9	2.5	8.3	38.4	31.9	5.1	5.6	8.3

source: INE (labour force survey II-87).
* see Table 24 for educational levels code numbers.

Table 28
Employed population, by branch of economic activity and level of education (thousands and percentages to the total in each branch) 1989

Levels of education *		0	1	2	3	4	5	6
Total	12 408.2	1.6	10.0	39.8	29.2	7.5	6.2	5.7
Agriculture	1 443.8	5.5	27.6	50.1	13.9	1.7	.6	.5
Fisheries	102.4	2.8	14.8	57.5	19.4	5.2	1.4	1.3
Fuel extraction	54.9	.3	1.4	52.9	25.7	9.9	4.1	5.7
Electricity & Gas	85.1	.7	4.8	39.7	25.8	12.5	8.6	7.9
Mining	278.9	1.1	10.3	47.6	26.0	9.6	3.0	2.3
Chemical industries	170.2	.7	6.8	30.0	34.8	12.5	4.8	10.3
Metallurgy, Machines	653.3	.2	5.8	40.9	30.5	15.9	3.7	3.0
Transport equipment	274.5	.1	7.6	45.3	26.1	16.3	2.3	2.4
Food industries	394.0	.8	9.4	45.8	33.8	6.6	2.0	1.6
Textile & Leather	471.6	.6	8.3	45.4	38.6	5.3	1.2	.6
Wood industries	250.0	.4	8.6	51.6	31.4	6.5	.8	.5
Paper & Printing	169.9	.2	5.9	34.7	36.8	11.0	3.1	8.3
Rubber & Plastics	138.1	.3	8.3	40.4	37.0	10.1	2.6	1.4
Building	1 176.8	1.5	14.1	52.8	22.9	6.1	2.0	.6
Commerce & Repairs	2 057.1	.8	6.8	41.3	38.4	7.8	2.7	2.2
Catering	640.4	1.4	8.8	50.7	32.9	4.5	1.2	.6
Transports	586.5	.3	9.9	48.4	27.4	8.3	2.8	2.9
Communications	140.6	.0	2.1	29.1	41.5	12.7	9.1	5.4
Finance, Insurance	325.7	.3	1.1	14.7	53.6	6.4	112.0	11.9
Services to enterprises	320.6	.1	.8	10.9	39.6	14.3	11.8	22.6
Education, Health	1 320.7	1.4	4.1	16.5	16.9	7.1	29.8	22.2
Other services	1 353.3	2.3	9.3	32.1	32.9	7.2	6.6	9.6

source: INE (labour force survey IV-89).
* see Table 24 for educational level code numbers.

Distribution by industry

The most important occupational category undoubtedly is "education, research, culture and health", where in 1989 46.5% of its employees were graduates. Well below this proportion are "other services" with 14.79%, "services to firms", with 7.46%, "commerce" with 6.85 per cent and "finance, insurance and real estate" 5.28%.

These five occupations, which accounted in 1989 for more than 80% of graduates in employment, already employed 79.8 per cent of all graduates just two years previously.

Research into the new graduate labour market

In 1984, the Secretary of State for Universities and Research commissioned a study of the labour market for university graduates in Spain. This showed that there are some well-established "shortcomings" in the education of Spanish students which hinder their ready entry into private sector employment; and that the position of graduates is different whether they are new graduates or already have work experience.

Companies look for certain "additional skills" (computer science, languages, accounting, etc.) which current courses either do not provide at all or else provide in too much depth (8). Ideally employers want a graduate with the skills to do the job offered, or failing this, they select a person on the basis of general and personal qualities (intelligence, maturity, etc.) or they seek a non-graduate with experience of the job.

The study showed that graduates without job experience, i.e. the newly qualified and those who have already been unemployed for a long time, are recruited by private companies primarily for their personal qualities (44.8%), followed by their academic record (23.3%), their additional skills (21.6%) and finally on the basis of personal recommendations (10.3%). Graduates with job experience are recruited on that basis alone and regardless of their degree subject and possession of any additional skills.

The recruitment method used by private companies, especially the large organisations, is to seek staff directly via their personnel department. This might be expected because it is the large companies who can afford their own selection board or personnel department. It is more common for smaller private companies (less than 1 000 employees) to turn to consultants to recruit the graduate personnel that they need. This is particularly so for transport and communication companies. However, small and medium companies also use a combination of direct first selection and advice from often consultants.

The majority of large companies provide training for their graduate recruits as soon as they join the company. Even the best graduates are normally unable to start work straight away. The university degree does not guarantee that graduates have the knowledge required for a specific job in a particular company. Graduates need specialized training for the job concerned because no two companies have exactly the same requirements and they also have differing training philosophies (9). In practice it is difficult to distinguish what is, strictly, training from the legally established "probationary period" for new employees. Thus, only 31.2% of employers provided entrants with "additional skills" and the average time of adjustment to the company -- a little over seven months -- is very close to the six months set by the Statute of Workers as the maximum trial period for technical staff with degrees.

This survey seems to show that there are no great "shortcomings" in Spanish University degrees. The education received by university students is general and therefore excludes specific skills such as accounting, languages, etc. but it is not very far away from what companies are asking for. As can be seen, the gaps in university education are skills which can be acquired later without great additional efforts. Employers seem to value university degrees in themselves and do not seek a close link between course and job which is typical of some parts of the economy: services, mining and much of the public sector.

The other large employer, public administration, mainly recruits graduates without work experience. Two thirds of the graduates who enter service in government, education, health or research, are newly qualified and only one third come from other jobs. There is also a wide range of public or semi-public services which provide work for a considerable number of higher and intermediate level engineers.

The Labour Force Survey shows that, between the second quarter of 1987 and the last quarter of 1989, the proportion of university graduates employed in the occupation group "Education, research, culture and health" rose from 46.7% to 47.22%, a current total of 393 700 first degree and 293 400 higher degree graduates. Following the waves of recruitment in the first two 'Public Employment Calls' in 1985 and 1986 graduate recruitment to government has run out of steam. Government is also suffering from a slow loss of senior management to private companies.

The well-established method of entry to the government employment was revised in 1984 in the Civil Service Reform Act. This initiated three routes: open competition, competitive competition and a mixture of the two. Approximately 66% of recruits enter through competitive competition and 22% are contracted workers who are normally recruited by means of open competition on merit. Only 11% of government officials and workers enter though open competition on merit.

University graduates selected for government employment do not usually need subsequent training to adjust their skills to the job, although in some cases there is a "learning period". The system of attributing functions to a defined group of professional officials means that there are high levels of equivalence between job/level of graduate (84%) and job/degree course studied (84.1%).

However there is no correlation between job/level/degree course in 15.6% of the government's officials. Two possible groups who might account for this are: a) persons who obtained their qualifications after entry to government and who have not been promoted to higher qualified jobs, and b) persons who knowingly accepted jobs with a lower level of qualifications than those for which they had been educated, in order to avoid being unemployed.

Government is an 'equal opportunity employer' and, by law, does not discriminate in its recruitment between men and women or between graduates and non-graduates. Nevertheless there are inequalities in promotion to higher levels which are well-known within government departments. (10).

Notes

1) The participation rate of first degree graduates stayed at its 1986 level. This suggests that the change introduced in the Labour Force Survey in the second quarter of 1987 had little effect on the consistency of the "working population" measure.

2) "It might be thought that there are too few higher level engineers and even fewer technical engineers and that there are too many doctors and lawyers and too few statisticians, biologists or opticians. But naturally these opinions must be based upon something more than just the total number of existing graduates: at least in the analysis of the labour market for each occupation". (FOESSA Report 75-83. E. Euramérica, Madrid, 1984, p. 320).

3) Table 29 shows that the proportion of graduates in the active population was 10.0 in 1987 and 11.4 in 1989. Although the survey methodologies are not completely comparable, as underlined above, we can say that over the 1980's, the proportion of graduates in the economically active population increased substantially (from 6.9 to 11.4 per cent) and among the employed (from 7.15 to 11.9 per cent), while unemployment among graduates, although it increased, increased less than the increase in employment (from 5.5 to 6.8 per cent).

4) Labour Force Survey. Detailed results. October, November, December, 1989, National Statistics Institute, p. 15.

5) Bosch, F. and Díaz, J.: "*La educación en España. Una perspectiva económica*". Ed. Ariel. Madrid, 1988, p. 223. In the work "*Las situaciones y perfil del desempleo y subempleo de los titulados universitarios*" it says however that: "a) normally the qualification and the job are matched, but nearly one fifth of working graduates "are not in their appropriate job". Some 198 200 graduates do work "inappropriate" to their qualifications. b) The inappropriateness is even greater between qualifications and job category. Around 220 000 graduates "put up with" positions lower than their qualifications. Youth, low social origins, low pay and precariousness and insecurity of employment are associated with these cases of inappropriateness..." (p. 116).

6) Jimenez Mañas, C.: "*La actividad económica de las mujeres en relación con su educación*", in "*Mujer y Educación*". Rev. of Education, n°. 290, Sept-Dec. 89, p. 173.

7) The Labour Force Survey does not provide unemployment data by university degree subject and this means that any attempt at this tends to be based on small surveys which are not nationally representative. Researchers have also used the unemployment figures recorded in the

Employment Offices, provided by the National Employment Institute. However these only record those graduates who have registered as unemployed and are not comprehensive. For example, the number of unemployed graduates recorded at computerized Employment Offices (which cover just 66.6% of all registered unemployed) was 59 705 persons in March 1990, a figure which contrasts noticeably with the estimate of more than 100 000 graduates quoted by the National Statistics Institute.

In 1989, the General Secretariat of the Universities Council published a study on underemployment, unemployment and how this varied by type of course, social class, age, sex, etc., based on surveys carried out on a sample of nearly 3 000 university graduates in mid 1987. This paper has drawn on part of the conclusions from that study, entitled "*Las situaciones y perfil del desempleo y subempleo de los titulados universitarios*".

8) Ministry of Education and Science: "*El mercado de trabajo de los titulados universitarios en España*". Madrid, 1987 (3rd. ed.), p. 125.

9) F. Bosch Font, in the preface to the work "*Educación y empleo*" (I.E.E., Madrid, 1981) points out that jobs have two essential characteristics which make it impossible to plan higher education in relation to work requirements: "1) There are no minimum educational requirements for each job, and 2) In jobs, there is a large degree of variation between types of training".

10) A system of recruitment by specific competition in the State Administration is at present being prepared to fill the more important and highest posts there. This system is a development of what has been established by the General Regulations for Provision of Posts and Job Promotion of Officials and is based, amongst other things, on the proper description of the post and job profile.

VI. POLICY FOR MATCHING UNIVERSITY GRADUATE SUPPLY AND DEMAND

The report prepared in 1987 by the International Council for Educational Development (I.C.E.D.) on Spanish university reform, warned that the most difficult and complex problem facing Spanish higher education at the moment, was that of "The ever growing imbalance between the number and types of graduates leaving the universities each year and the ability of the economy to assimilate them and use them productively". According to the report, one of the causes of this situation in the 1970's and early part of the 1980's was the constant obstruction, the continual blocking which the university system experienced "through the rapid expansion of higher education which followed the coming into force of the 1970 General Education Act", coinciding with the economic boom "which had been developing throughout the 1960's creating an increase in employment and developing optimistic expectations that growth would continue in the future" (1).

The situation seems to have been repeated following publication of the 1983 Reform of Higher Education Act, although this has not been fully put into effect. The Spanish economy experienced sustained economic growth in the second half of the 1980's and there were optimistic prospects for future growth, bolstered by Spain's admission to the European Community. In addition individuals sought a university degree as protection against unemployment. All this meant that the situation has not changed substantially between the period covered by the I.C.E.D. report and the end of 1980's. The annual inflow of over two hundred thousand students into Spanish universities determines the resources which have to be devoted to improving the quality of education and means new universities and buildings. This encourages short and medium term planning which has to be reviewed each year. In the same way, the annual addition of nearly one hundred thousand graduates to the already existing "stock", in spite of the current economic boom, does not help policies for balancing supply and demand and puts pressure on the labour market.

However, the imbalance is not only in terms of numbers. It also has a significant qualitative ingredient. The harsh reality is that, already, university graduates "will never again reap the market rewards that their scarcity gave them in past elitist times" (2). It is no less harsh a reality that there will be restrictions on the numbers who can follow certain courses of studies because, in short, university graduate unemployment is education lying idle. It is a charge on the taxpayer (nationally and locally) and the aim should be its reduction and ultimate elimination. This is the task for two responsible bodies: the public authorities who must guarantee equality of opportunity for all students, and the universities whose job it is to select and educate the most able.

The cost to the State of graduate unemployment

It is not easy to calculate what the current cost per student is in Spanish universities, mainly because some local authorities ('Autonomous Communities') have assumed powers on university education and include headings in their budgets which previously appeared in consolidated form in the State Budgets. In spite of all the difficulties and with suitable caveats, a recent study, based on 1984 figures, has estimated the cost at between 100 000 and 191 500 pesetas per student per year (3). At 1989 prices, using the consumer price index, this range of costs is 139 000 to 267 500 pesetas.

So, disregarding private costs, opportunity costs and any other type of costs which might be as large as public costs or larger (4), and which can be measured as much in economic terms as political ones, the State has spent, not very efficiently, the following on each unemployed university graduate:

- between 695 000 and 1 337 500 pesetas in the case of higher degrees;
- between 417 000 and 802 500 pesetas in the case of first degrees.

These figures, which already seem high, are even more striking when they are multiplied by the number of graduates who spend more than two years seeking employment -- unemployment which can be considered almost entirely to reflect a genuine, structural imbalance in supply and demand. The resulting amounts (from 50 000 to 100 000 million pesetas) are equivalent to between 0.4% and 0.8% of the State expenditure budget for 1990. These sums would pay for the total planned expenditure of the Ministry of Culture and half of the total allocated to the Ministry of Industry and Energy.

Measures for matching the number of graduates and the needs of the economy

Measures to match the number of university graduates to the needs of the economy must act at three specific points: admission to university, course content and graduates' entry to the labour market.

Admission

The university system is currently growing because of the pressure of demand for higher education and because the combination of the University Preparation Course and the selective entrance tests has functioned effectively albeit that it has its shortcomings. The straight abolition of this scheme would disrupt the universities and would produce more problems than advantages.

The imposition of ceilings on access to universities for new applicants has partly managed to channel student demand into degree courses with better employment prospects. But this procedure, which was intended to be provisonal until there could be an objective assessment of the capacity of individual institutions, is in danger of ceasing to be effective. This is first, because it is provisional and will not necessarily get public acceptance. Second, there are conflicting forces at work. There is local pressure to expand the university system even with unnecessary or poorly attended degree courses. On the other hand, there are calls to limit access in employable subjects by certain professions who want to defend their privileged position in the labour market which reflects a shortage of certain types of graduate.

There are two measures which together can achieve a better adjustment of the number of students to the capacity of the system with a greater degree of equality of access to higher education. First is the establishment of a unified system, namely, the recognition of the right to follow a course of studies in any university of the State. Second is the introduction of a new selection examination which overcomes the academic and social drawbacks of the present scheme. In addition, development of the system has to be planned so that it reflects the pattern of student demand and not simply where it is easiest to expand the supply of places. And expansion should be in areas where there are good job prospects and not simply in those subjects that happen to be best known in the employment offices.

Courses

Spanish university degree courses have been strongly criticised by the majority of education researchers. They have been described as inadequate with little or nothing to do with the needs of the economy. The subjects offered reflect the internal imperatives of the universities. The course content has been described as simply composed of lists of subjects which do not develop abilities such as those of relating theoretical knowledge to real life problems and situations. There is also a lack of appreciation of the importance of science and technology. However some commentators have questioned whether graduate unemployment is because of the apparent irrationality of the university structure and have put the main blame on employers.

Spain chose to modify the structure and contents of the higher education levels with the 1983 Reform of Higher Education Act. This provided for university departments to become the main bodies charged with organizing and developing research and education appropriate to their respective areas of learning. The Act also established the procedure for subsequent award of degrees and the general guidelines for degree courses which should be followed in order to justify their degree status. It can confidently be predicated that the number of recognised degree courses will increase considerably (approximately double the present number). Courses will be modular and flexible, more in line with those current in Europe and, above all, they will be more closely linked to employment.

Spanish university education must be reformed, not because it is particularly inadequate but rather because of its inflexibility, which is sometimes excessive, and because of its lack of orientation towards the labour market (5). However this reform will certainly not guarantee an automatic decrease in first and higher degree graduate unemployment. This is partly because of the structural causes of this unemployment and partly because a large number of private employers are guided by subjective criteria and give more weight to job applicants' sex and age than to the education they have received.

Access to jobs

University graduate unemployment is almost entirely dependent on the economy's ability to generate jobs requiring high qualifications. The worst aspect of this matter is not that it leaves the education system passive, but rather the difficulty in understanding what determines the current and future supply of jobs for graduates. The first difficulty is to assess which occupations will require graduate skills -- a qualitative problem. The second difficulty, quantitative, is rooted in the near impossibilty of predicting the medium and long term work force requirements. A third difficulty, related to the first one, but not completely identical, concerns the great "variety of educational and training levels" (6) which is apparent in jobs.

All of these problems mean that any policy for balancing the supply and demand for highly qualified workers should be based on research studies and should operate both in the growth phase and the downswing of the business cycle. Here it very important that the public authorities can offer unemployed graduates "job conversion programmes aimed at less saturated areas or with greater growth potential" (7). The universities should intensify collaboration programmes with other bodies (the government, companies, research organizations, etc.) in order to improve the links between the final part of students' degree courses and the start of their careers.

Notes

1) International Council for Educational Development: "*La reforma universitaria española. Evaluación e informe*". Ministry of Education and Science; Universities Council. Madrid, 1988 (2nd. ed.), p. 131.

2) I.C.E.D., op. cit., p. 135.

3) Bosch, F. and Diaz, J. op. cit., p. 150.

4) "It is not only the collective endeavour which is lost with unemployment, the "damnum emergens", as classical jurists would say, but also the "lucrum cesans", the cultural or financial wealth not earned, that should worry us". (Lamo, E.: op. cit., p. 163).

5) "Our students leave university with a good stock of knowledge but a poor stock of abilities. They know sufficient or a lot, but they know how to do very little, and that encourages a passive attitude which directs them towards seeking a ready created job and not towards attitudes with more initiative or self-employment". (Lamo, E.: op. cit., p. 169).

6) As can be seen, they agree with those stated by F. Bosch Font in the preface of the work "*Educación y empleo*" (I.E.E., 1981) which we cite in note 8 of chapter IV.

7) Ministry of education and science: "*Las situaciones y el perfil...*": op. cit., p. 180.

ANNEX

Figure 1a
Diagramm of the Spanish education system

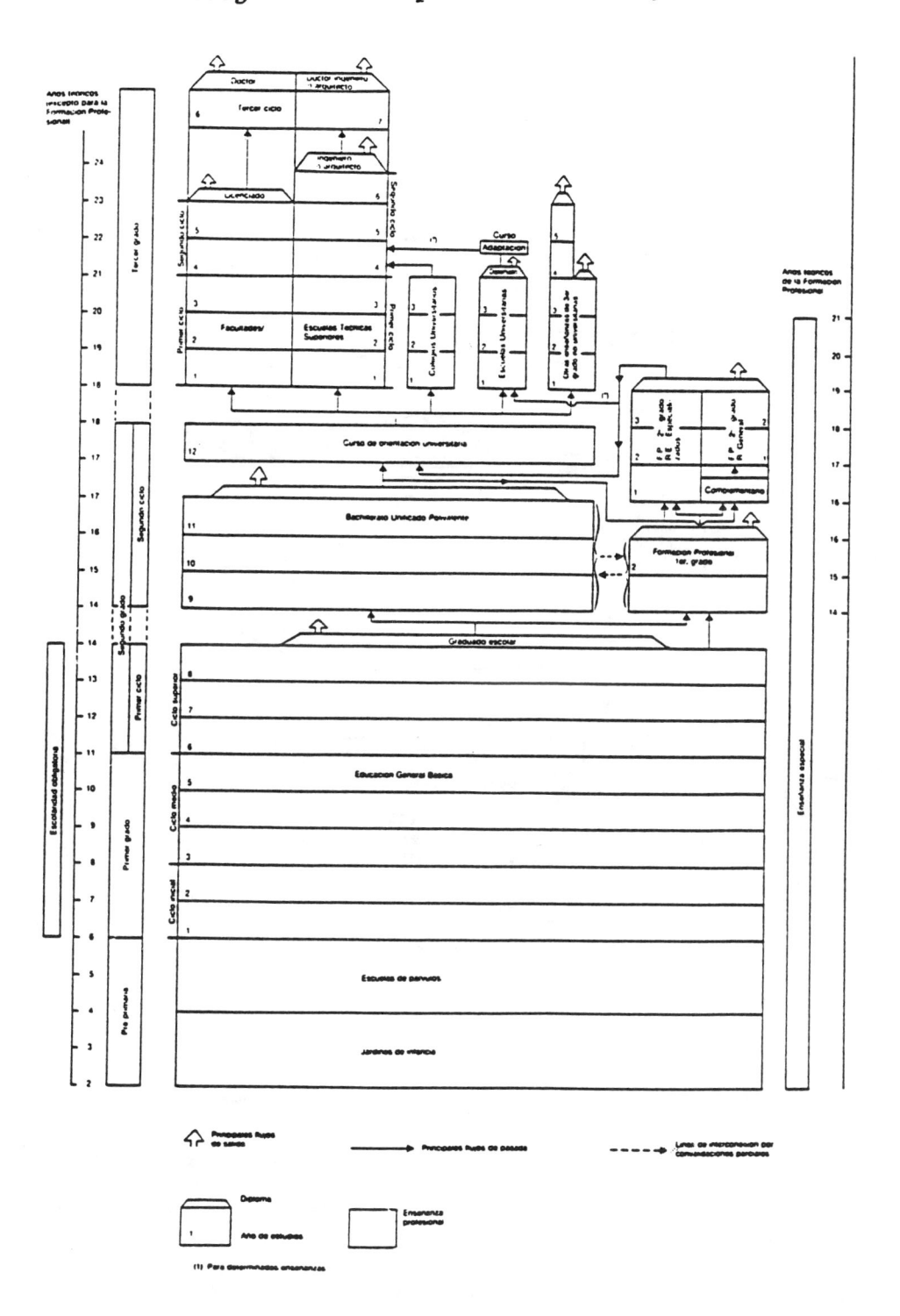

Figure 1b
Diagramm of the Spanish education system

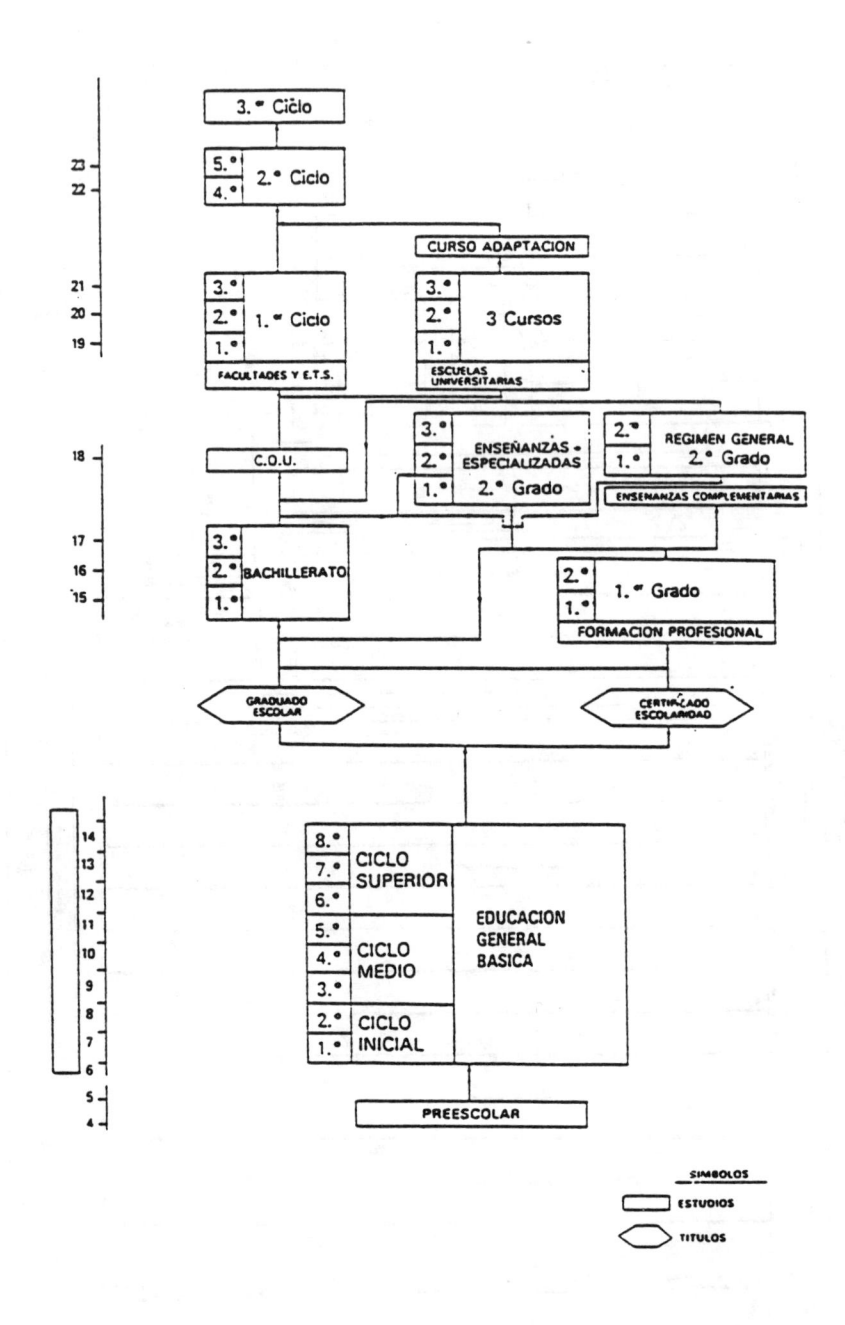

ETATS-UNIS

—

UNITED STATES

E. Stephen Hunt

Office of Educational Research and Improvement
U.S. Department of Education

Contents

Introduction   131

Chapter 1
From high school through higher education:
Trends in the flow of post-secondary students, 1977-1987   134

    An aggregate overview   134
    Entry into post-secondary education   140
    Financing undergraduate studies   144
    Patterns of undergraduate enrolments   152
    Undergraduate degree completions   163
    Undergraduate degree earners on the labour market   167
    Pursuing graduate education   172
    Conclusion   191

Chapter 2
Trends in the major and its relation to work   195

    The liberal arts and occupational concepts   195
    Majors at the less-than-four-year level   197
    Bachelor's degree trends   203
    First-professional degree trends   215
    The master's degree   217
    Trends in doctoral fields of study   224
    After the doctorate   237
    Conclusion   239

INTRODUCTION

This report consists of two chapters. Chapter One, **From High School Through Higher Education**, discusses the flow of students from secondary school graduation (or the equivalent), through postsecondary education, and into the workforce. The data presented in Chapter One are in the form of aggregate descriptive statistics. Various postsecondary issues and experiences are discussed, including different degree levels, the financing of higher education, the experiences of women and minorities, persistence from initial enrollment to diploma, and initial work experiences after leaving higher education.

Chapter Two, **Trends in the Major and Its Relation to Work**, focuses on the different subjects that postsecondary students study, and relates information about how choices of subject have fluctuated over time and what types of experience different majors have had in the workforce. As with Chapter One, data in Chapter Two are presented for minorities, women, and different degree levels as appropriate.

In each Chapter, data are presented for the period 1977-1987. This time period was selected in order to illustrate changes during an important period in recent U.S. educational history, particularly in terms of policy changes toward higher education at all political levels. More recent data than those or 1987 are too fragmented and/or preliminary to include in this Report.

The Chapters of this report comprise a description of the trends in U.S. postsecondary education in terms of who attends, who finishes, what they study, and what experiences they have in initial employment. Unless otherwise indicated, the source for all data is the National Center for Education Statistics of the U.S. Department of Education. Most of the raw data used are publicly accessable on tapes; the presentations contained in this report were largely developed for it, however, and thus may not be readily available.

A Note About U.S. Education Data

Researchers and policy-makers who have occasion to use U.S. data on education topics often note differences in the data presented on similar themes by different organizations. This fact is not surprising; such variations are universal where data collectors use different methodologies, samples, instruments, and time frames -- not to mention having different purposes for data presentation. A few examples will suffice to illustrate the problem.

Some data collectors have limited purposes, such as a researcher interested in a narrow question of behavior or policy, or an agency of government interested in tracking its specific activity (such as expenditures or assistance disbursements). Others have limited resources, such as private researchers or foundations, and cannot produce comprehensive national data. Resource limits also mean that data are not always collected regularly, and changing interests means that data collection instruments may change over time, thus limiting comparability. The purposes for which data are collected also tend to determine the method used, and this can also result in divergent outcomes. For example, a survey of students asking them what they did in school, a survey of faculty asking about their students' experiences, and an analysis of institutional records (such as transcripts) concerning student experiences are likely to result in three different answers -- even about the same students. These are fairly well-known limitations to social research. Two other facts, however, relate specifically to U.S. data, and need to be understood.

First, the federal system in the United States, and the consequent limited role assigned to national agencies such as the Department of Education, means that national data collection in the U.S. is not a function of central regulatory authority. States, local governments, and private organizations are not compelled by law to report data to the Department except in certain limited circumstances (such as enforcement of the civil rights acts). Data collection is voluntary, not mandatory. Furthermore, the data that may be requested are limited by strong policies and oversight bodies (such as the Office of Management and Budget and the Reduction in Paperwork Act), not to mention a customary suspicion of governmental inquisitiveness that is ingrained in the American political character. Thus the data available from national agencies in the United States may be less extensive, less regular and consistent, and less penetrating (in terms of analytical depth) than what might be expected from societies with a tradition of tolerating both more centralized authority and more detailed governmental examination of education issues.

Lack of such Federal power, however, does not mean that the data available are inaccurate, merely that they are limited in scope and often episodic in nature, as political leaders seek to repond to specific concerns which -- once dealt with -- are not transformed into ongoing, regular data collection demands.

State governments do the real work of close regulation in U.S. education, and their data on local practices are usually quite detailed -- closer to what many other national governments might do. Unfortunately, turning to U.S. state data for the information unavailable from Federal sources is no solution, since no state has data collection jurisdiction beyond its territory, and each state has education regulations, traditions, political interests, and socio-ecomomic concerns of its own. California data, for example, cannot serve as a representative of U.S. national practice, since California operates a highly regulated (by U.S. state standards) education system, and has demographic, economic and cultural characteristics that make it unrepresentative of the whole country. (The same could be said of any other state.) Equally important is the fact that each state sets its own legal definitions of education concepts, so that compiling a national picture requires knowing each of these systems and how to reconcile the various statistical procedures employed.

The problem is further compounded at the postsecondary level by the tradition of institutional autonomy. This means that each individual institution -- and in many cases individual campuses and departments or divisions within institutions -- designs and implements its own data collection policies and mechanisms, including specific definitions of crucial concepts such as full-time and part-time registration. Publicly controlled institutions have somewhat less latitude in these matters than do private institutions, but most of them are much freer to set their own internal standards of data collection than are many of their foreign counterparts. Efforts to reconcile data reporting methods, and to adopt uniform (or at least consistent) definitions and procedures, have met with some success, as well as resistence. Furthermore, institutions obey the same laws and customs regarding individual privacy and organizational intrusiveness as do governments. They, too are limited in terms of how much data they can gather and report, and in what formats.

The second major point is really the conclusion that follows from the first. Ours is a decentralized educational system -- an informal "system" resulting from the sum of many formal systems that share crucial features and that collaborate and compete extensively in a common educational marketplace. Several threads of national policy and law weave through this informal system and tie portions of it more or less closely together, but this does not now -- and might never -- evolve into a truly formal system in which power is vested in any central Federal apparatus. Such a decentralized system means that any overview of its behavior -- such as the present report -- is a description based on aggregated data rather than a depiction of a prescribed and regulated process. The data employed in this report may at best only approximate the actual personal experience of any randomly selected U.S. student.

Chapter 1

*FROM HIGH SCHOOL THROUGH HIGHER EDUCATION:
TRENDS IN THE FLOW OF POSTSECONDARY STUDENTS, 1977-1987*

This Chapter addresses the topic of general trends in the flow of students from secondary school through the various levels of postsecondary education and into the workforce. As does Chapter 2, it deals with developments from 1977 through 1987, the most recent decade for which complete final data are available. After a brief overview of the size and shape of U.S. postsecondary education in general, Chapter One presents and discusses data on each stage of the academic journey, beginning with the transition from secondary school to postsecondary education. Information on trends in initial enrollment, persistence, degree completion, and transition to either further education or work is provided, with the data broken out by gender, race/ethnicity, and citizenship/residency status. Developments at each level of postsecondary education are discussed. Chapter One does not examine what happens to students concentrating in different subject matter fields; this issue is addressed in detail in the next chapter.

The data presented here are largely drawn from annual comprehensive surveys of U.S. postsecondary institutions. Two of these have been used: the Higher Education General Information System (HEGIS), which was in use until 1981, and the Integrated Postsecondary Education Data System (IPEDS) that has been in use since 1981. IPEDS (and its HEGIS predecessor) amount to a census of non-profit accredited postsecondary institutions. While the data thus collected have longitudinal value at the institutional level, they provide no information on how individual students fare in their academic and work careers. To find out how students actually move through the system the Department of Education has initiated a series of longitudinal studies of cohorts of students, each of which takes a large national sample (over 15,000 in each study) of high school students and follows them, via follow-up surveys, across their lives. Data from the first of these studies, the National Longitudinal Study of the High School Class of 1972 (NLS 72), is used in this Chapter, as are some data from the second such study, High School and Beyond (HSB 80 and 82, covering the high school classes of 1980 and 1982).

AN AGGREGATE OVERVIEW

Postsecondary education is a major industry in the United States, and the various components of the informal national system generate a tremendous annual volume in terms of inputs (income, enrolling students, hiring, purchasing) and outcomes (graduates, research products, services rendered, expenditures). Prior to discussing the flow of students into and through this system, it is important to put the nature of the enterprise into perspective.

TABLE 1:
**U.S. National Expenditures on Different Levels of
Education as Percents of All Educational
Expenditures and of Annual GNP,
Academic Years 1976-77 - 1986-87**

| | | Educational Expenditures (Mil. $) and Percents (GNP, Ed.) ||||||||
| Year | Annual GNP (Bil.$) | All Education || Primary & Secondary ||| Postsecondary |||
		Amount	%GNP	Amount	%GNP	%All	Amount	%GNP	%All
1977	1,991	137,042	6.9	86,544	4.3	63.2	50,498	2.5	36.8
1978	2,250	148,308	6.6	93,012	4.1	62.7	55,296	2.5	37.3
1979	2,508	165,627	6.6	103,162	4.1	62.3	62,465	2.5	37.7
1980	2,732	182,849	6.7	112,325	4.1	61.4	70,524	2.6	38.6
1981	3,053	197,801	6.5	120,486	3.9	60.9	77,315	2.5	39.1
1982	3,166	212,081	6.7	128,725	4.1	60.7	83,356	2.6	39.3
1983	3,406	228,597	6.7	139,000	4.1	60.8	89,597	2.6	39.2
1984	3,772	247,657	6.6	149,400	4.0	60.3	98,257	2.6	39.7
1985	4,015	269,485	6.7	161,800	4.0	60.0	107,685	2.7	40.0
1986	4,232	291,823	6.9	175,200	4.1	60.0	116,623	2.8	40.0
1987	4,524	313,600	6.9	187,900	4.2	59.9	125,700	2.8	40.1
77-87	+127.2%	+128.8%	0.0	+117.1%	-0.1	-3.3	+148.9%	+0.3	+3.3
11 YR Avg.	3,377	227,656	6.7	138,221	4.1	61.0	89,435	2.6	39.0

NOTE: All figures and percentages have been rounded and are based on current dollars.

SOURCE: U.S. Department of Education, National Center for Education Statistics, *Digest of Education Statistics 1990*, (Washington: U.S. Government Printing Office, February 1991), Table 28, p. 33.

Economics.

Table 1 illustrates the place of postsecondary education in the U.S. economy, relative to total GNP and to total expenditures on all levels of education. While the figures are based on annual compilations expressed in current dollars, they are useful for identifying relative changes in emphasis in each year.

It is apparent from Table 1 that postsecondary education had a good decade, economically speaking, relative to primary/secondary education and to education in general. While total expenditures on education rose one percent faster than GNP, postsecondary expenditures increased at a faster rate than either GNP or total education expenditures. By comparison, the rate of spending on primary/secondary education failed to keep pace with either GNP or postsecondary expenditures. Even though the amounts spent on both primary/secondary and postsecondary education have more than doubled over 1977-1987, the relative rates of increase, and the proportionate shares of the total, have differed considerably.

Postsecondary education's share of the total national education expenditure during 1977-1987 was especially large in relation to the population served. For example, in 1987 the proportion of all education expenditures spent on postsecondary education -- some 40.1 percent -- supported the services rendered to 12.8 million postsecondary students, while the 45.5 million students enrolled in the primary and secondary grades divided the remaining 59.9 percent. Based on these data, the 1987 postsecondary *per capita* expenditure thus works out to have been over $9,800.00 per enrolled student, or about 2.4 times that for the corresponding *per capita* primary/secondary expenditure of over $4,100.00 (1).

These figures show the significant size of the educational enterprise in the United States, and the real dollar amounts illustrate that the scope of educational activity is actually greater than the percentages alone indicate. The question of whether Americans get an adequate return on their education dollar -- specifically their postsecondary dollar -- is an issue of considerable controversy in the United States, but an answer to it lies outside the scope of this report. Certainly, the expenditures on different levels of education have been one factor informing the current national education reform movement, especially the recent emphasis on improving primary and secondary education (2).

Institutions

Postsecondary education is delivered by many providers, including but by no means limited to colleges and universities. Traditional colleges and universities -- two- and four-year institutions operating on a non-profit basis and providing both full- and part-time instruction -- are, however, the largest and most important group of providers that deliver courses for formal academic credit. Table 2 shows something of the diversity of this sector in the United States, as well as the pattern of openings and closings over the period 1977-1987.

TABLE 2:

Trends in the Number of U.S. Postsecondary Institutions, by Level and Control, Fall 1977 - Fall 1987/88

Year	Inst. Total	Two-Year Institutions			Four-Year Institutions		
		All	Public	Private	All	Public	Private
1977	3,095	1,157	921	236	1,938	552	1,386
1978	3,134	1,193	924	269	1,941	550	1,391
1979	3,152	1,195	926	269	1,957	549	1,408
1980	3,231	1,274	945	329	1,957	552	1,405
1981	3,253	1,274	940	334	1,979	558	1,421
1982	3,280	1,296	933	363	1,984	560	1,424
1983	3,284	1,271	916	355	2,013	565	1,448
1984	3,331	1,306	935	371	2,025	566	1,459
1985	3,340	1,311	932	379	2,029	566	1,463
1986	3,406	1,336	960	376	2,070	573	1,497
87/88	3,587	1,452	992	460	2,135	599	1,536
Closed, 77-88	92	25	1	24	67	2	65
Opened, 77-87	584	320	72	248	264	49	215
Change, 77-87	+15.9%	+25.5%	+ 7.7%	+94.9%	+10.2%	+ 8.5%	+10.8%

SOURCE: U.S. Department of Education, National Center for Education Statistics, <u>Digest of Education Statistics 1990</u>, (Washington: U.S. Government Printing Office, February 1991), Tables 216 and 219, pp. 228 and 231.

Net increases have occurred in every category of institutional level and control for which data are available. The increase has been largest in the two-year college sector, which experienced a 25.5 percent growth over 1977-1987, and within that sector, the privately controlled junior college subsector, which nearly doubled in size. It is noteworthy that the private two-year subsector also experienced the most institutional failures of the two-year sector, accounting for all but one closing. Growth rates in the numbers of four-year institutions have also been significant, but not so great as in the two-year sector. Institutional failure rates have been far greater comprising nearly 73 percent of all institutional failures during 1977-1987. As with the two-year sector, private four-year institutions were much more likely to fail than were public institutions (all but two four-year closings were private).

These numbers demonstrate the general health of the U.S. postsecondary institutional population, and confirm the growth of this sector of education in recent years. They also indicate both the size of the private sector in U.S. postsecondary education and the considerable vulnerability of many of these institutions to various economic factors. A calculation based on data in Tables 2 and 3 (see below) shows that the average Fall, 1987 enrollment of a private two-year institution was 509; of a private four-year institution, 1,665. Such enrollments are not large enough to ensure institutional financial security through tuition and fee payments alone. Other income sources are usually required, such as endowment interest, gifts, research contracts, property, sales (such as institutional memorabilia to alumni), and the like. The small size and precarious economics of private postsecondary institutions contribute to the continual turnover in the private sector institutional population, even as new institutions (often with equally problematic chances of survival) are constantly being established.

Students

Table 3, as stated above, provides a picture of the scope of total participation in U.S. postsecondary education. The size of the population thus served is not news to anyone, since the United States has long had a reputation for making serious efforts to expand access to postsecondary study. As of Fall 1987, over 12.8 million students were enrolled in some form of postsecondary education in accredited public and private institutions. Like the data on institutions and national expenditures, however, these enrollment totals do not include persons enrolled in short, non-credit courses in non-traditional settings such as work sites, conference centers, community centers, or via distance learning networks. The totals also undercount the number of persons enrolled in what are called proprietary institutions (private, for-profit schools providing various programs of study, usually occupationally oriented), since only a sample of such institutions is normally included in annual Federal data collection efforts.

It is clear from the data in Table 3 that enrollments in postsecondary education have expanded during 1977-1987. Two-year enrollments have expanded nearly twice as fast as have four-year enrollments, but the total number of Americans participating in programs in four-year institutions was still 40 percent greater than the total in two-year institutions as of 1987 -- a four

TABLE 3:
Trends in Aggregate Enrollments in U.S. Postsecondary Education, by Level and Control of Institution, Fall 1977 - Fall 1987

Year	Two-Year Institutions Total	%Pub	%Prv	Four-Year Institutions Total	%Pub	%Prv
1977	4,042,942	96.5	3.5	7,242,845	68.3	31.7
1978	4,028,141	96.2	3.8	7,231,951	67.9	32.1
1979	4,216,666	96.2	3.8	7,353,233	67.7	32.3
1980	4,526,287	95.6	4.4	7,570,608	67.7	32.3
1981	4,716,211	95.0	5.0	7,655,461	67.5	32.5
1982	4,771,706	94.7	5.3	7,654,074	67.6	32.4
1983	4,723,466	94.4	5.6	7,741,195	67.5	32.5
1984	4,530,773	94.5	5.5	7,711,167	67.4	32.6
1985	4,531,077	94.2	5.8	7,715,978	67.5	32.5
1986	4,679,548	94.3	5.7	7,823,963	67.7	32.3
1987	4,776,222	95.1	4.9	7,990,420	68.0	32.0
Change 77-87	+18.1 %	-1.4	+1.4	+10.3 %	-0.3	+0.3

NOTE: Pub = Public institutions; Prv = private institutions.

SOURCE: U.S. Department of Education, National Center for Education Statistics, <u>Digest of Education Statistics 1990</u>, (Washington: U.S. Government Printing Office, February 1991), Table 158, p. 168.

Note by the Secretariat

Data on total enrolments that will be presented below in Table 10 are not comparable to those in this Table. This discrepancy is due to the fact that data in Table 10 are drawn from the annual reports from higher education institutions, while those in Table 3 are the result of a revision of all 1977-87 data. This particularly affects the years 1986 and 1987. All NCES data published today carries with it a note for 1986-on: "Data have been revised from previously published figures".

percent decline in the margin of difference since 1977. Such numbers indicate that bachelor's degree-granting institutions remain the choice of most students who aspire to postsecondary education, even though two-year institutions have increased in popularity.

Another trend indicated in Table 3 is a modest increase in enrollments in private postsecondary education as opposed to public. The number of students enrolled in private two-year institutions increased nearly 40 percent between 1977 and 1987, which translated into a 1.4 percent increase in the private subsector's share of all two-year students. Enrollment share in private four-year institutions also increased faster than the total increase at that level, but not by as much. The number of private four-year students increased by ten percent (from around 2.3 million in 1977 to 2.6 million in 1987), which amounted to a slight increase in overall enrollment share for that subsector.

ENTRY INTO POSTSECONDARY EDUCATION

Because the whole U.S. student population is not comprehensively tracked, it is only possible to gain an impression of the frequency and pattern of individuals' transition from secondary to postsecondary education. This may be done in two ways: by interpolating from aggregate data on educational activities reported via means such as the Census or institutional enrollment reports, or by extrapolating to the population as a whole from one or more of the national longitudinal study samples.

Initial Enrollment

The transition from secondary to postsecondary education is the point at which a detailed analysis of the flow of students must begin. Traditionally, most students who enrolled in any postsecondary education did so immediately after high school graduation and followed a standard track to the associate or bachelor's degree. This picture has been changing since the end of World War II and is no longer valid for many who participate in postsecondary level studies. Today's postsecondary student is frequently an adult learner either entering college later in life or re-entering after stopping out for anywhere from a semester to many years. Students are also more likely to be studying part-time than previously, and working either full- or part-time while attending school. A majority of postsecondary students still tend to follow the traditional pattern, but U.S. educators are increasingly aware of the changing demographics of college attendance and their implications for the ways in which instruction is designed and delivered, and how institutions themselves are organized and managed.

Table 4 presents data on students who entered (enrolled for the first time) postsecondary institutions immediately after high school graduation, which is defined as enrolling in the same year as, or within six months of, receiving their secondary diplomas or equivalency certificates. These data have been collected from the initial and follow-up surveys for the National Longitudinal Study (NLS-72) and the High School and Beyond Study (HSB-80 and -82).

NLS-72 began as a survey of a stratified national sample of 22,652 twelfth-graders (seniors) in U.S. secondary schools. The original (Base Year) sample has been followed up in subsequent surveys in 1973, 1974, 1976, 1979, and 1986. HSB consists of a data base founded upon a stratified national sample of 30,030 tenth graders (sophmores) and 28,240 twelfth graders (seniors) in 1980. Follow-Ups were conducted in 1982 (the scheduled year of high school graduation for the HSB-82 subsample), 1984, and 1986. Three noteworthy developments are revealed by these data. First, there was a rapid increase in the female postsecondary entrance rate between the 1972 and 1980 high school classes, and the female enrollment rate in 1982, although less than 1980, was still higher than twelve years before. Women were also enrolling pattern continued in 1982. By contrast, the rate for men in 1982 had fallen to less than it was in 1972. Second, the initial enrollment rate for black students rose between 1972 and 1980, and then fell for the 1982 high school class. A similar but less volatile fluctuation pattern was registered by hispanic students. Neither minority enrolled in postsecondary education at the same rate as white students in any year studied. The third development appears to be a general fall-off in initial postsecondary enrollment rates by the early 1980s.

At present, there are no longitudinal data for more recent years. The Department of Education has begun a new study, the National Education Longitudinal Study of 1988 (NELS 88), but data on postsecondary entrance will not be available until after 1992, when the eighth graders being surveyed are due to graduate from high school.

TABLE 4:
A Comparison of Initial Postsecondary Enrollment Data for NLS 72 and HSB 80/82 Secondary School Graduates

(Entrance Into Postsecondary Education Immediately)

STUDY, STATUS	TOTAL	SEX		RACE/ETHNICITY		
		MALE	FEM.	WHITE	BLACK	HISP.
72 Imm.	47.5	49.2	45.9	49.4	38.0	29.5
80 Imm.	52.6	50.2	54.8	53.7	46.7	42.3
82 Imm.	49.9	47.3	52.3	52.6	38.5	40.9

NOTE: Imm. = Immediate Enrollment after High School Graduation. Percentages are rounded and refer to percent of all surveyed individuals who entered postsecondary education immediately (same year as graduation).

SOURCE: Eva Eagle and C. Dennis Carroll, <u>Postsecondary Enrollment, Persistence, and Attainment for 1972, 1980, and 1982 High School Graduates</u>, (Washington: U.S. Government Printing Office, December 1988), pp. 2-3 and 28.

Characteristics of Entrants

Data from postsecondary enrollment surveys provides some information on the characteristics of those individuals who enter postsecondary education. These data are collected via the Department of Education's Integrated Postsecondary Education Data System (IPEDS), a series of coordinated survey instruments sent to all postsecondary institutions on an annual basis. The Fall Enrollment Survey of the IPEDS series provides the most complete and accurate source of nationwide information on official institutional records of student enrollment behavior and characteristics.

TABLE 5:
Trends in the Characteristics of First-Time
Enrollees in Postsecondary Institutions,
Selected Years 1977 - 1987

		\ All First-Time Undergraduate Enrollment (Fall Semester)							
Year	Total	% by Sex		% by Level		% by Status		% by Control	
		Male	Fem.	2 Yr	4 Yr	FT	PT	Pub.	Priv.
1977	2,394	48.3	51.7	52.3	47.7	70.2	29.8	80.3	19.7
1978	2,390	47.8	52.2	52.2	47.8	69.1	30.9	80.0	20.0
1979	2,503	47.1	52.9	53.1	46.9	68.2	31.8	80.5	19.5
1980	2,588	47.1	52.9	54.3	45.7	67.6	32.4	80.3	19.7
1981	2,595	46.9	53.1	54.8	45.2	67.0	33.0	79.9	20.1
1982	2,505	47.9	52.1	54.7	45.3	67.4	32.6	79.2	20.8
1983	2,444	47.4	52.6	53.7	46.3	68.7	31.3	78.5	21.5
1984	2,357	47.2	52.8	52.6	47.4	68.4	31.6	78.2	21.8
1985	2,292	47.0	53.0	51.3	48.7	69.9	30.1	77.5	22.5
1986	2,219	47.2	52.8	49.9	50.1	71.7	28.3	77.1	22.9
1987	2,246	46.6	53.4	48.3	51.7	72.4	27.6	77.4	22.6
Change 77-87	- 6.2	-1.7	+1.7	-4.0	+4.0	+2.2	-2.2	-2.9	+2.9

NOTE: Totals are in thousands; percentages are rounded.

SOURCE: U.S. Department of Education, National Center for Education Statistics, Digest of Education Statistics 1990, (Washington: U.S. Government Printing Office, February 1991), Table 165, p. 176.

Referring to Table 5, it can be seen that the majority of first-time enrollees have been women in every year studied, and that the proportion of first-time women has increased even as the overall postsecondary enrollment total has decreased. Across 1977-1987, postsecondary enrollments at first bulged from around 2.4 million to nearly 2.6 million (as of 1981), then fell to 2.2 million by decade's end. During this same period, female enrollment climbed twice, once between 1977-1981, and again between 1982-1987. The female enrollment patterns reported by institutions via the IPEDS surveys support the evidence from the longitudinal studies (see Table 4) showing that women tend to enter postsecondary education at higher rates than do men.

The enrollment status of first-time students has also exhibited changes between 1977 and 1987. Individuals enrolled on a part-time basis (as defined by reporting institutions) accounted for just under 30 percent of all first-timers in 1977, and very nearly the same proportion in 1987 (approximately 28 percent). (Real mumbers declined during this time, so there were actually even fewer part-time enrollees in 1987 than the percent suggests.) However, the data on part-time versus full-time enrollment actually described a curve in the intervening years, with one-third of all first-time students enrolled on a part-time basis in 1981 -- the highest proportion recorded during the time period under study.

Table 5 data also illustrate the relative volatility, in terms of enrollment data, of two-year colleges. These institutions comprise two types of entity: private (and some public) junior colleges offering mainly associate's degrees and preparing most of their students for transfer to four-year institutions (generally with very small enrollments and privately sponsored); and public community colleges (sometimes called vocational/technical colleges) that enroll students in a wide variety of less-than-four-year programs (usually with large, fluctuating enrollments of local commuters who often attend part-time). Enrollments in two-year institutions peaked in 1981, when such schools accounted for almost 55 percent of all first-time postsecondary students. Since then, two-year enrollments have fallen off, and stood at less than 50 percent of the total by 1987. Since actual numbers also fell during this period, the enrollment decline was absolute as well as relative. Two-year enrollments in 1987 stood at 169,000 less than in 1977; four-year enrollments had meanwhile increased slightly, by 21,000.

Paralleling the decline in enrollment at two-year institutions has been a similar fall-off in enrollments at all publicly controlled institutions, both two- and four-year. Private institutions have increased their share of initial postsecondary enrollments by some three percent, corresponding to an actual increase of approximately 37,000 enrollees in 1987 as compared to 1977. Public enrollment fell 89,000 between the same two years.

Before addressing the next chronological step, it is important to briefly divert attention to consider a critical issue influencing the progress of U.S. students through postsecondary education (and the health of U.S. postsecondary institutions). That issue is the financing of undergraduate studies by individuals and families. It is important to address this issue before continuing because, as in real life, affordability concerns exert influence over who continues and completes postsecondary studies, as well as who enters.

FINANCING UNDERGRADUATE STUDIES

It is a well-known fact that postsecondary education is not considered a social entitlement in the United States, although it is considered an important benefit to the economy and society worthy of public support. This means that postsecondary students in the U.S. have to finance their own educations, both as regards academic tuition and fees (the price institutions charge students for providing instruction, allowing use of research facilities, and awarding degrees) and other costs (including such items as room and board charges, fees for using recreational facilities, parking permits for commuters, and other expenses). These costs vary tremendously among institutions and types of education, as well as from year to year (3).

Self-financing does not mean a situation nearly as stark as it implies, however. All levels of government and nearly all postsecondary institutions, not to mention independent foundations and financial institutions as well as employers, provide different types of assistance to aspiring students and to those already enrolled. There is a myriad of public assistance programs at the local, state and Federal levels designed to help deserving individuals attend college (as well as graduate school), and there are even more private sources of such support. In addition, publicly controlled institutions are subsidized by the governments which operate them, and thus can charge students less money than most private institutions. (In some states the price public institutions can set is limited by law; in others it is regulated by oversight boards or through other means.)

Most postsecondary financial assistance may be defined as either need-based or talent-based. Need-based programs are intended for persons who demonstrate an inability to pay for their educations but who are otherwise qualified to enroll in postsecondary studies. Talent-based programs are competitive postsecondary scholarships available to the most academically qualified applicants regardless of financial need. In addition to these programs, which are generally in the form of grants that do not require repayment, there are loan programs available from all levels of government as well as private sources. Some financial assistance programs also carry other types of conditions with them, such as requiring that recipients take part-time jobs provided by the cooperating institution, that they enroll in certain institutions or programs of study, that they be residents of certain states (to qualify for state assistance), or that they agree to work in certain jobs (such as providing rural or inner-city services) for a time after graduation.

The aggregate data already discussed in this Chapter demonstrate that the U.S. tradition of treating postsecondary education as an economic opportunity rather than a subsidized right has not prevented the continued growth of a diverse, extensive and generally accessable range of postsecondary education options. Indeed, few countries in the world enroll such a high percentage of their populations in postsecondary studies, and few others manage to enroll such a wide mix of their population subgroups or socio-economic classes.

The General Cost of Postsecondary Education

To put the financial situation into perspective it is necessary to show how postsecondary education costs, and their increase over time, compare with family incomes. Table 6 presents data on the median family income of U.S. households over the years 1977-1987, and compares these figures with the average cost of full-time postsecondary education at public and private institutions in each of the same years. The median family income represents the point at which half of all American households earn above that figure, and half less, and is derived from calculations based on a family of four persons. It is used here to show what constitutes midlevel resources for a fairly large household (by contemporary standards) -- a deliberately generous estimate. By comparison, using average amounts for institutional costs illustrates what U.S. families would most likely encounter among the thousands of postsecondary institutions that they might look at in the process of making decisions about college.

As can be seen, in recent years Americans have been in for a growing "sticker shock" as they shop for affordable postsecondary education. While median family income has been declining in terms of relative purchasing power, college costs have been rising at even greater rates than the decline in incomes. Nor has this disequilibrium been confined to expensive private schools, allowing citizens to rely on affordable public institutions. While private costs have indeed skyrocketed -- at nine times the adjusted median income rate of change over the same decade this is not too sweeping a description -- public costs have also managed to increase by nearly four times the median income rate over the same period.

From these data it would appear that private institutions have become priced out of reach of at least half of all citizens, and that public institutions are rapidly becoming as unaffordable as private institutions were already in the late 1970s. One might also expect students and their families to seek less expensive alternatives, such as part-time study, delayed entry, and enrolling initially in less expensive two-year degree programs. As has been shown previously and will be illustrated again shortly, however, this shift does not appear to have taken place.

What might cause such an apparently counterintuitive result? One factor may be the extensive financial assistance available to students. Another factor is that the U.S. social custom of paying for one's own postsecondary education is widely accepted and is a perennial ritual for which individuals and families prepare. Yet another factor is the role that institutional pricing appears to play in advertising and validating a school's quality and attractiveness to consumers. While such a phenomenon may be unfamiliar to those who are used to national systems where educational quality is determined by non-market factors, and unattractive to those who view higher education as ethically and aesthetically "above" capitalism, it is a real factor in a system which accepts inter-institutional competition, depends to a great degree on consumer payments to finance operations, and has no nationally accepted authority to independently judge or decree which schools are the best. Evidence exists that institutional costs play such a role, and that U.S. consumers tend to use price as a significant factor in judging institutional quality (4).

TABLE 6:
Trends in the Cost of U.S. Postsecondary Education and the Relationship to Median Family Income, 1977 - 1987

Year	Median Family Income	Average Tuition, Room & Board			
		Public	%MFI	Private	%MFI
1977	$ 39,012	$ 3,832	9.8	$ 8,440	21.6
1978	39,383	3,701	9.4	8,378	21.3
1979	39,893	3,545	8.9	8,044	20.2
1980	36,391	3,480	9.6	8,025	22.1
1981	35,368	3,604	10.2	8,354	23.6
1982	34,550	3,813	11.0	8,963	25.9
1983	34,385	3,942	11.5	9,379	27.3
1984	35,025	4,096	11.7	9,859	28.2
1985	36,334	4,187	11.5	10,360	28.5
1986	36,645	4,429	12.1	11,157	30.5
1987	37,524	4,423	11.8	11,501	30.7
Change 77-87	- 3.8%	+15.4%	N/A	+36.3%	N/A

NOTE: Numbers and percentages have been rounded; table is keyed to constant 1989 U.S. dollars.

SOURCE: U.S. Department of Education, National Center for Education Statistics, *The Condition of Education 1990, Vol. 2: Postsecondary Education*, (Washington: U.S. Government Printing Office, 1990), p. 22.

Another way of looking at the changes in postsecondary costs, and one that has been of even more concern to policy makers than the steep increase in prices, is to examine the relationship between what institutions charge students and what it costs for them to deliver the educational services for which they charge. Table 7 presents a cost-price index based on the average public and private institutional educational expenses in each year 1977-1987, together with average tuition, room and board charges. Both indices are pegged to 1984 constant dollars. As one would expect, both types of index increased over the period examined, but with one difference noted. While public institutions were able to keep their charges in line with increases in their expenses, private institutions were not. It is this apparent excess of income over expenses that has created the current interest of state and Federal agencies, as well as various consumer groups, in the finances of private postsecondary education -- a sector that is partially tax-exempt under non-profit corporation statutes.

Table 7 also illustrates a second point. Postsecondary education is expensive, and this expense becomes most apparent in a system that operates as a consumer market and demands disclosure of actual costs. Much of the increase in costs documented over 1977-1987 has been the legitimate consequence of inflation and increased operating expenditures, and as such has tended to follow the pattern of the rest of the U.S. economy.

TABLE 7:
Postsecondary Education Cost Index Comparing
Student Charges to Institutional Expenses,
1977 - 1987

Year	Comparative Index (1971=100)			
	Public Institutions		Private Institutions	
	Operating Expenses	Student Charges	Operating Expenses	Student Charges
1977	101	92	103	99
1978	101	93	102	99
1979	103	90	101	99
1980	100	85	100	95
1981	96	83	98	95
1982	94	87	100	97
1983	97	92	101	107
1984	99	99	105	112
1985	108	104	112	118
1986	114	109	117	125
1987	116	112	124	134
Change 77-87	+ 15	+ 20	+ 21	+ 35

NOTE: Expenses = Average Institutional Expenditures on Educational Services and Operation; T, R & B = Average Tuition, Room and Board Costs Charged to Students.

SOURCE: U.S. Department of Education, National Center for Education Statistics, *The Condition of Education 1990, Vol. 2: Postsecondary Education*, (Washington: U.S. Government Printing Office, 1990), p. 88.

Financial Assistance

Students may apply for and receive assistance at any time in their academic careers; they may be approved for aid but not enroll for some reason or another; and they may (and usually do) receive more than one type of assistance from more than one source -- called an "aid package" in the parlance of U.S. academia. These realities make tracking the flow of aid by individual student a most difficult statistical exercise, with the result that most public figures are based on total amounts per type of aid or type of institution, often tabulated by student characteristics (level of enrollment, age, status, etc.). To get some idea of how aid is actually distributed to real people, it is necessary once again to turn to longitudinal studies that track cohorts of individuals over time or study similar types of students over time.

Table 8 presents data on student assistance from the Fifth Follow-Up (1986) to the National Longitudinal Study (NLS-72). This follow-up surveyed 12,841 individuals who had been NLS-72 participants. (Complete data are not yet available for HSB 80/82 postsecondary students.)

Several interesting points emerge from the NLS-72 financial aid data. First, a majority of respondents who attended college did not receive any assistance at any time between 1972 and 1986. This was true for all men, all women, and all white students, as well as all students whose family income levels placed them in either the middle or upper class. By contrast, a majority of black and hispanic students, and those of a lower-class socio-economic background, did receive some form of assistance. Such an observation is important, for it shows that -- at least for the NLS-72 cohort of students -- financial assistance programs really did help the groups at which they were aimed (5).

Students who enrolled in postsecondary programs but earned no credential (did not complete), or who enrolled in and completed a less-than-four-year program, tended not to receive assistance. Those who enrolled in four-year programs and who completed bachelor's degrees, however, tended to receive assistance more often than students in two-year institutions, while those enrolled in graduate studies received aid most often. As far as numbers go, bachelor's degree earners clearly received more financial assistance, as a group, than did any other category. They constituted around 34 percent of the sample. Students who earned no credential at all, at any level, constituted 39 percent; less-than-four-year degree earners 14.5 percent; and graduate students over 12 percent. Graduate students, though more likely than other groups of students to receive aid, were only a small percentage of the total sample.

To explore the types of financial assistance going to students it is necessary to track the assistance itself across time, noting how it flows to students in different types of institutions. This may partially be done via the U.C.L.A. data for traditional freshmen. These data, collected annually on the full-time freshman population, ignore part-time students and undergraduates enrolled beyond the first year. Incomplete as they may be, however, these data show definite changes in the pattern of financing postsecondary education over time, and are worth examining.

TABLE 8:
Financial Assistance Patterns for 1972 Secondary School Graduates Who Attended Postsecondary Institutions Between 1972 and 1984

Characteristic	Aid at Any Time 1972-74	Aid Only 1975-79 (Any Time)	Never Received Aid
All (N=12,332)	27.9%	16.4%	55.7%
Men	26.6	18.0	55.4
Women	29.3	14.8	55.9
White	26.4	15.7	57.9
Black	39.6	24.1	36.3
Hispanic	35.8	16.5	47.7
Low SES	37.2	18.6	44.2
Medium SES	28.6	15.8	55.6
High SES	23.0	15.8	61.2
No Degree Earned	19.1	14.7	66.2
Certificate/Lic.	14.3	18.1	67.6
Associate Degree	26.2	16.3	57.5
Bachelor's Degree	37.9	17.7	44.4
Graduate Degree	49.3	20.7	30.0

SOURCE: Clifford Adelman, *A College Course Map: Taxonomy and Transcript Data*, (Washington: U.S. Government Printing Office, October 1990), p. 246.

Table 9 presents data from the Cooperative Institutional Research Program (CIRP) database for full-time, first-time undergraduate students at two-year and four-year institutions. CIRP, based at the University of California at Los Angles and co-sponsored by the American Council on Education, conducts a survey of college freshmen (as first-year undergraduates are traditionally called in the U.S.) on an annual basis. These data help to clarify the patterns in assistance that have occurred over the 1977-1987 period. Comparing the two-year and four-year percentages, it is apparent that students in two-year institutions do indeed tend to receive less assistance overall than their four-year counterparts. They also spend less money on their educational programs in the first place (6). There also important differences in how two-year and four-year students pay for their educations. Over 1977-1987, family and personal resources are the only sources of money that most two-year students have tended to rely on. The third largest source of funds has tended to be work of some kind, followed by Federal grant and loan programs. These proportions have been fairly consistent over time, and support the profile of the typical two-year student as being older, more self-supporting, more likely to be holding a regular job, and more likely to be a part-time student than his or her four-year counterpart.

Data on four-year students themselves are equally revealing. As Table 9 illustrates, four-year college freshmen have historically tended to rely most heavily on family resources and savings to finance their educations, and less so on holding jobs. This observation is consistent with the profile of the traditional four-year student, who has generally been younger than his or her two-year counterpart, more likely to still be dependent on parental support, more likely to be a full-time student, and less likely to be holding a regular job.

However, the four-year data in Table 9 also show the profound shift that has been occurring in recent years in both the sources of college assistance and the nature of four-year students. Reliance on Federal grant assistance used to be the third most important source of funding for the majority of four-year freshman. It is no longer, a consequence of Federal policy shifts during the 1980s. As intended and predicted by these policy shifts, four-year students have fallen back on their own resources to a great extent, including a significant rise in the proportion who work at least part-time to finance their educations. Institutional and state government programs have taken up some of the gap created by a decline in available Federal support, but most of it has been absorbed by individuals and their families. Americans' determination to attend college may be gauged from the fact that a higher proportion of students and their families have been dipping into their savings and taking out private sector loans, despite tight economic times and the much higher interest rates charged by private lenders.

These data lend further weight to the importance of current American debates on how to deal with these rising costs in a period of general economic retrenchment. Obviously, the shift from a policy of mainly Federal assistance to one of shared responsibility for aid, coupled with more reliance of private/individual resources, has been achieved. But if costs continue to rise, at some point individuals and private sources will not be able to pay more -- or a much greater share -- in the absence of an economy that expands even more rapidly than college costs increase.

TABLE 9:
Trends in the Proportion of Freshmen Undergraduates Reporting Receiving Various Forms of Financial Assistance, 1977 - 1987

YEAR	\multicolumn{4}{c}{LOANS}				\multicolumn{3}{c}{GRANTS}			\multicolumn{3}{c}{FAMILY/SELF}			OTH.

FULL-TIME, FIRST-TIME ENROLLEES IN TWO-YEAR INSTITUTIONS

YEAR	\multicolumn{4}{c	}{LOANS}	\multicolumn{3}{c	}{GRANTS}	\multicolumn{3}{c	}{FAMILY/SELF}	OTH.
	Fed	S/L	Col	Prv	Fed	S/L	Col	Rel	Sav	Job	
1979	15.9	----	2.6	3.0	47.1	13.2	6.4	61.3	51.0	33.2	13.1
1981	31.0	----	3.1	3.9	43.6	12.9	6.5	63.1	55.1	29.3	14.8
1983	27.0	----	3.2	3.8	44.5	14.8	7.2	65.6	50.5	29.8	9.5
1985	27.6	----	3.4	3.8	35.5	12.4	10.2	61.5	61.3	33.9	7.4
1987	25.5	----	4.4	4.8	33.9	12.7	6.8	66.7	73.8	47.9	2.5
Change 79-87	+9.6	----	+1.8	+1.8	-13.2	-0.5	+0.4	+5.4	+22.8	+14.7	-10.6

FULL-TIME, FIRST-TIME ENROLLEES IN FOUR-YEAR INSTITUTIONS

YEAR	\multicolumn{4}{c	}{LOANS}	\multicolumn{3}{c	}{GRANTS}	\multicolumn{3}{c	}{FAMILY/SELF}	OTH.
	Fed	S/L	Col	Prv	Fed	S/L	Col	Rel	Sav	Job	
1979	24.3	----	3.9	3.8	53.6	16.3	14.5	75.8	67.5	21.9	18.3
1981	35.8	----	4.0	4.3	45.5	14.4	14.7	75.2	67.6	23.1	17.2
1983	29.5	----	4.0	4.1	49.0	16.1	17.2	76.7	65.0	22.8	15.4
1985	29.3	----	3.9	3.8	36.1	15.0	23.4	76.0	76.3	32.4	13.2
1987	26.8	----	5.8	5.1	34.9	17.9	16.2	84.0	88.9	42.4	17.6
Change 79-87	+2.5	----	+1.9	+1.3	-18.7	+1.6	+1.7	+8.2	+21.4	+20.5	-0.7

NOTE: Fed = Federal; S/L = State/Local Government; Col = Institution; Rel = Relatives (Parents/Spouse); Sav = Savings; Job = Full- or Part-Time Work While Enrolled; Oth = Other Public/Private Source. Percentages are rounded and do not add to 100 because of multiple responses.

SOURCE: Cooperative Institutional Research Program, U.C.L.A./American Council on Education, Annual College Freshman Survey Reports.

PATTERNS OF UNDERGRADUATE ENROLLMENT

Among the reasons that transition enrollment data are not reliable are that so many students enter postsecondary education at different points, transfer from one institution to another, stop out (leave school for a time), and drop in (re-enter school after a temporary absence). These patterns can produce errors in counts, but in the absence of definite national data standards the cost of controlling for them is often prohibitive. A good argument can also be made that the changing character of the student population (older, more part-timers, etc.) increasingly renders traditional statistics problematical, since these counting methods presuppose a student who enters postsecondary education at a fixed point, stays with the program until he or she graduates or drops out, and does not complicate the researcher's life with an undue amount of variation as to major, sequence of events, or interfering outside activity.

Perhaps the best way of treating these problems is to examine aggregate enrollment data. This is a count, to the extent possible in a non-mandatory census, of all registered students. Such data can provide a picture of enrollment patterns that takes into consideration all possible variations in registration behavior, and can be compared to graduation data. In addition, longitudinal study data can be referenced to to get a good idea of actual persistence patterns, that is, who continues in their studies after initial enrollment.

Aggregate Enrollment Trends

Table 10 presents comprehensive data on U.S. undergraduate enrollments over the period under study. Data are provided by raw count (in thousands), by percentages, and by gender (7). Several observations can be drawn from these data that help illuminate current postsecondary education policy debates in the U.S.

As with other data, figures on aggregate enrollment show that the size of the U.S. postsecondary student population has tended to increase in recent years, despite some predictions that enrollments would decline due to the end of the "baby boom" population cycle. The aggregate totals also demonstrate something else -- that the numbers of enrolled students in every surveyed minority population category have increased as well. The increases in numbers of enrolled hispanic, Asian-American, and foreign students have been particularly significant, but black and Native American enrollments have also gone up.

It is equally apparent that the record of across-the-board increases in enrolled numbers of students, by population sub-group, has not been matched when these raw totals are converted into percentages. Whites and blacks, for example, lost ground in terms of proportionate share of all enrollments relative to their position at the beginning of the period in question. Asian-Americans and hispanics, by contrast, gained significantly in terms of their percentage of all enrollments over the same period. The percentage of Native American and foreign enrollments also increased, but not by so much.

TABLE 10:
Trends in Undergraduate Fall Enrollments by Student Characteristics, 1976-1986

TOTAL NUMBER OF ENROLLED STUDENTS							
Year	Undergraduate Enrollment (2- and 4-Year, Thousands)						
	Total	White	Black	Hisp.	Asian	Nat.A.	Foreign
1976	9,419	7,741	943	353	169	70	143
1978	9,666	7,871	967	384	203	72	170
1980	10,469	8,481	1,019	433	249	78	210
1982	10,789	8,676	1,020	480	308	81	223
1984	10,611	8,484	995	495	343	78	216
1986	10,798	8,558	996	563	393	84	205
76-86	+14.6%	+10.6	+ 5.6	+59.6	+132.5	+20.0	+43.4
PERCENTAGE OF TOTAL, BY CHARACTERISTIC							
1976	100.0	82.2	10.0	3.8	1.8	0.7	1.5
1978	100.0	81.4	10.0	4.0	2.1	0.8	1.8
1980	100.0	81.0	9.7	4.1	2.4	0.8	2.0
1982	100.0	80.4	9.5	4.5	2.9	0.8	2.1
1984	100.0	80.0	9.4	4.7	3.2	0.7	2.0
1986	100.0	79.3	9.2	5.2	3.6	0.8	1.9
PERCENTAGE OF WOMEN, BY CHARACTERISTIC							
Year	Total	White	Black	Hisp.	Asian	Nat.A.	Foreign
1976	48.0	47.6	54.4	45.6	46.2	50.0	32.9
1978	50.9	50.7	56.9	49.5	47.3	52.8	31.8
1980	52.3	52.2	58.0	51.3	48.2	55.1	33.3
1982	52.4	52.4	58.3	51.7	47.1	55.6	33.2
1984	52.9	52.8	59.3	52.7	46.9	55.1	34.3
1986	53.5	53.5	59.6	53.1	47.3	56.0	36.1

NOTE: Numbers and percentages have been rounded.

SOURCE: U.S. Department of Education, National Center for Education Statistics, HEGIS/IPEDS Fall Enrollment Surveys, Annual tabulations in various editions of the Digest of Education Statistics.

The comparison between actual and proportional enrollments relates directly to critical questions of educational policy. Is it more important to cite improvements in aggregate numbers of enrolled students as evidence of equal opportunity for access to postsecondary education, or should policy makers be concerned with fluctuations in the proportionate share of all enrollments that a particular sub-group's members represents? If numbers are the key, then the position of all population groups has improved relative to the situation over a decade ago. But if the issue is perceived as one of proportionate representation, then both black and white Americans will -- as many have done -- voice concern over recent trends.

Turning to gender, Table 10 reveals equally important enrollment trends. Women have come to be the majority of all postsecondary students. It is noteworthy that this trend has been true of all population sub-groups in America except Asian-Americans and foreign students. In the former case, it is possible that family cultural traditions continue to inhibit female postsecondary enrollment rates. If this were true, though, it is interesting that such a factor appears not to have restricted hispanic female enrollment trends. On the other hand, the relatively low percentage of foreign students who are female is unquestionably a reflection of the generally low rate of female postsecondary enrollment in many countries that send students to the United States.

Another point revealed by the percentage of female enrollees is the growing predominance of females among all black and Native American postsecondary students. Females have long been a majority of black students in U.S. colleges, and by 1986 they accounted for nearly 60 percent of all such students. (Preliminary reports suggest that that trend has continued since 1986.) This is an enrollment rate considerably in excess of the female share of the black population, and is indicative of the current concern in the United States over the status, opportunities, and future of the current generation of college-age black males. The fact that the black female percentage has increased even as the overall percentage of enrolled blacks has declined (and the total expanded) makes the issue only more significant. Women are somewhat less predominant among Native American enrollees than among blacks, but their percentage of the small Native American student population is still quite large, and may point up similar patterns of enrollment for members of that minority group.

Table 11 points to the ways in which the age and enrollment status of undergraduate students have varied over the period 1975-1986. These percentages demonstrate the degree to which students in community and junior colleges (two-year programs) are part-timers, and the contrast between them and their four-year counterparts, who are mainly full-time students. The proportions mirror each other: approximately two-thirds of all two-year students tend to be part-time students, while a little less than one-third of all four-year students are part-time. Both percentages have risen slightly in recent years.

Part-time students tend to be older than the traditional undergraduate college age range, as can be seen from the age data presented in Table 11. Around 20 percent of traditional college-age students (from under 18 to 24) have tended to be part-time, while nearly three-fourths of undergraduate adult learners (students over 25) enroll as part-time students. It is significant that the proportion of traditional-age students in the undergraduate population has been shrinking, for this trend is likely to result in more part-time students as well. These data also permit the inference that many female students, who tend to be part-time more often than male students, and most two-year undergraduates, the majority of whom are part-timers, are older than the traditional age of college attendance.

TABLE 11:
Trends in the Age and Enrollment Status of U.S.
Undergraduates, by Level and Sex,
Selected Years 1975-1986

CHARACTERISTIC	PERCENT OF TOTAL IN REPORTING YEAR			
	1975	1980	1985	1986
ENROLLMENT IN ALL TWO-YEAR INSTITUTIONS				
% PT of All Students	55.6	61.3	62.7	63.8
% Male PT (of All PT)	51.1	42.1	41.4	41.4
% Female PT (")	48.9	57.9	58.6	58.6
% PT of All Males	51.2	59.4	60.5	61.7
% PT of All Females	59.8	64.7	65.8	66.7
ENROLLMENT IN ALL FOUR-YEAR INSTITUTIONS				
% PT of All Students	29.6	29.4	30.2	30.7
% Male PT (of All PT)	51.2	45.7	44.4	43.7
% Female PT (")	48.8	54.3	55.6	56.3
% PT of All Males	27.4	26.6	27.1	27.4
% PT of All Females	32.2	32.3	33.3	33.8
AGE AND STATUS FOR ALL UNDERGRADUATES				
% 24 Years and Under	63.1	62.5	58.4	57.9
% 24/Under PT	20.5	20.2	19.9	20.7
% 25 Years and Older	36.9	37.5	41.6	42.1
% 25/Older PT	70.2	76.5	73.5	73.7

NOTE: Percentages are rounded; not all columns add to 100.

SOURCE: U.S. Department of Education, National Center for Education Statistics, <u>Digest of Education Statistics 1990</u>, (Washington: U.S. Government Printing Office, February 1991), Tables 159 and 163, pp. 169 and 173.

Persistence Patterns

Among the most important questions relative to progress through postsecondary education are those addressing the issue of who stays the course and finishes. This is particularly important at the undergraduate level, since undergraduate degrees and certificates (what much of the rest of the world calls "first-university degrees and diplomas") are the markers that both justify the expense and time devoted to such study, and certify an individual's preparation for either further study or a chance at a job with advanced career potential.

The best current American source of information about undergraduate persistence and attainment patterns is the PETS 1984 transcript study undertaken as part of the National Longitudinal Study of the High School Class of 1972. (In 1993 similar data for the High School Class of 1982 will be available.) Data from PETS 84 are available for students who undertook both two-year and four-year studies (sometimes continuing from one level to the other), and are summarized here in Tables 12A and 12B.

Turning first to Table 12A, it will be seen that most of the sample of respondents who earned two-year degrees did so within four and one-half years of graduating from high school, and the majority of that group earned their degrees in two and one-half years. When the sample was broken out by various subcategories, however, it emerged that a significant proportion of two-year degrees were also earned much later, after six to eight years, and might indicate adult students who either began their studies after a delay or returned to school after a lengthy stopout period. This pattern was particularly true of minority group respondents and persons with a high socio-economic status background. The data also indicate that persons who delayed entry into postsecondary education tended to take longer to finish, and were less likely to do so that those who began immediately and did not interrupt their studies.

Data for four-year degree earners, presented in Table 12B, reveals a predictable pattern except at two points. A significant number of bachelor's degree earners took longer than four and one-half years to earn their degrees, and a significant number of hispanic bachelor's degree earners appeared to have delayed their educations considerably. Such a delay was also apparent in the case of some high- and low-socio-economic background respondents. Delayed studies, as with two-year degree earners, tended to lengthen the time taken and reduce the chances of finishing.

The issue of how long it takes U.S. undergraduates to complete their studies is further illuminated by the data presented in Table 13, which compares average time-to-degree in months for the different subsamples of the PETS 84 bachelor's degree recipients. These data confirm that the "other minority" subsample, mainly hispanic students, tended to delay or stretch out their studies in comparison with other respondent groups. It also, and most importantly, demonstrates that the typical American bachelor's degree earner has been taking over 4.5 years to complete his or her program and earn a degree, regardless of background or other characteristics. This observation runs counter to the assumption that, since most four-year students are traditional full-time students, they ought to be pursuing a sequence of studies

TABLE 12A:
Persistence and Attendance Patterns for Students
Participating in the Postsecondary Education
Transcript Study, NLS/72, 1984
(ASSOCIATE DEGREE EARNERS)

Category	Percent of Earners	\multicolumn{7}{c}{Year/Range in Which Degree Earned}
		72-74	1975	1976	1977	1978	79-80	81-84
All (N=1055)	100.0%	38.4	19.7	10.7	5.9	5.9	9.6	9.9
Men	45.4	34.6	20.6	13.7	5.1	5.9	11.0	9.0
Women	54.6	41.5	18.9	8.1	6.5	5.8	8.3	10.7
White	90.2	40.0	19.0	10.8	6.2	5.1	9.2	9.8
Black	5.9	21.4	28.0	7.5	1.1	14.3	13.1	14.6
Hispanic	3.9	28.4	23.4	13.2	5.8	11.3	12.4	5.4
Low SES	18.0	34.0	21.9	9.2	4.8	10.3	13.0	7.0
Medium SES	55.4	44.0	17.7	10.6	5.3	4.5	8.0	9.9
High SES	25.6	30.1	22.5	11.8	8.1	5.5	10.0	12.0
0- 6 Delay	75.6	49.3	20.6	10.2	5.2	3.8	5.6	5.4
7-18 Delay	9.0	11.0	39.5	14.0	7.5	4.7	17.0	6.4
19-30 Delay	5.2	5.2	11.2	32.5	9.5	11.7	15.0	15.0
31-54 Delay	5.7	---	---	0.9	13.3	29.6	28.8	27.5
55+ Delay	4.9	---	---	---	1.5	7.2	29.1	62.3

NOTE: Percentages are rounded; rows add to 100. Delay refers to the number of months between secondary school graduation and initial enrollment in postsecondary education.

SOURCE: Clifford Adelman, <u>A College Course Map: Taxonomy and Transcript Data</u>, (Washington: U.S. Government Printing Office, October 1990), p. 249.

TABLE 12B:
Persistence and Attendance Patterns for Students
Participating in the Postsecondary Education
Transcript Study, NLS/72, 1984
(BACHELOR'S DEGREE EARNERS)

Category	Percent of Earners	\multicolumn{7}{c}{Year/Range in Which Degree Earned}
		pre76	1976	1977	1978	1979	1980	81-84
All (N=4927)	100.0%	4.8	55.2	19.9	7.8	4.1	3.3	5.0
Men	53.0	3.8	50.9	22.7	9.6	4.5	3.7	5.5
Women	47.0	6.7	60.1	16.7	5.7	3.7	2.8	4.4
White	92.7	4.7	56.1	19.8	7.5	3.9	3.1	4.9
Black	5.6	5.6	48.7	21.2	8.7	5.2	3.8	6.7
Hispanic	1.8	3.8	32.6	17.5	16.0	11.8	12.2	5.6
Low SES	10.1	4.7	48.0	18.2	9.0	6.9	6.3	6.9
Medium SES	48.8	3.8	54.6	19.7	7.5	4.8	3.8	5.7
High SES	41.1	5.6	57.4	20.2	7.6	2.9	2.2	3.9
0- 6 Delay	88.4	5.2	59.3	19.5	6.9	3.3	2.3	3.5
7-18 Delay	6.1	2.1	30.0	32.7	16.0	6.6	5.2	7.3
19-30 Delay	2.5	3.5	38.5	14.2	15.4	7.5	9.1	11.9
31-54 Delay	2.3	---	2.6	12.7	12.6	23.2	24.7	24.3
55+ Delay	0.8	---	---	---	2.5	8.1	15.0	74.4

NOTE: Percentages are rounded; rows add to 100. Delay refers to the number of months between secondary school graduation and initial enrollment in postsecondary education.

SOURCE: Clifford Adelman, <u>A College Course Map: Taxonomy and Transcript Data</u>, (Washington: U.S. Government Printing Office, October 1990), p. 248.

that gets them through within the time that a four-year degree is supposed to take. This is in fact not the case.

Further evidence that American undergraduates are taking longer to complete their studies than conventional wisdom assumes is provided by data from the Recent College Graduates Survey (RCG), a survey of individuals one year after graduating from college that is periodically conducted by the National Center for Education Statistics. In Table 14, data from the RCG Surveys conducted in 1977 (of 1976 bachelor's degree recipients) and 1986 (of 1985 bachelor's degree recipients) are compared.

In nearly every category in Table 14 for which adequate data were collected a similar pattern emerged. The proportion of students earning the bachelor's degree within four years fell between 1977 and 1986, and the proportion taking longer -- sometimes much longer -- rose. The only exception to this pattern was, once again, hispanic students, but data for them indicate that the tendency toward delayed enrollment and completion detected for them in the NLS 72 data has recently begun to change, and more hispanic students are now entering college earlier. This can be viewed as a positive development, since earlier entry has been associated with a greater likelihood of completing a degree program.

TABLE 13:
Time to the Bachelor's Degree
for NLS/72 PETS Respondents
With Selected Characteristics

CHARACTERISTIC	AVERAGE TIME TO DEGREE
All Bachelor's Recipients	54.2 (months)
Male Bachelor's Recipients	55.6 "
Female Bachelor's Recipients	52.7 "
White Bachelor's Recipients	54.0 "
Black Bachelor's Recipients	55.8 "
Other Minority Recipients	56.9 "
Low SES Bachelor's Recipients	55.7 "
Medium SES Bachelor's Recipients	54.7 "
High SES Bachelor's Recipients	53.5 "

NOTE: Average times are for all respondents in each category who had earned a bachelor's degree by 1984.

SOURCE: Paula R. Knepper, Student Progress in College: NLS-72 Postsecondary Education Transcript Study, 1984, (Washington: U.S. Government Printing Office, February 1989), pp. 42.

TABLE 14:
Comparison of Time to the Bachelor's Degree from Secondary Graduation, by Characteristic, 1977 and 1986

Characteristic	Percent Obtaining Bachelor's Degree In:			
	4 Years	5 Years	6 Years	Over 6
1977 Total	53.8	17.1	6.2	22.9
1986 Total	45.5	20.0	7.5	27.0
77-86 Change	- 8.3	+ 2.9	+ 1.3	+ 4.1
1977 Men	47.8	17.8	7.9	26.5
1986 Men	41.4	22.0	9.5	27.1
77-86 Change	- 6.4	+ 4.2	+ 1.6	+ 0.6
1977 Women	61.2	16.1	4.1	18.6
1986 Women	49.4	18.0	5.8	26.8
77-86 Change	-11.8	+ 1.9	+ 1.7	+ 8.2
1977 White	55.2	17.2	5.8	21.8
1986 White	47.1	20.2	7.2	25.5
77-86 Change	- 8.1	+ 3.0	+ 1.4	+ 3.7
1977 Black	42.3	15.9	9.1	32.7
1986 Black	31.8	19.8	10.0	38.4
77-86 Change	-10.5	+ 3.9	+ 0.9	+ 5.7
1977 Hispanic	31.4	17.0	7.3	44.3
1986 Hispanic	33.5	18.1	11.3	37.1
77-86 Change	+ 2.1	+ 1.1	+ 4.0	- 7.2
1977 Asian	48.2	18.3	10.4	23.1
1986 Asian	35.4	22.0	9.3	33.3
77-86 Change	-12.8	+ 3.7	- 1.1	+10.2
1977 Native Amer.	--.-	--.-	--.-	--.-
1986 Native Amer.	42.4	16.1	5.1	36.4
77-86 Change	N/A	N/A	N/A	N/A
1977 Other Min.	--.-	--.-	--.-	--.-
1986 Other Min.	31.9	14.2	11.7	42.2
77-86 Change	N/A	N/A	N/A	N/A

NOTE: Blank cells for 1977 data indicate too few sample observations for reliable analysis.

SOURCE: U.S. Department of Education, National Center for Education Statistics, The Condition of Education 1991, (Washington: U.S. Government Printing Office, 1991), p. 30.

What about actual completion (graduation) rates? Data to answer this question exist in two forms: crude comparisons of initial enrollment rates for certain years with degree completion rates a given number of years later, and comparatively good longitudinal data about the experiences of single sample cohorts of students (such as the NLS 72 data).

The first of these data sets can give only a vague impression of completion rates, but may be briefly examined in the absence of any other comprehensive national tracking data. Table 15 presents comparisons of the bachelor's degrees reported earned in the U.S. during 1977-1987 with reported initial postsecondary enrollment counts five years earlier (1972-1982). Such a comparison must be viewed with great caution, since its crudity ignores variables such as transfers and part-time status, and there is no way to know what proportion of the same people are being captured by these ratios. Furthermore, the choice of five years' difference is not precisely reflective of what is known about actual average time-to-degree (4.5 years is closer), but reflects dependence on annual institutional reports for the source of raw data.

The ratios indicate that between 50 and 60 percent of full-time freshmen entering four-year colleges in the United States have, in recent years, tended to graduate within five years of their initial enrollment. This result is not very different from that suggested by the PETS 84 (NLS-72) and RCG data.

Much more powerful data on completion rates are available for the NLS-72 sample, although these data are reflective of only one generation of American college students. Since the NLS-72 (and PETS 84) data have shown considerable congruity with data patterns derived more recently, however, this is not a great obstacle to using NLS-72 data for making general observations about recent historical trends. Using the NLS-72 data also allows for in-depth exploration of different variables that may or may not be associated with different rates of degree completion.

TABLE 15:
Ratio of Individuals Earning Bachelor's Degrees to Full-Time, First-Time Freshmen Five Years Earlier, 1977 - 1987

Year (Ending)	Ratio
1977	0.573
1978	0.585
1979	0.573
1980	0.556
1981	0.530
1982	0.573
1983	0.577
1984	0.590
1985	0.574
1986	0.565
1987	0.570

SOURCE: U.S. Department of Education, National Center for Education Statistics, The Condition of Education 1990, (Washington: U.S. Government Printing Office, 1990), p. 36.

Data presented in Table 16 indicate that, overall, around 41 percent of 1972 high school graduates who began a four-year program immediately after secondary school actually completed a degree. Varying the traditional pattern of undergraduate studies did not make for academic success, however, according to these data. The drop-off in completion rates for persons who delayed the start of their postsecondary studies was truly striking. This result has caused policy makers who notice the trend of more recent data (see Table 13) to be very concerned about current completion rates, and also has implications for the financing of postsecondary studies in view of the increasing tendency of students to work part-time, which may mean even more delay in their postsecondary student careers.

Table 16 also indicates that PETS 84 respondents who attended public four-year institutions during their undergraduate careers were less likely to graduate than were their counterparts at private institutions. This finding may in part be due to the fact that many public institutions are required by state laws to be less selective in admissions at the undergraduate level, even though their graduation requirements may be as rigorous as any. The discrepancy between public and private graduation rates was maintained by those respondents who transferred from public to private institutions or the reverse.

Interestingly, however, the graduation rate for respondents who progressed from a two-year to a four-year program was higher for those continuing in public institutions. No clear reason for this finding suggests itself, but two possibilities -- both consistent with the rest of the sample data -- might be candidates. Many public institutions have articulation agreements with local public community college systems, which promote the transfer of qualified two-year students and which try to ensure that such students take courses that adequately prepare them for the demands of four-year programs. Private four-year institutions do not often have such arrangements with two-year institutions, and their entry-level academic demands are often high due to their ability to carefully select their students. These factors could concievably account for two-year transfers having a higher rate of success at public four-year institutions than at private ones. A second possible reason for the discrepancy is money, irrespective of preparation. Public institutions are less expensive than private ones, and many persons who can afford the price and time demands of two-year colleges (whose schedules are often arranged to accomodate part-time adults with responsibilities other than schoolwork) may find that private four-year programs, often oriented toward traditional undergraduates, are simply too expensive and/or inconvenient to manage. Neither possibility excludes the other.

UNDERGRADUATE DEGREE COMPLETIONS

The key measure of success in any educational program is satisfying the requirements and graduating with an earned credential. In American undergraduate postsecondary education, there are three types of credentials that can be earned: postsecondary certificates, associate degrees, and bachelor's degrees.

Postsecondary certificates are of two kinds: less-than-four-year vocational or technical diplomas certifying completion of an occupationally specific program of training, and specialist certificates awarded along with associate and bachelor's degrees that certify competency in a certain subject, such as foreign languages or computer skills. Completion data for neither type of certificate program are presented here, but information on earners of these awards will be discussed later on in the section on employment outcomes.

Associate and bachelor's degrees are the recognized U.S. undergraduate academic degrees. Associate degrees are awarded for the successful completion of two-year programs, and bachelor's degrees for successfully completing

TABLE 16:
Bachelor's Degree Completion Rates
for NLS/72 PETS Respondents
With Selected Characteristics

CHARACTERISTIC	DEGREE COMPLETION RATE
Immediate PSE Entry	40.6 %
2-3 Year Delay in Entry	21.0 %
More Than 3 Years Delay	11.6 %
Earned at Public Institution	57.6 %
Earned at Private Institution	61.5 %
Transferred, Private to Public	65.0 %
Transferred, Public to Private	69.0 %
Progressed, 2- to 4-Year, Public	67.2 %
Progressed, 2- to 4-Year, Private	61.8 %

NOTE: Percentages are rounded and refer to all respondents in each category who began a degree program and who completed it, as of 1984. PSE Entry = Initial enrollment in a postsecondary institution; Public/Private refers to control of institution; Transferred = moved from one 4-year institution to another prior to earning degree; Progressed = transferred from a 2-year to a 4-year institution en route to the bachelor's degree.

SOURCE: Paula R. Knepper, Student Progress in College: NLS-72 Postsecondary Education Transcript Study, 1984, (Washington: U.S. Government Printing Office, February 1989), pp. 43.

four-year programs or the equivalent (8). While these degrees can be awarded for the study of either professional or traditional academic subjects (what Americans call "liberal arts" or "general studies" subjects), they are called academic degrees to distinguish them from shorter training programs that do not require students to cover a subject in so much depth (including related theory), nor require students to master as broad a range of related knowledge.

Associate Degree Completions.

The associate degree is considerably less common than the bachelor's degree as a credential, even taking into account the fact that the two-year student population is smaller than the four-year population. Recent data indicate that the number of students completing this degree has been rising, however. Table 17 shows aggregate data on associate degree completions during 1985-1987 (9).

Two interesting pieces of information emerge from the data in Table 17. First, it is noteworthy that the proportion of associate degrees awarded to foreign students appears to be falling, for -- as will be demonstrated

TABLE 17:
Trends in Associate Degrees Earned by U.S. Students,
by Race/Ethnicity and Sex, 1985 and 1987

Year	Number of Degrees Conferred by Category						
	Total	White	Black	Hispanic	Asian	N.Amer.	Foreign
1985	426,870	355,343	35,799	19,407	9,914	2,953	6,407
1987	433,112	361,819	35,466	19,345	11,794	3,196	4,688
85-87	+ 1.5%	+ 1.8	- 0.9	- 0.3	+19.0	+ 8.2	-26.8
Degrees Conferred by Category as a Percent of Total								
1985	100.0	83.2	8.4	4.6	2.3	0.7	1.5
1987	100.0	83.5	8.2	4.5	2.7	0.7	1.1
Percent of Degrees Conferred on Females in Each Category								
1985	55.7	55.7	60.4	55.9	44.6	59.4	42.3
1987	56.2	56.3	60.7	54.7	47.7	60.5	45.4

NOTE: Detailed data on Associate Degree Earners are only available for the academic years ending in 1985 and 1987.

SOURCE: U.S. Department of Education, National Center for Education Statistics, HEGIS/IPEDS Program Completions Survey, Annual tabulations in Digest of Education Statistics. (Breakouts are prepared for odd-numbered years only).

TABLE 18:
Trends in the Award of Bachelor's Degrees to U.S. Students, by Race/Ethnicity and Sex, Selected Years 1977 - 1987

Year	Number of Degrees Conferred by Category						
	Total	White	Black	Hispanic	Asian	N.Amer.	Foreign
1977	915,131	805,186	58,515	18,663	13,745	3,319	15,703
1979	916,226	799,617	60,125	20,029	15,336	3,404	17,715
1981	934,800	807,319	60,673	21,832	18,794	3,593	22,589
1985	968,311	826,106	57,473	25,874	25,395	4,246	29,217
1987	991,260	841,820	56,555	26,990	32,618	3,971	29,307
77-87	+ 8.3%	+ 4.6	- 3.3	+ 44.6	+137.3	+ 19.7	+ 86.6
Degrees Conferred by Category as a Percent of Total							
1977	100.0	88.8	6.4	2.0	1.5	0.4	1.7
1979	100.0	87.3	6.6	2.2	1.7	0.4	1.9
1981	100.0	86.4	6.5	2.3	2.0	0.4	2.4
1985	100.0	85.3	5.9	2.7	2.6	0.4	3.0
1987	100.0	84.9	5.7	2.7	3.3	0.4	3.0
Percent of Degrees Conferred on Females in Each Category							
1977	46.3	45.9	57.2	45.1	44.8	45.9	27.8
1979	48.4	48.1	59.2	48.3	46.6	49.2	27.9
1981	49.8	49.7	59.6	50.5	46.2	52.7	27.7
1985	50.8	51.0	60.0	52.1	46.6	52.9	31.2
1987	51.5	51.7	60.2	52.3	47.1	54.2	33.1

SOURCE: U.S. Department of Education, National Center for Education Statistics, HEGIS/IPEDS Program Completions Survey, Annual tabulations in *Digest of Education Statistics*. (Breakouts are prepared for odd-numbered years only).

throughout this section -- this runs counter to the general trend for awards to foreign students. And second, it is apparent that (except for a significant increase in the relatively small number of Asian-Americans earning associate degrees) this degree is predominantly popular with white students. Any notion that minority groups earn two-year degrees more frequently than they earn four-year degrees is not borne out by the reported data (see also Table 18).

Bachelor's Degree Completions.

Data on bachelor's degree completions are available for the period 1977-1987. These data, presented in Table 18, show that the total number of bachelor's degrees awarded increased modestly to significantly for all population subgroups except blacks. Bachelor's degrees awarded to foreign students, Asian-Americans, hispanics, and Native Americans increased significantly, while the number awarded to whites managed to increase even as the white percentage of all awards declined. Black bachelor's degree recipients, on the other hand, not only declined in absolute numbers but also as a percentage of the total. The proportion of degrees awarded to Native Americans could not be accurately determined because the total number remained so small in all years studied, but an examination of the actual count of Native American bachelor's degrees shows that this number did significantly increase in size from 1977 to 1987, even though representing a tiny share of the total number awarded.

During 1977-1987 females moved from earning a minority of all U.S. bachelor's degrees to earning a majority. This milestone happened around 1982 for the total population of bachelor's degree earners, although the pattern varied by subgroup. Black females earned a disproportionate share of black bachelor's degrees throughout the 1977-1987 period, winding up the period with over 60 percent of the total. Native American women passed men in earning bachelor's degrees around 1980, and hispanic women by 1981. Neither of these female cohorts represented as disproportionate a share of their subgroup's bachelor's degree earners as did black women. Native American female undergraduate enrollments tended to be a larger proportion of that subgroup's representation than did actual degree earners (compare with Table 9). Asian-American women, by contrast, were still a minority of that subgroup's bachelor degree earners as of 1987, as were foreign women.

These points conclude the findings from available data on the aggregate progress of United States students into and through undergraduate postsecondary education. (Refer to Chapter Two of this report for data on specific subjects studied at this level.) Two tasks remain, examining information on those students who pursue further postsecondary education, and examining how undergraduates and graduate students fare once they leave school and enter the workforce. Because graduate study is really preparation for a specific occupation (whether academic research and teaching or professional practice), and because data on the pursuit of graduate studies are commonly grouped together with other types of employment data, we will consider graduate study to be a subset of post-bachelor's degree employment. Before considering graduate study, therefore, we will first direct attention to the general question of what happens to undergraduate degree earners as they enter the labor market.

UNDERGRADUATE DEGREE EARNERS IN THE LABOR MARKET

A considerable degree of attention has been focused on the employment prospects and opportunities for holders of U.S. bachelor's degrees, with the conventional wisdom holding that such graduates are increasingly unlikely to find satisfactory work, or even any work at all in some cases. To a great extent this debate can only be settled by looking at employment experiences by specific major field of study, since prospects vary quite at bit from field to field. Chapter Two of this report does just that. Nevertheless, aggregate data can shed light on general employment trends and answer some important questions about how we define employment, thus clarifying the issues.

General Trends and Definitions.

The Recent College Graduates (RCG) Survey, which was conducted in various years on national samples of bachelor's degree recipients one year after graduation, provides a comparison of post-graduation employment experiences for students at either end of the decade being examined in this report. Table 19 presents data from the RCG on general employment characteristics, including earnings and status, for these graduates.

Table 19 helps demonstrate several important points. First, the structure of the table itself shows that United States national employment data typically distinguish full-time work for an employer, including self-employment, from all other types of work and non-work. Furthermore, other work includes graduate study as well as part-time employment, and later on it will be shown that these categories are often related. When appropriate elements of the "other" category are added to the employment column -- as they should be -- the proportion of employed bachelor's degree recipients changes dramatically. As for unemployment, this concept is also complex and is subdivided into two types of unemployment: those unemployed and seeking work, and those who are unemployed but not seeking work (not in the labor force). Only the former subcategory constitutes genuine unemployment.

Average earnings have tended to follow the same pattern as the full-time employment rate, and have always been low for those just starting out. This result is partly due to the differences in initial earning power for graduates in technical and non-technical fields (lumped together in this presentation), partly a reflection of nationwide costs of living (which affect pay levels and vary widely by region and urban/rural mix), and partly a reflection of the fact that a bachelor's degree in most professions is not a guarantee of instant financial well-being. It is a ticket to future opportunity (often involving further education) rather than a confirmation of success.

Another interesting point demonstrated by the RCG data is that most bachelor's degree earners do not immediately begin working in fields related to their undergraduate studies. Only around one-third of RCG respondents who are employed full-time reported work related to their undergraduate major. Half of them reported working in a job that made use of their degree qualification but had little or nothing to do with what they actually studied, while the remainder, between 10 and 15 percent, reported that they held a job that did not even require a bachelor's degree of any kind. The latter percentage, together with the low starting earnings, indicates that underemployment is a

TABLE 19:
Trends in the Employment Status and Average Salary of U.S. Bachelor's Degree Recipients One Year After Graduation, Selected Years 1976 - 1987

Survey Year	Mean* FT Salary	Employment Status		Type of Work (Full-Time Only)		
		F-Time	Other*	Related*	Unrelated*	Non-Prof.*
1976	$15,500	67 %	33 %	35 %	55 %	10 %
1981	$19,200	71 %	29 %	38 %	50 %	12 %
1985	$18,700	73 %	27 %	38 %	49 %	13 %
1987	$20,300	74 %	26 %	38 %	48 %	14 %
Change 78-87	+ 31.0%	+ 7	- 7	+ 3	- 7	+ 4

NOTE: Figures and percents are rounded. Mean* Full-Time (FT) Salary refers to persons with full-time jobs and not enrolled in school. Other* Employment Status refers to the sum of respondents who reported part-time employment, were seeking work, were enrolled in further education, or were unemployed but not seeking work. Under Type of Work, Related = Work Related to the Major Field of Study; Unrelated = Professional or Managerial-Level Work Not Related to the Major Field of Study; and Non-Prof. = Work that is Non-Professional in Character and Did Not, in Respondent's Opinion, Require the Level of Education She/He Possessed. Salaries are given in constant 1987 dollars.

SOURCE: U.S. Department of Education, National Center for Education Statistics, *Digest of Education Statistics 1990*, (Washington: U.S. Government Printing Office, February 1991), Tables 348 and 352, pp. 368 and 371.

more significant problem for bachelor's degree recipients who enter the workforce than actual unemployment.

The relatively low relationship of undergraduate studies to job type points up a significant difference between U.S. undergraduate education and that of many other countries -- here the first postsecondary degree is not necessarily intended to prepare a person for a career path unless it is earned in a field for which it actually fulfills a credentialing requirement. The bachelor's degree is a general capstone to preparatory education in most cases, and is designed as much to equip a person with a general education -- or preparation for further specific study -- as it is to serve as a job qualification.

The Experience of One Generation.

Data from the National Longitudinal Study of 1972 provide another opportunity to examine how education and work experience interact. While the high school class of 1972 began to enter the labor market long before the decade that is the subject of this report, the data reported by them are nevertheless useful both as a comparison to the more recent RCG data and as a much more powerful set of numbers, in view of the nature of the longitudinal study itself.

Table 20 presents data on NLS-72 respondents' work experience between 1979 (the year of the Fourth Follow-Up) and 1986 (the year of the Fifth Follow-Up), broken out according to the level of education completed as of the latter year. These data were collected somewhat differently from those for the RCG, in that the NILF category included those seeking work as well as those not seeking work. Aside from this difference, the categories are similar.

The salient point in Table 20 is the low percentage of respondents who held continuous full-time jobs, even as long as twelve years after completing school. Much of this is the consequence of continuing in school after the 1972 high school graduation, since full-time enrollment in any year would, according to the definitions used here, take one out of the full-time employment category at least temporarily. It also accounts for why the percentage of intermittent full-time employed tends to increase as the postsecondary degree level increases, and why the proportion in this category is so high for those with two-year and graduate degrees (both groups tend to attend school, and work, intermittently). The steady shrinkage in the NILF category across degree levels, however, indicates increased success in either finding work or enrolling in further education, or both.

TABLE 20:
Employment Status of Participants in the NLS/72 Study
Who Possessed at Least a Secondary Diploma,
Between 1979 and 1986 (Fifth Follow-Up)

Employment Status	Level of Education Attained (% by Status)					
	Total	H.S.	Some PS	1-2yr	Bach.	Grad.
Total	100.0	100.0	100.0	100.0	100.0	100.0
Continuous FT	39.0	33.1	41.8	39.7	44.1	39.6
Intermit. FT	33.7	30.0	32.7	37.0	35.0	46.0
Part-Time	6.8	7.8	6.1	9.1	5.7	5.0
NILF	20.4	29.2	19.4	14.2	15.3	9.4

NOTE: H.S. = Possessed a High School Diploma; Some PS = Recorded Some Postsecondary Credits but Earned No Degree; 1-2yr = One- or Two-Year Degree/Certificate; Bach. = Bachelor's Degree; Grad. = First-Professional, Master's, or Doctorate Degree. For Employment Status, Continuous FT = Employed Continuously Full-Time Between 1979 and 1986; Intermit. FT = Employed Intermittently Full-Time; Part-Time = Steady Work, but Not Full-Time; NILF = Not in Labor Force.

SOURCE: Eva Eagle, et. al., A Descriptive Summary of 1972 High School Seniors: Fourteen Years Later, (Washington: U.S. Government Printing Office, August 1988), pp. D-7.

An even more informative record of experience is presented in Table 21, where the mean hourly earnings of NLS 72 respondents are broken out by both degree level and socio-economic characteristics. Table 21 confirms the observation indicated by Table 20, that increased educational attainment translates into better overall employment prospects. In the case of Table 20 it was employment rates; of Table 21, wage rates. But the data are far more significant even than that, for they help to confirm or explain several phenomena in U.S. postsecondary education that are matters of ongoing concern.

First, Table 21 makes obvious the considerable difference in earnings that can be expected by male and female graduates, a difference that is consistent across all degree levels and that cannot be entirely explained away by such variables as the nature of the subjects studied, enrollment patterns (delay, stopping out. etc.), or the percent of women who are not in the labor force (Table 21 refers only to respondents who were employed full-time). There remains a bias in the labor market wage rates that works against women, regardless of other factors (10). Across the board, women respondents tended to earn an average of 13 percent less than men. The gap was widest for those with only a high school diploma (23 percent); closed to nearly the same rate for those with an associate degree (less than one percent difference); and widened again at the higher degree levels (15 percent for a bachelor's and nine percent for a graduate degree). Such a pattern suggests that the earnings ratio of college-educated women is likely to worsen despite more education,

TABLE 21:
Average Hourly Earnings Reported by Respondents to the NLS/72 Fifth Follow-Up Who Were Employed Continuously Full-Time, by Level of Education Attained, Spring 1986

Category	Average Hourly Earnings by Education Level Attained					
	Secondary	Some PSE	1-2 Year	Bachelor	Graduate
Total	$ 7.01	$ 7.17	$ 7.59	$ 8.71	$ 10.80
Men	7.57	7.62	7.61	9.23	11.17
Women	5.80	6.39	7.55	7.87	10.19
White	7.11	7.32	7.70	8.76	10.86
Black	5.89	5.85	6.58	7.97	10.66
Hispanic	7.26	7.28	6.87	8.94	-----
Low SES	6.48	6.67	6.71	7.97	9.74
Medium SES	7.16	7.21	7.53	8.39	10.46
High SES	8.02	7.54	8.62	9.16	11.19

SOURCE: Eva Eagle, et. al., <u>A Descriptive Summary of 1972 High School Seniors: Fourteen Years Later</u>, (Washington: U.S. Government Printing Office, August 1988), pp. C-3, D-10, D-13/14, and D-17/18.

and that the women who do comparatively the best in the labor market (vis a vis men) are those who obtain less-than-four-year credentials and work in jobs without significant career potential.

The data on minority respondents is just as fascinating and reavealing as that for women. For both black and hispanic respondents, a little postsecondary education did no good, but a lot could lead to significant rewards. Indeed, the data indicate that blacks who begin limited postsecondary education (not enough credits for any degree), and hispanics who stay for a two-year degree or certificate, may have had actual disincentives in terms of relative earning power. In the case of hispanics in the NLS 72 sample, it was far more rewarding in the near term to go to work after high school than to continue their educations, which could help account for relatively low hispanic postsecondary enrollment rates. On the other hand, both blacks and hispanics appear to have had positive economic incentives to obtain advanced degrees -- assuming they could afford the time and expense required.

Since these data were derived from 1972 high school graduates, the correspondence between the earnings performance of males and persons of high socio-economic status may not be surprising. The demographics of American postsecondary education have changed in the meantime, so it will be interesting to compare these statistics with those forthcoming for later high school classes.

Enrollment as Employment

Throughout this section of Chapter One we have mentioned that oft-reported unemployment statistics for U.S. college graduates need to be viewed critically unless they clearly separate unemployed job-seekers from persons not working for other reasons, and unless they add those who are attending graduate school to the number employed. Why the latter? Because graduate school, regardless of subject studied, is essentially the same as employment for persons who are either enrolled full-time or who must complete an advanced degree in order to be hired or licensed in a specific field. And since many graduate students also work full- or part-time, adding them to the pool of employed persons reduces the categories of "intermittently employed" and "employed part-time" to those persons who are truly unable, for whatever reason, to hold a continuous job for reasons other than concentration on preparing for their real careers.

Table 22 presents data on the employment status of college graduates that accounts for graduate study as a category of employed activity, as well as distinguishing unemployed job-seekers from persons not seeking work, and separating part-time workers who are attending graduate school from those who are not. The results, as suggested earlier, show that fewer than five percent of American college graduates, on average, actually cannot find any work. Slightly under five percent are not looking for work at all, and seven percent tend to locate only part-time work. Those attending graduate school on whatever basis (whether also working or not) are as occupied on a career path as anyone who is out of school and in a full-time job. These data result in a recent figure of 11 percent (1986) of U.S. college graduates who can be said to be either unemployed or only occasionally employed. Such data, taken together with that in Table 18, indicate that the real problem of college graduates and work is underemployment (too many part-time and unrewarding jobs), not unemployment.

TABLE 22:
Trends in the Adjusted Employment Status of
U.S. Bachelor's Degree Recipients One
Year After Graduation, Selected
Years 1978-1987

EMPLOYMENT STATUS	1980 (%)	1984 (%)	1986 (%)
ALL RESPONDENTS	100	100	100
Employed (Full-Time)	71	73	74
Enrolled (Graduate Study)	13	13	11
TOTAL EMPLOYED/ENROLLED	84	86	85
UNEMPLOYED, SEEKING WORK	6	3	4
(NOT IN LABOR FORCE)	3	5	4
(OTHER) [Part-Time Not Enrolled]	7	7	7

NOTE: Enrolled = persons employed part-time while attending graduate school as well as those attending but not employed; Other = persons not enrolled but working part-time or intermittently; Unemployed, Seeking = persons not enrolled or employed but looking for work; NILF = persons not enrolled, employed, or seeking work.

SOURCE: U.S. Department of Education, National Center for Education Statistics, The Condition of Education 1990, Vol. 2: Postsecondary Education, (Washington: U.S. Government Printing Office, 1990), pp. 131-133.

PURSUING GRADUATE EDUCATION

Graduate study is the term used in the United States to refer to what is often called postgraduate study elsewhere (postgraduate study in the U.S. refers to further study or research after earning a Ph.D.). As a further complication, graduate study is subdivided by level and type of work pursued, into "professional" and "academic" studies and corresponding degrees.

Professional studies in some subjects are graduate-level studies in the U.S. Schools and departments (faculties) in those subjects require a prospective student to already possess either a bachelor's degree or a specified number of undergraduate credits. This requirement exists in those fields of study because it has been mandated by the authority (governmental agency, professional association, or religious body) charged with licensing practicing professionals, or because it is the custom of the field and graduate study is typically required in order to be hired for the best jobs. Examples of the former type, where graduate study is mandated by licensure requirements, include law, ordination degrees in theology, and medicine and related health professions (dentistry, veterinary medicine, etc.). These degrees constitute a special case in U.S. data reporting and will be discussed separately. By contrast, examples of professions in which graduate study is often required for advancement, but not as a prerequisite for entry-level hiring, include engineering, education (teacher training), business management, accounting, architecture, and nursing.

Those professional fields for which graduate study is a mandatory prerequisite are few: law, divinity/ministry (preparation for full ordination in the various Christian churches), rabbinical/Talmudic studies (preparation for Jewish congregational leadership), and several of the health professions (medicine, dentistry, veterinary medicine, osteopathy, chiropractic, pharmacy, optometry, and podiatry). They have been specially recognized by the U.S. Department of Education, and data on them are reported in a separate category called "first-professional programs". Students who enroll in and complete instructional programs in these professions receive what are called first-professional degrees. These degrees are often called doctorates of one kind or another, but they are not research doctorates inasmuch as candidates for them are not required to demonstrate advanced independent research competencies, nor does the instructional content of the programs emphasize the theoretical and conceptual aspects of the subject studied except as this may relate to practice (11).

American postsecondary institutions also offer programs of study leading to master's degrees and research doctorates, which are more familiar degree types than the first-professional category. These degrees may be awarded in both academic and professional subjects, depending only upon how a particular field of study has developed (some subject fields do not offer any graduate-level work, and others only limited work at that level). Outside the licensed professional fields (those regulated by a designated authority), no regulations determine the nature or form of graduate study other than accreditation rules and the traditions of the disciplines as reinforced by institutional practices. Accreditation rules govern which institutions are qualified to offer graduate-level programs, and long-standing traditions and practices within disciplinary fields influence the nature of graduate study in a particular field across different institutions.

Since virtually all graduate students are adult learners who pursue such education on their own as time and money permit, and since the total number of such students at any time is quite small (around ten percent of the student population), it is not normally cost-effective to develop comprehensive statistical data that tracks the flow of such students. Such data have been collected in some cases, however, and where available it will be presented here. The examination of graduate studies data will begin with the transition from undergraduate to graduate study, and will then progress through the successive degree levels: first-professional, master's, and the doctorate.

The Transition to Graduate Study

The choice of pursuing graduate study is generally determined by an individual's interests and ambitions, as well as -- in many fields -- by the requirements of professional qualification or advancement. Since a great many U.S. four-year undergraduate programs (and their enrolled students) aim at preparation for further study, it is not surprising that a considerable proportion of students take one of the several standardized aptitude examinations designed to assist in screening graduate school applicants. The most important of these tests include the Graduate Record Examination (GRE) and associated Achievement Tests, the Law School Admissions Test (LSAT), the Medical College Admissions Test (MCAT), and the Graduate Management Admissions Test (GMAT - for business students). Table 23 shows how the proportion of enrolled undergraduates taking one such test, the GRE, has fluctuated over 1977-1987. (The GRE is the aptitude test widely used to evaluate applicants for graduate study in the academic disciplines.)

As can be seen from the data presented, the absolute number of test-takers was falling at the beginning of the decade and continued to do so until 1982, when the numbers began rising again.

TABLE 23:
Undergraduates Taking the Graduate Record Examination, 1977-1987

YEAR	NUMBER OF BACHELOR'S EARNERS TAKING GRE	PERCENT OF ALL BACHELOR'S
1977	287,715	31.3
1978	286,383	31.1
1979	282,482	30.7
1980	272,281	29.3
1981	262,855	28.1
1982	256,381	26.9
1983	263,674	27.2
1984	265,221	27.2
1985	271,972	27.8
1986	279,428	28.3
1987	293,560	29.7
Change, 77-87	+ 2.0 %	- 1.6

SOURCE: U.S. Department of Education, National Center for Education Statistics, <u>The Condition of Education 1990, Vol. 2: Postsecondary Education</u>, (Washington: U.S. Government Printing Office, 1990), p. 129.

TABLE 24:
Further Postsecondary Education Activities of 1985-86 Bachelor's Degree Recipients, as of Spring 1987

EDUCATIONAL ACTIVITIES	% TOTAL	% STATUS
Did Not Apply for Further Education	64	(100)
(Reasons for Not Applying) - Wanted to Work - Wanted Time Off - Could Not Afford Further Education - No Plans for Further Education - Other Reason(s)	34 6 5 16 3	(53) (9) (8) (25) (5)
Applied for Further Education	36	(100)
Proportion of Applicants Who Attend	(78)	N/A
Actually Pursuing Further Education	28	(100)
(Type of Further Education Pursued) - Miscellaneous Courses Only - Second Bachelor's Degree - Post-Bachelor's Certificate - First-Professional Degree - Master's Degree - Doctorate - Other	3 1 1 4 15 1 2	(11) (4) (4) (15) (54) (4) (7)
Not Enrolled in Further Education	72	(100)

SOURCE: U.S. Department of Education, National Center for Education Statistics, Digest of Education Statistics 1990, (Washington: U.S. Government Printing Office, February 1991), Tables 350 and 351, p. 370.

By 1987 more students were taking the GRE than had done so in 1977, but they represented a smaller percentage of all students earning bachelor's degrees. In the case of the GRE, this trend can be attributed in part to the economic saturation suffered by most academic disciplines during the late 1970s and most of the 1980s, a phenomenon which received wide publicity in the news media and caused much concern on college campuses. While a more favorable job market for academic graduate degree-holders is forecast by some sources for the 1990s, this forecast comes after nearly a generation of poor employment prospects and has not yet created a major turn-around in graduate school applications.

The data on GRE test-taking also indicates the degree to which such tests have become popular among students who may not intend to actually attend graduate school. Evidence from the national longitudinal studies, particularly the NLS 72/PETS data, show that some 42 percent of all bachelor's degree earners in that sample took one or more graduate school aptitude test (the GRE plus others), while only 12.7 percent actually enrolled in and completed any graduate-level studies by age 30 (12).

Another picture of graduate school transition is provided by data from the Recent College Graduates Survey. Table 24 presents the responses of the 1987 sample to questions about their plans for further education. The 1987 RCG Survey indicated that slightly over one-third of the college seniors (degree candidates) in that year had applied for admission to some form of graduate education. Of that proportion, over three-quarters (28 percent of the entire sample) actually had enrolled in graduate school as of the Spring of 1987. Some 22 percent had either been rejected by graduate schools or had not enrolled for some other reason. By far the largest number of those attending graduate school were there to obtain a master's degree (mainly in business or education -- see Chapter Two); first-professional degrees were second in popularity, but a very distant second. Very few respondents indicated that they were pursuing a research doctorate.

These data on the transition to graduate school indicate that the numbers involved are small in comparison to undergraduate study, that they are mainly candidates for a master's degree, and that graduate school application is not something that is done lightly -- those who go are a large percentage of those who apply, indicating a large degree of self-selection and determination. In the analysis that follows first-professional programs will be considered first, followed by other types of graduate study.

First-Professional Programs - Enrollment

First-professional degree programs include the highly selective fields of law and medicine, areas of study that promise significant socio-economic rewards for many who complete the courses of study and enter practice. Such programs have been popular in recent years, so much so that the number of applicants has greatly exceeded the available places. Also included in this degree category are the master's degrees in theology and rabbinics that are required for full ordination as ministers, pastors, priests and rabbis (depending on the faith community concerned). More will be said about these programs in Chapter Two; here the purpose is to examine aggregate enrollment trends across all programs at this degree level.

As with undergraduate enrollment data, the figures for first-professional enrollments are presented both as headcount numbers and as percentages. Table 25 presents the number of enrollees in each reported year, rounded to thousands, as well as percentages of each year's total by selected characteristics.

Total enrollments in first-professional degree programs increased over much of the 1977-1987 period, as the data for 1978-1986 in Table 25 show. The most recent years, however, have seen a levelling off -- even a slight decline -- in the numbers of students engaged in these studies. (This enrollment fall-off largely reflects a trend in law school attendance, as will be demonstrated in Chapter Two.)

First-professional students are overwhelmingly full-time. The very small total number of part-time students did rise between 1978 and 1986, but the proportion of part-time to full-time students actually fell over the same period. The main reason for this consistently low number of part-time students has to do with the requirements of the schools offering first-professional programs, as well as with the regulations of the professional bodies that accredit such programs and license the graduates. Full-time study is required, or at least strongly preferred, by nearly every organization that oversees legal, medical, and theological education. The intensity of the curricular programs of study, the co-curricular requirements of professional socialization and practica, and the standards required to pass the eventual licensing examinations combine to restrict the desireability and the opportunities for part-time study.

In addition to being traditional in the sense of enrolling full-time, first-professional students are traditional -- or at least anachronistic -- in another way: they are overwhelmingly male. In no other type of postsecondary education in the United States are males still as predominant as they are in first-professional studies. Table 25 demonstrates that the number of females enrollees rose by nearly 50 percent between 1978 and 1986, while the number of males fell by almost 10 percent; and the proportion of males to females also changed by over 10 percentage points in womens' favor. But the Table also shows that the number of first-professional women was so small to begin with that this significant set of shifts in male/female enrollment patterns has only served to increase women from around one-fourth of all students to just over one-third (13). Despite gains, the image of American law and medicine (but only

TABLE 25
Trends in Enrollments in First-Professional Degree
Programs, Fall 1978 - Fall 1986

VARIABLE	1978	1980	1982	1984	1986	Change, 78-86
Total	256.9	277.8	278.4	278.6	270.4	+ 5.3%
Male	192.2	199.3	191.2	185.0	173.9	- 9.6
Female	64.7	78.4	87.2	93.7	96.6	+ 49.3
Full-Time	232.5	251.4	252.1	249.7	245.7	+ 5.6
Part-Time	24.4	26.4	26.3	28.9	24.8	+ 1.6
White	229.3	247.7	246.2	243.4	230.5	+ 0.5
Black	11.4	12.8	12.9	13.4	14.1	+ 23.7
Hispanic	5.4	6.5	7.4	8.0	9.1	+ 68.5
Asian	4.8	6.1	7.7	9.3	11.4	+137.5
Nat. Amer.	1.1	0.8	0.9	1.0	1.1	0.0
Foreign	3.0	2.9	3.1	3.4	4.1	+ 36.7
Unclassified	1.9	1.0	0.4	0.1	0.1	- 94.7

(Table 25 continued next page.)

Table 25, Continued:

ENROLLMENTS BY CHARACTERISTIC AS A PERCENTAGE OF ANNUAL TOTALS						
VARIABLE	1978	1980	1982	1984	1986	78-86
Total	100.0	100.0	100.0	100.0	100.0	N/A
Male	74.8	71.7	68.7	66.4	64.3	- 10.5
Female	25.2	28.3	31.3	33.6	35.7	+ 10.5
Full-Time	90.5	90.5	90.6	89.6	90.9	+ 0.4
Part-Time	9.5	9.5	9.4	10.4	9.1	- 0.4
White	89.3	89.2	88.4	87.4	85.2	- 4.1
Black	4.4	4.6	4.6	4.8	5.2	+ 0.8
Hispanic	2.1	2.3	2.7	2.9	3.4	+ 1.3
Asian	1.9	2.2	2.8	3.3	4.2	+ 2.3
Nat. Amer.	0.4	0.3	0.3	0.4	0.4	----
Foreign	1.2	1.0	1.1	1.2	1.5	+ 0.3
Unclassified	---	0.1	---	0.1	---	----
PERCENT OF TOTALS IN SELECTED CATEGORIES WHO WERE FEMALE						
Full-Time	24.8	27.8	31.0	33.4	35.5	+ 10.7
Part-Time	29.1	32.2	34.6	35.3	38.3	+ 9.2
White	24.6	27.5	30.6	32.8	34.9	+ 10.3
Black	38.6	43.0	44.2	47.0	48.2	+ 9.6
Hispanic	25.9	29.2	32.4	35.0	37.4	+ 11.5
Asian	31.3	32.8	35.1	37.6	38.6	+ 2.6
Nat. Amer.	27.3	37.5	33.3	40.0	45.5	+ 18.2
Foreign	20.0	20.7	25.8	26.5	26.8	+ 6.8

NOTE: Numbers are given in thousands; numbers and percents have been rounded.
SOURCE: U.S. Department of Education, National Center for Education Statistics, Digest of Education Statistics 1990, (Washington: U.S. Government Printing Office, February 1991), Table 191, p. 200.

certain types of medicine -- see Chapter Two), not to mention theology, as bastions of maleness is unlikely to change in the near future unless these numbers begin shifting much more rapidly.

The percentages of women within the various racial/ethnic categories further underscore the anomalous character of female enrollment at the first-professional level. Unlike every other degree level, women do not predominate in the first-professional enrollment patterns of any racial/ethnic group, not even blacks. Indeed, first-professional programs were, as of the mid-1980s, the only place in American postsecondary education where black males still outnumbered black females, or even came close to proportionate enrollment. Even so, the proportion of black females stood at just under 50 percent by 1986, and may have shifted to the majority since then. For black females to account for nearly half of all black enrollments at a degree level characterized by low overall female participation is remarkable (Native American women also have high enrollments at this level within their population subgroup). Female enrollments within other racial/ethnic groups also increased over 1978-1986, but these increases were much closer to the overall proportion of women in the first-professional student population.

First-professional students are predominantly white as well as male, but the predominance of the former characteristic is not so anomalous as the latter, given American demographic patterns. Perhaps the most noteworthy development revealed in the racial/ethnic data was the steadily rising number and proportion of black students, which ran counter to the situation at the undergraduate level. (There the numbers rose but the proportion fell.) At the same time the proportion of white first-professional students fell, from around 90 percent of the total in 1978 to about 85 percent by 1986. White student numbers, however, stayed virtually the same over this period.

First-Professional Programs - Completions.

A comparison of first-professional enrollment data with data on who completes such programs conveys a rough idea of the flow pattern in such programs. The data presented in Table 26 show that the numbers and relative percentages of persons graduating from first-professional programs are close to the proportions who enroll. They indicate that the number and proportion of both female and minority graduates have increased over the period in question in patterns that appear to parallel those for enrollment, although usually at rates slightly below their respective proportions of total enrollment. The percent of 1987 first-professional graduates who were female, for example, is, at 35 percent, very close to the 1986 female enrollment proportion of 35.7 percent. Since first-professional students do not graduate the year after they enroll, these data imply that the female persistence and graduation rates in these programs are actually quite high in relation to males, since female enrollments rates in prior years were lower than 35 percent. By comparison, the performance of enrolled minority students also appears to be good, based on similar comparisons between Tables 25 and 26. Minority women appear to form slightly smaller proportions of the graduating classes than they do of all enrolled students.

TABLE 26:
Trends in the Award of First-Professional Degrees in the United States, 1977 - 1987

Year	Number of Degrees Conferred by Category						
	Total	White	Black	Hispanic	Asian	N.Amer.	Foreign
1977	63,949	58,411	2,536	1,076	1,021	204	701
1979	68,503	62,430	2,836	1,283	1,205	216	533
1981	71,340	64,551	2,931	1,541	1,456	192	669
1985	71,057	63,219	3,029	1,884	1,816	248	861
1987	71,617	62,688	3,420	2,051	2,270	304	884
77-87	+ 12.0%	+ 7.3	+ 34.9	+ 90.6	+122.3	+ 49.0	+ 26.1
Degrees Conferred by Category as Percent of Total							
1977	100.0	91.3	4.0	1.7	1.6	0.3	1.1
1979	100.0	91.1	4.1	1.9	1.8	0.3	0.8
1981	100.0	90.5	4.1	2.2	2.0	0.3	0.9
1985	100.0	89.0	4.3	2.7	2.6	0.3	1.2
1987	100.0	87.5	4.8	2.9	3.2	0.4	1.2
Percent of Degrees Conferred on Females in Each Category							
1977	18.7	18.2	30.6	17.0	24.0	18.1	12.4
1979	23.6	22.9	37.1	22.9	28.6	30.6	19.7
1981	26.8	26.2	39.5	26.6	31.9	30.2	19.7
1985	33.2	32.6	46.4	34.2	36.6	29.0	20.9
1987	35.0	34.4	46.4	36.5	37.5	39.8	28.5

SOURCE: U.S. Department of Education, National Center for Education Statistics, HEGIS/IPEDS Program Completions Survey, annual tabulations in the *Digest of Education Statistics*. (Breakouts are prepared for odd-numbered years only).

As with enrollment data, graduation numbers and proportions have increased for nearly every racial/ethnic group. As with enrollments, however, the small numbers of minority group students involved make these increases (as well as those for women graduates) reflect how far first-professional education has yet to go to be comparable to the rates of enrollment and completion reached elsewhere in U.S. postsecondary education.

One final note: as would be expected, recent data on completion rates does not yet reflect the fall-off in first-professional enrollments indicated by recent data. It will be two or three years before the students who are part of that trend, and who have by now completed their studies, have their completion data recorded and analyzed.

Graduate Studies - Enrollment

Data on graduate program enrollment are not broken out by degree level (master's and doctorate), although completion (degree production) data are. This is because there is no way to know who, when beginning graduate school, will stop and at what point, and who -- also at what point -- will continue (including returning to school) all the way to a doctorate and beyond. Enrollment counts for master's programs thus get hopelessly confused with those for doctoral programs; indeed, the one may become the other and thus get counted twice. To avoid this, the data presented in Table 27 include all graduate enrollment that is not first-professional, including unclassified students (those not enrolled in a degree program) as well as those enrolled in master's and doctoral programs (classified students).

It can immediately be seen that graduate enrollment is very large in comparison to first-professional enrollment (compare with Table 25), and that graduate school enrollments have increased rather modestly, contrary to some accounts. Generally speaking, the data on graduate enrollments exhibit patterns closer to those at the undergraduate level than to those at the first-professional level.

The numbers of enrolled graduate students have increased over 1978-1986 for every category of student except blacks and, apparently, Native Americans and unclassified students. Hispanic, Asian-American, and foreign graduate enrollments increased significantly: 60, 50, and 70 percent, respectively. Turning to the percentage data, it can be seen that the growth registered by Hispanics, Asian-Americans, and foreign students have been both absolute and relative, since these groups also increased their proportionate share of all graduate enrollments.

TABLE 27:
Trends in Enrollments in Graduate Degree
Programs, Fall 1978 - Fall 1986

VARIABLE	ACADEMIC YEAR BEGINNING					Change, 78-86
	1978	1980	1982	1984	1986	
Total	1,312	1,343	1,322	1,345	1,435	+ 9.4%
Male	682	675	670	672	693	+ 1.6
Female	630	670	653	673	742	+ 17.8
Full-Time	468	485	485	501	522	+ 11.5
Part-Time	844	860	838	844	913	+ 8.2
White	1,094	1,105	1,075	1,087	1,133	+ 3.6
Black	76	75	69	67	72	- 5.3
Hispanic	28	32	32	32	46	+ 64.3
Asian	28	32	35	37	43	+ 53.6
Nat. Amer.	5	5	5	5	6	----
Foreign	80	92	105	115	136	+ 70.0
Unclassified	1	2	1	2	0	----
ENROLLMENTS BY CHARACTERISTICS AS PERCENTAGES OF ANNUAL TOTALS						
	1978	1980	1982	1984	1986	78-86
Total	100.0	100.0	100.0	100.0	100.0	N/A
Male	52.0	50.3	50.7	50.0	48.3	- 3.7
Female	48.0	49.7	49.3	50.0	51.7	+ 3.7
Full-Time	35.7	36.1	36.7	37.3	36.4	+ 0.7
Part-Time	64.3	63.9	63.3	62.7	63.6	- 0.7
White	83.4	82.3	81.3	80.8	79.0	- 4.4
Black	5.8	5.6	5.2	5.0	5.0	- 0.8

(Table 27 continued next page.)

Table 27, Continued:

Hispanic	2.1	2.4	2.4	2.4	3.2	+	1.1
Asian	2.1	2.4	2.7	2.8	3.0	+	0.9
Nat. Amer.	0.4	0.4	0.4	0.4	0.4	----	
Foreign	6.1	6.9	7.9	8.6	9.5	+	3.4
Unclassified	0.1	0.2	0.1	0.2	0.0	----	
PERCENT OF TOTALS IN SELECTED CATEGORIES WHO WERE FEMALE							
Full-Time	40.2	42.1	42.3	42.9	43.7	+	3.5
Part-Time	52.4	54.2	53.3	54.4	56.3	+	3.9
White	49.2	51.2	51.1	52.1	54.1	+	4.9
Black	61.8	62.7	62.3	64.2	63.9	+	2.1
Hispanic	50.0	50.0	53.1	53.1	54.4	+	4.4
Asian	39.3	40.6	40.0	40.5	41.9	+	2.6
Nat. Amer.	49.0	51.9	53.7	54.2	58.2	+	9.2
Foreign	23.8	26.1	24.8	26.1	27.2	+	3.4

NOTE: Numbers are given in thousands for each cell, and have been rounded, so columns may not add to totals. Percentages have been rounded, columns in categories add to 100.

SOURCE: U.S. Department of Education, National Center for Education Statistics, <u>Digest of Education Statistics 1990</u>, (Washington: U.S. Government Printing Office, February 1991), Table 191, p. 200.

Table 27 clearly shows that graduate students, unlike first-professional students, tend to be enrolled on a part-time basis. A consistent two-thirds of all graduate students (around 64 percent) were part-timers during 1978-1986, a higher proportion than for any other group of students except those attending two-year institutions. And these part-time graduate students were mainly females (also like the two-year student population), whereas the full-time graduate students were primarily male in every year studied.

The total number of female graduate students increased by nearly 18 percent during 1978-1986, and females became a majority of all U.S. graduate students after 1984. In addition to dominating the ranks of part-time students, female graduate students were distributed across the different racial/ethnic categories in patterns reminiscent of undergraduate distributions. In 1978, most white, hispanic, and Native American graduate students were male. By 1986 females were the majority in each group. As with enrollments at all other levels, females have never become a majority (or even reached a fifty-fifty split) among Asian-American or foreign graduate students. And, as at the undergraduate level, black females dominate black graduate school enrollments in disproportionate numbers.

These data indicate that enrollment patterns in graduate school somewhat parallel the patterns in undergraduate programs, although the total numbers are far smaller. Later on, in Chapter Two, we will see what the patterns look like when examined by specific subject field.

Graduate Programs - Completions

No comparison is possible between aggregate graduate school enrollment and completion statistics, since too many variables (such as type of degree and time to complete it) are mixed together. There are data available on the time taken to complete research doctorates, however, and these will be examined shortly. First, however, it is necessary to deal with completion data for students taking master's degrees.

Master's Degrees

Table 28 presents numerical and percentage data on U.S. students completing master's degree programs during 1977-1987. As with the doctorate, it is only at the point of degree production that we can separate graduate-level data by degree program. When we do so, as in Table 28, it becomes apparent that master's-level students make up a definite majority of all graduate students.

Another obvious point is that the number of master's degrees awarded has been steadily shrinking in recent years, although 1987 data indicate that this decline may have stopped. But the decline in the award of master's degrees has not been consistent across all groups of students. While awards to whites and blacks have declined (by one-third in the case of blacks), awards to females, hispanics, Asian-Americans, Native Americans, and foreign students have increased. The most significant percentage change is that of foreign students, who accounted for over 10 percent of all U.S. master's degrees as of 1987 (up from just over five percent in 1977).

While total female graduate enrollment did not pass that of men until after 1984 (see Table 27), the female share of master's degrees awarded had already passed mens' by 1981. As with enrollment and undergraduate data, females had risen to account for a majority of master's degrees earned by students from all racial/ethnic groups by 1987 -- except Asian-Americans and foreign students. And, as before, black females consistently dominated black master's degree production throughout the decade, although their degree of dominance, interestingly, declined slightly rather than continuing to rise. The graduation rate percentages of female Asian-American and foreign master's students resembled the proportions for first-professional degrees (a little over one-third and one-fourth, respectively) rather than for graduate study.

The Doctorate

The total number of research doctorates awarded annually by U.S. postsecondary institutions is but a tiny fraction of all postsecondary degree production, approximately the same amount as would constitute the enrollment of a single large university. As of 1987 the number of doctorates awarded equalled only 1.9 percent of all degrees conferred, the same proportion as in 1977 (14).

TABLE 28:
Trends in the Award of Master's Degrees in the United States, 1977-1987

Year	Number of Degrees Conferred by Category							
	Total	White	Black	Hispanic	Asian	N.Amer.	Foreign
1977	315,660	265,147	21,024	6,069	5,115	967	17,338
1979	301,707	249,051	19,993	5,544	5,985	999	20,135
1981	294,183	241,216	17,133	6,461	6,282	1,034	22,057
1985	280,421	223,628	13,939	6,864	7,782	1,256	26,952
1987	289,341	228,870	13,867	7,044	8,558	1,104	29,898
77-87	- 8.3%	- 13.7	- 66.0	+ 16.1	+ 67.3	+ 14.2	+ 72.4
Degrees Conferred by Category as Percent of Total							
1977	100.0	84.0	6.7	1.9	1.6	0.3	5.5
1979	100.0	82.5	6.6	1.8	2.0	0.3	6.7
1981	100.0	82.0	5.8	2.2	2.1	0.4	7.5
1985	100.0	79.7	5.0	2.4	2.8	0.4	9.6
1987	100.0	79.1	4.8	2.4	3.0	0.4	10.3
Percent of Degrees Conferred on Females in Each Category							
1977	47.3	47.8	63.1	46.2	39.1	46.1	22.2
1979	49.3	50.3	64.8	50.0	44.5	50.5	22.5
1981	50.5	52.1	64.1	53.7	39.9	51.6	24.8
1985	50.3	52.6	62.7	55.4	37.8	53.6	27.0
1987	51.2	53.9	62.9	52.7	38.8	53.2	28.2

SOURCE: Henry Gordon and Patricia Q. Brown, <u>Degrees Conferred in Institutions of Higher Education, by Race/Ethnicity and Sex: 1976-77 through 1986-87</u>, (Washington: U.S. Government Printing Office, October 1990), pp. 32-34.

For many years the Federal Government has researched the award of doctorates via an annual survey conducted by the National Research Council on behalf of the Department of Education, the National Science Foundation, and other interested agencies. The Survey of Earned Doctorates, as it is called, has built up a data base which enables analysts to develop reliable longitudinal data on the characteristics of students earning U.S. doctorates, including the time it takes to complete such studies, the fields in which degrees are earned, and post-doctoral activities (including employment and further supported research). These data will be presented here in order to illustrate the progress and prospects of students at the top end of U.S. postsecondary education, and may be usefully compared with the data for undergraduates that have already been discussed.

Time to the Doctorate

The annual surveys sent to all candidates for the doctorate asks respondents to indicate the year they completed their undergraduate degree (or first-university qualification for foreign students). Other questions in the survey instrument ask for information on students' activities between the end of the undergraduate period and the completion of doctoral studies, including such items as other degrees or credentials earned, funding assistance received, time registered as a student, time spent out of school (or not registered), interim employment, and the like. The aggregate information pertaining to the time it takes students to complete the doctorate is summarized in Table 29, expressed as an average of students' responses across all fields of doctoral study (field-specific data are presented in Chapter Two). The study from which these data are taken was a major research project conducted in 1987-1990 on the question of how long U.S. students take to obtain research degrees, and what implications this may have for educational policy (15).

TABLE 29:
Mean Time to the Doctorate from Date of Bachelor's Degree, 1967 and 1986 Compared

Year	Mean Times for All Fields of Study (In Years)			
	Mean TTD	Mean TPGE	Mean RTD	Mean TNEU
1967	8.2	0.9	5.6	1.7
1986	9.8	0.2	7.0	1.6
Change 67-86	+ 1.6	- 0.7	+ 1.4	- 0.1

NOTE: TTD = Total Time to the Doctorate; TPGE = Time Prior to Graduate School Entrance; RTD = Registered Time to the Doctorate (time actually registered as a student); TNEU = Time Not in University (time not registered).

SOURCE: Howard Tuckman, Susan Coyle, and Yupin Bae, On Time to the Doctorate, (Washington: National Academy Press, 1990), pp. 116-117.

The data in Table 29 show that the average doctoral program in the United States takes around seven years to complete, but that students often take nearly ten years to finish because of delays in enrolling (the time between earning the bachelor's degree and starting a doctoral program) and stopping out en route. Stopping out (time not enrolled, but after initial enrollment in a doctoral program) may be related to various factors, including family obligations, the need to earn money to pay for further study, a desire to obtain work experience, or other variables.

The data further indicate that the increased time required to finish a doctoral program has been almost entirely due to students being registered longer. This observation, in turn, implies that changes in the academic requirements for doctoral degrees, or in the characteristics of graduate study, are in some way responsible for the increased time taken. Such changes could -- depending on the field of study and other factors -- derive from diverse causes, including but not limited to: increases in the subject matter content required to be mastered; toughened standards for graduation; poor preparation of students resulting in more introductory coursework; incentives for students to remain in school rather than finish; possible faculty tendencies to prolong enrollment; and difficulties in scheduling the sequence of seminars and other activities required to complete degrees. More will be said about time-to-the-doctorate in Chapter Two, where data will be examined by subject field.

Doctoral Program Completions

Table 30 shows the distribution of earned doctorates in terms of major graduate student population subgroups across the 1977-1987 period. The total number of degrees awarded fell until the latter part of the decade under study, but appears to have increased significantly in recent years. The number of doctorates awarded to women, hispanics, Asian-Americans, Native Americans, and foreign students increased considerably, while the number awarded to white and black graduate students fell. Asian-Americans and foreign students registered the largest increases, nearly 67 percent in the former case and 75 percent in the latter. Hispanic and Native American students also earned significantly more doctorates by 1987 than they had in 1977.

Women improved their share of doctorate production in every category although, as with first-professional degrees (but not as extreme), they began the decade with a low proportion of students at this degree level. By 1987 women accounted for over one-third of all earned doctorates in the U.S., up from under one-fourth in 1977. Black women were earning the majority of all doctorates awarded to blacks by the end of the decade, further confirming a trend within that racial group noted across virtually all of U.S. postsecondary education. Asian-American and foreign women were once again exceptions to the otherwise consistent trend of rapid improvement in female enrollment and graduation rates. By 1987 Asian-American women were earning over one-fourth of the doctorates awarded to this group, but women accounted for only 17 percent of the growing number of doctorates awarded to foreign students. The small counts of doctoral awards to females in these two rapidly growing subgroups managed to significantly lower the total percent of female doctorates in relation to other subgroups.

TABLE 30:
Trends in the Award of Doctorates in the
United States, 1977 - 1987

Year	Number of Degrees Conferred by Category						
	Total	White	Black	Hispanic	Asian	N.Amer.	Foreign
1977	33,109	26,836	1,253	522	658	93	3,747
1979	32,664	26,128	1,267	439	811	104	3,915
1981	32,839	25,908	1,265	456	877	130	4,203
1985	32,307	23,934	1,154	677	1,106	119	5,317
1987	34,033	24,435	1,060	750	1,097	104	587
77-87	+ 2.8%	- 8.9	- 15.4	+ 43.7	+ 66.7	+ 11.8	+ 75.8
	Degrees Conferred by Category as Percent of Total						
1977	100.0	81.1	3.8	1.6	2.0	0.3	11.3
1979	100.0	80.0	3.9	1.3	2.5	0.3	12.0
1981	100.0	78.9	3.9	1.4	2.7	0.4	12.8
1985	100.0	74.1	3.6	2.1	3.4	0.4	16.5
1987	100.0	71.8	3.1	2.2	3.2	0.3	19.4
	Percent of Degrees Conferred on Females in Each Category						
1977	24.4	25.4	38.9	26.6	17.9	28.0	13.3
1979	28.1	29.5	42.2	33.0	20.4	33.7	15.4
1981	31.2	33.2	45.1	39.3	25.3	26.9	15.2
1985	34.1	37.3	51.4	36.3	27.5	46.2	16.9
1987	35.2	39.4	54.0	41.5	27.5	44.2	17.0

SOURCE: Henry Gordon and Patricia Q. Brown, <u>Degrees Conferred in Institutions of Higher Education, by Race/Ethnicity and Sex: 1976-77 through 1986-87</u>, (Washington: U.S. Government Printing Office, October 1990), pp. 35-37.

Postdoctoral Employment

As with undergraduates in the U.S., there is some perception that holders of doctorates encounter difficulties upon entering the labor market. To examine this supposition in detail is beyond the scope of this report, but general information on the postdoctoral plans of students who earn doctorates may be obtained from survey data.

Table 31 presents data from the Survey of Earned Doctorates on degree-earners during the 1977-1987 period who indicated that they had postdoctoral plans, or did not. Many doctorate earners, especially in the sciences (see Chapter Two), undertake postdoctoral research fellowships after obtaining their degrees rather than going directly into the workforce. Postdoctoral fellowships are considered virtual requirements of professional socialization in some disciplines, since it is the successful completion of a postdoctoral research apprenticeship that qualifies the graduate for the best job opportunities. A doctorate in these cases is considered only an essential qualifying step on the road to professionalization, not the confirmation of full-fledged competence. Therefore, as with the undergraduate data presented earlier, plans for further study need to be considered the same as full-time employment for those doctorate earners who go that route. Those indicating no plans whatever, however, may be roughly considered to equate with "unemployed", although the category also captures those who are not in the labor force.

Considered in this way, it can be seen from Table 31 that, in recent years, around 90 percent of all doctorate recipients have had employment plans of some kind by the dates of their graduation. The proportion with such plans declined slightly across the decade, however, from 93 percent in 1977 to just under 90 percent as of 1987. These percentages compare favorably with the overall prospects of undergraduates during the same period, but they do indicate signs that all is not well with the employment picture for doctoral students. The proportion of doctorate recipients with firm job plans (offers in the case of this survey) has declined, as has the overall percent of such students with any plans at all. Meanwhile, the proportion who report no idea of what they will do has risen, as has the number staying in research institutions -- often the same ones that awarded them the doctorate.

Equally significant is the shift in the type of job taken. Fewer doctoral candidates were planning academic careers in 1987 than had done so in 1977. Based on the trend revealed by these data, one might expect that half of all doctorate recipients will very shortly be going into non-academic work. The degree to which these non-academic jobs reflect, or make use of, the research knowledge and skills such students obtain is another interesting question.

TABLE 31:
Employment Status and Plans of U.S. Doctorate Recipients, 1977 - 1987

Year	Postdoctoral Plans			Type of Employment	
	Study	Employment	Unknown	Education	Other
1977	17.5 %	75.5 %	7.5 %	65.4 %	34.6 %
1978	17.9	74.4	7.7	63.8	36.2
1979	17.8	75.0	7.2	61.3	38.7
1980	18.4	75.4	6.3	60.1	39.9
1981	18.3	75.4	6.4	58.8	41.2
1982	18.6	74.6	6.8	42.8	57.2
1983	19.3	74.4	6.3	58.9	41.1
1984	20.5	72.5	7.0	58.6	41.4
1985	20.8	71.2	8.0	58.0	42.0
1986	22.0	69.0	9.0	58.1	41.9
1987	22.8	67.1	10.1	59.3	40.7
Change 77-87	+ 5.7	- 8.4	+ 2.6	- 6.1	+ 6.1

SOURCE: National Academy of Sciences/National Research Council, Survey of Earned Doctorates, Annual Summary Reports.

CONCLUSION

This brings the report to the end of the cycle of American postsecondary education. At this point it may be useful to summarize data on post-degree economic prospects for U.S. postsecondary students across all degree levels. This will allow a comparison to be made between different levels. To do this, we will use data from the Bureau of the Census on average monthly earnings, broken out by degree level (as reported by respondents to census data collectors) and characteristics, and indexed to the aggregate average earnings of the entire population as of 1984.

Table 32 presents the indexed figures described above. The data show how different degree levels are actually associated with differences in earning power. It can clearly be seen that there are significant differences in average earnings by degree level, an unsurprising fact, perhaps, but one that deserves reiteration in a period when the value of education is being critically examined. The data show that, in general, the higher the degree the higher the earning capacity. The only consistent exception to this rule is that holders of first-professional degrees tend to earn more than do holders of either master's or doctoral degrees, although all graduate degree holders do significantly better than persons holding only lower-level degrees or none at all. Of the subgroups included in this analysis, whites, blacks, and women appear to have the largest differences in earnings by degree level -- if graduate degree holders are compared with others. The difference is not so great for men in general or for persons in the traditional college age range.

Table 32 indicates both the potential incentives and frustrations that attend postsecondary education. On the one hand, there appear to be rewards for obtaining higher degrees, especially at the graduate level. But on the other, the prospects for women, minorities, and young people just starting out remain relatively limited, despite significant societal commitment to assisting these groups and despite important improvements in recent years. No one, of course, can claim that indexes like that of the Bureau of the Census equate to causal analyses. The data presented in this report do not confirm a firm link extending from schooling to labor market success, for no such analysis has been attempted here. However, the remarkable consistency of associated data from all sources, which continually reveals the parallel relationship of advanced education and high earnings (as well as good employment rates), certainly argues for the presence of a connection between education and work that is not merely accidental.

The picture of flow patterns through American postsecondary education that is presented by aggregate data depicts a very large enterprise involving large segments of the youth and adult populations. This enterprise has undergone changes in recent years in terms of those who enroll in and complete degree programs, and these changes in turn have socio-economic implications for the larger society. The tradition of self-financing of postsecondary education is also showing some signs of strain as costs continue to climb but assistance resources do not. Those who do earn degrees appear to be taking longer to complete them (and are increasingly doing so on a part-time basis). Once finished, graduates are finding that the probability of finding employment is still high but not quite as good as in the past, and the type of work available

TABLE 32:
Comparative Index of Monthly Average Earnings, by Selected Characteristics and Education Levels, Spring 1984

SELECTED CHARACTERISTICS INDEXED TO LEVEL OF EDUCATION									
Category	All	Sec.	Some	V/T	Assoc.	Bach.	1-Prof	Mast.	Doct.
All	1.00	0.93	1.05	1.08	1.30	1.68	3.75	2.13	3.00
Men	1.00	0.96	0.97	1.16	1.16	1.56	2.81	1.85	2.27
Women	1.00	0.95	1.17	1.35	1.58	1.70	3.36	2.54	----
White	1.00	0.91	1.04	1.06	1.26	1.64	3.64	2.04	2.94
Black	1.00	1.09	1.28	1.25	1.69	2.04	----	3.00	----
18-24	1.00	1.12	0.92	1.37	1.42	1.65	----	----	----
24-34	1.00	0.86	1.01	0.97	1.14	1.35	2.42	1.66	----

NOTE: The categories of Characteristics used are all respondents, sex, race, and age cohort. The Educational Levels used are all respondents, secondary school graduates (Sec.), some postsecondary education/no degree (Some), vocational/technical certificate (V/T), associate degree (Assoc.), bachelor's degree (Bach.), first-professional degree (1-Prof), master's degree (Mast.), and doctorate (Doct.).

SOURCE: U.S. Department of Commerce, Bureau of the Census, Survey of Income and Program Participation, What's It Worth? Educational Background and Economic Status: Spring 1984, in Current Population Reports - Household Economic Studies, Series P-70, Number 11, (Washington: U.S. Government Printing Office, September 1987), pp. 8-14.

is not always related to their educations or aspirations. This picture of a system undergoing change is fascinating, but it lacks one important detail -- how people who study different subjects fare, both in school and afterwards. That detail will be supplied in Chapter Two of this report, and it is to that Chapter that we now turn.

NOTES:

1. The data reported here measure the activity reported from school systems and traditional postsecondary institutions and systems. They do not include a complete accounting of other important educational activities such as employer training, basic and continuing education (often non-credit) offered by non-school-based providers, community education activites outside the education system, and the activities of proprietary schools (schools managed on a profit-making basis).

2. See The National Commission on Educational Excellence, A Nation at Risk, 1983, pp. 32-33;

3. There are very few free postsecondary institutions in the United States. The five Federal armed services academies are entirely free, and include stipends paid to students. Most other "free" institutions are really tuition-free only, and do charge modest sums for general expenses. The list is short and includes such schools as Berea College in Kentucky, Berry College in Georgia (both serving poor students in the Southern Appalachian Highlands), General Motors Institute (for employees of General Motors Corporation) in Michigan, and The Cooper Union, an art and engineering school in New York City.

4. See Jeffrey L. Gilmore, Price and Quality in Higher Education, Office of Research, Office of Educational Research and Improvement, U.S. Department of Education, October 1990. The research was conducted as part of an ongoing project to analyze the costs and benefits of postsecondary education in the U.S. While many well-known reputational measures of institutions exist, these do not appear to count for any more, and perhaps less, that the consumer notion that "you get what you pay for".

5. See Clifford Adelman, A College Course Map: Taxonomy and Transcript Data (Washington: U.S. Government Printing Office, October 1990), p. 242.

6. Average costs at two-year institutions were $1,590 in 1977, some 22 percent less than the average four-year cost of $2,038. By 1987 the difference was over 30 percent ($3,066 two-year versus $4,403 four-year) in favor of two-year institutions. These cost figures can be roughly calculated by taking data on the tuition and fee income (including boarding charges) of all institutions of a given type in a selected year and dividing the total by the number of such institutions.

7. The Department of Education's National Center for Education Statistics collects and reports data on postsecondary enrollments in even-numbered years, and completions in odd-numbered years.

8. Some professional programs award bachelor's degrees for longer periods of study, such as architecture and pharmacy. Several groups within the engineering community are currently studying the possibility of extending the time required to earn a Bachelor of Science (B.S.) in Engineering. Naturally, all these times-to-degree refer to the theoretical amount of time that a student needs to complete the program if registered full-time for a full schedule of coursework. Such theoretical times differ friom the actual time that most students take to finish, as has already been shown.

9. Data for earlier years were collected via different survey instruments, and are not compatible with more recent data.

10. Further support for this observation is found in Adelman, <u>Women at Thirtysomething: Paradoxes of Attainment</u>, Office of Research, OR 91-530 (Washington: U.S. Government Printing Office, June 1991), pp. 18-31.

11. A United States first-professional degree in law, for example, is generally called a J.D. -- <u>Juris Doctor</u> -- and qualifies its holder to sit for the bar examination given in each state that determines who will be licensed to practice law. It is not a doctorate in law, despite occasional claims to the contrary. The actual American research doctorate in law is called an S.J.D. or J.S.D. (depending on the school awarding it), and is very rarely awarded -- usually fewer than 50 per year across the whole country. A J.D. degree is not even considered the equivalent of a master's degree in law, as is demonstrated by the requirement that students enrolled for an LL.M. (Master of Laws) or M.C.L. (Master of Comparative Law) must already possess a J.D. or the equivalent first degree in law from a foreign institution. Similar observations could be made about the various medical first-professional degrees termed doctorates -- M.D., D.V.M., D.D.S., etc.

12. Adelman, <u>A College Course Map</u>, pp. 242 and 252.

13. For further evidence of female underenrollment in first-professional study, as well as a breakdown by subject field based on the NLS-72 database, see Adelman, <u>Women at Thirtysomething</u>, pp. 32-33.

14. These percentages are calculated by dividing the total reported number of doctorates awarded in a given year by the sum of all degrees awarded in that year.

15. Howard Tuckman, Susan Coyle, and Yupin Bae, <u>On Time to the Doctorate: A Study of the Increased Time to Complete Doctorates in Science and Engineering</u>, National Research Council Special Study (Washington: National Academy Press, 1990), summary tables and definitions in Appendices. This study has generated controversy in academic research circles in the U.S., some experts claiming that it overstates the increase in time-to-degree. All sides agree, however, that the time taken to earn doctorates has increased.

Chapter 2

TRENDS IN THE MAJOR AND ITS RELATION TO WORK

This chapter addresses the topic of the fields of study in which U.S. postsecondary students concentrate and the initial work experiences of individuals with different concentrations (called majors in the U.S.). Patterns of study across the 1977-1987 period are presented, so that the data in Chapter Two are comparable with those in Chapter One. In most cases, the data in both Chapters of the report are derived from the same sources and were collected using the same surveys. Chapter Two is organized like Chapter One, by level of study, from less-than-four-years to the doctorate.

This Chapter will not present fine-grained detail on the various population sub-groups that participate in U.S. postsecondary education. Relatively little insight would be gained by so doing that has not already been presented via the aggregate data in Chapter One, since the patterns are fairly consistent throughout the data. Chapter Two will, however, analyze variations in field of study by gender, since this particular question is of timely interest both in the U.S. and abroad, and since the numbers concerned are large enough to allow reliable statistics to be produced. At the graduate level, we will also present data on the field-specific study patterns of foreign students, since non-U.S. citizens make up a significant and growing proportion of postsecondary students at this level.

THE LIBERAL ARTS AND OCCUPATIONAL CONCEPTS

Before beginning to examine U.S. data on postsecondary majors, it is necessary to explain two terms that recur with great frequency throughout the literature, not always with clarity. The first, liberal arts, is a derivative term evoking ideas of the classical university curricula of the Middle Ages and/or the Englightenment, while the second, occupational, is a term coined to blend together a group of subjects pertaining to vocational themes.

The Liberal Arts

Originally, this term referred to the Medieval *trivium* and *quadrivium*; then to the post-Renaissance curriculum which added modern languages, natural philosophy, and history; and finally, in the United States particularly, to the academic subjects in the undergraduate college curriculum that did not aim toward preparation for a specific occupation or profession. This report uses the term liberal arts in the latter sense, and defines it to include the fine and performing arts (usually studied as humanistic subjects, not for professional qualification), the humanities (literature, languages, area studies, philosophy, and religion), the social sciences (including history and psychology), and the natural sciences (including the biological and physical sciences, and mathematics).

Generally, the number of American undergraduates studying these subjects greatly exceeds the number who intend, or who would be qualified, to practice them professionally. A graduate degree would be required to be considered professionally qualified in nearly all of these fields except the fine and performing arts. The term liberal arts, for that reason, is often restricted to the undergraduate study of these subjects. An undergraduate major in one of these subjects is part of a degree that also involves a broad range of work in a variety of other subjects, nearly all at or near the introductory level. It is on the graduate level that U.S. students concentrate on a single subject in the focused and advanced way that characterizes university-level education in many other countries.

Occupationally Specific Programs

Occupational curricula refer to any subject the study of which prepares a student to practice a work-related specialty, or sit for a licensing examination, immediately upon completing a program -- whether on the undergraduate or the graduate level. Thus, the term "occupational," incorporates both the vocational and professional concepts in education. "Vocational" typically refers, in the U.S., to less-than-four-year programs that prepare people for work and that do not require any postsecondary academic study. "Professional," by comparison, refers to a work-related field requiring the possession of a postsecondary academic degree as a prerequisite for studying it. The academic degree in question usually means an undergraduate bachelor's degree, often with a major in one of the so-called liberal arts.

The key characteristics of occupationally specific educational programs are focus, which involves concentration on a single subject and its practical application; and immediacy, which orients the program toward that which practicioners currently need to know in order to succeed, as opposed to the theoretical, analytical, or reflective study of the subject. (Occupational subjects are studied in the latter ways, but this is usually at an advanced level, either in a graduate research degree program in a professional field or via a program in one of the liberal arts disciplines (such as history, philosophy, or the natural sciences) that focuses on applications of theoretical knowledge to the solution of problems encountered in professional or vocational practice.) The narrow focus of occupationally specific programs allows students who major in them, even on the undergraduate level, to attain enough knowledge and skill to qualify as entry-level practicioners of that particular occupation.

Both of these terms are used throughout Chapter Two in order to separate data on postsecondary degree output into two groups by type of major. The fields grouped under the liberal arts remain the same across all degree levels examined; occupationally specific fields change somewhat, because some fields are offered only (or mainly) at certain levels.

MAJORS AT THE LESS-THAN-FOUR-YEAR LEVEL

As was pointed out in Chapter One, there are two types of less-than-four-year credential offered by U.S. postsecondary institutions: postsecondary certificates and the associate degree. The former consist of a group of credentials earned for completing programs of study ranging from less than one year to three years, and are usually vocational in orientation (the U.S. Federal term for this is "occupationally specific"). These programs are not, however, academic degrees, even though students who complete them may earn transferable credit. The associate degree, a two-year program, is the recognized less-than-four-year academic degree. It may be awarded in an occupationally specific field or an academic field, and much of the work done for this degree carries credit that students can transfer to a more advanced program. Each of these program types will be examined in turn.

Less-Than-Four-Year Certificate Programs

Less-than-four-year certificates are primarily awarded for completion of programs in the postsecondary vocational area, chiefly in fields for which a credential is useful or necessary in order to become licensed or to get a relatively good job. Table 1 presents data on field-of-study patterns at the postsecondary certificate level, and the data confirm the overwhelmingly vocational orientation of students who complete programs at this level. (Data are only available for the 1984-1987 period due to changes in the data elements and instruments used to report information on specific majors) (1).

Table 1 shows that the chief fields in which postsecondary certificates are awarded include engineering-related technologies, trades, health care, and business. Engineering-related technologies consist of a group of fields that prepare students to either assist engineers or to perform complex technological operations that do not require an engineering qualification but do require considerable advanced training. The trades include the traditional skilled vocational crafts as well as training for skilled work in industries such as transportation, manufacturing, and maintenance. Certificate programs in health care include training for most functions that do not require scientific educations or professional licensure, such as medical office workers, nurses' assistants, aides and orderlies. Programs awarding certificates in business are mainly concentrated in the secretarial and general office clerk categories.

Less-than-four-year certificates range from brief programs lasting a few weeks (such as sports officiating) to those that take up to three years to complete (some of the engineering technology programs, for example). Awards of postsecondary certificates have been declining in recent years, and the proportion earned in technical fields (engineering-related, computers, trades, and health occupations) has been declining in favor of those earned in service-oriented fields (public service, education, business, communications). The service fields involve occupational training for jobs such as secretaries, clerks, receptionists (business); teacher's aides (education); police officers and firefighters (public service); and technicians for broadcasting facilities and the publishing industry (communications). Very few individuals earn less-than-four-year certificates in academic subjects, and this type of credential is not generally considered to be preparation for further study.

TABLE 1:
Postsecondary Certificates Awarded by Field, 1984-1987

NUMERICAL TOTALS					
Field	1983-84	1984-85	1985-86	1986-87	84-87
ALL FIELDS	124,964	124,066	120,813	110,357	-11.7
LIB. ARTS (TOT)	2,753	2,641	3,706	2,199	-20.1
General	1,394	1,482	1,888	943	-32.3
Arts	844	727	771	629	-25.5
Humanities	251	178	514	315	+25.5
Soc.Sci./Psy.	62	53	233	180	+190.3
Bio. Sciences	88	82	81	6	-----
Phys. Sciences	86	101	120	107	+24.4
Mathematics	28	18	99	19	-32.1
OCCUPAT. (TOT)	122,211	121,425	117,107	107,926	-11.7
Eng/Technology	14,001	13,151	12,177	12,898	- 7.9
Computer Sci.	2,327	2,453	1,889	1,977	-15.0
Trades	32,424	31,948	29,201	28,019	-13.6
Agric/Nat.Res.	2,970	2,969	2,891	1,640	-44.8
Health Fields	28,376	27,220	25,789	22,310	-21.4
Public Service	2,641	2,948	3,203	3,167	+19.9
Home Economics	3,991	3,762	4,099	3,603	- 9.7
Business	33,080	34,293	34,127	29,989	- 9.3
Communications	331	386	433	744	+124.8
Education	532	561	573	661	+24.3
Other Occupat.	1,538	1,734	2,725	2,918	+89.7
UNDESIGNATED	0	0	0	232	-----

(Table 1 continued next page.)

Table 1, Continued:

FIELDS AS PERCENTAGES OF ANNUAL TOTALS					
Field	1983-84	1984-85	1985-86	1986-87	84-87
ALL FIELDS	100.0	100.0	100.0	100.0	N/A
LIB. ARTS (TOT)	2.2	2.1	3.1	2.0	- 0.2
General	1.1	1.2	1.6	0.9	- 0.2
Arts	0.7	0.6	0.6	0.6	- 0.1
Humanities	0.2	0.1	0.4	0.3	+ 0.1
Soc.Sci./Psy.	---	---	0.2	0.2	---
Bio. Sciences	0.1	0.1	0.1	---	---
Phys. Sciences	0.1	0.1	0.1	0.1	0.0
Mathematics	---	---	0.1	---	---
OCCUPAT. (TOT)	97.8	97.9	96.9	98.0	+ 0.2
Eng/Technology	11.2	10.6	10.1	11.7	+ 0.5
Computer Sci.	1.9	2.0	1.6	1.8	- 0.1
Trades	26.0	25.8	24.2	25.4	- 0.6
Agric/Nat.Res.	2.2	2.4	2.4	1.5	- 0.7
Health Fields	22.7	21.9	21.4	20.2	- 2.5
Public Service	2.1	2.4	2.7	2.9	+ 0.8
Home Economics	3.2	3.0	3.4	3.3	+ 0.1
Business	26.5	27.6	28.3	27.2	+ 0.7
Communications	0.3	0.3	0.4	0.7	+ 0.4
Education	0.4	0.5	0.5	0.6	+ 0.2
Other Occupat.	1.2	1.4	2.3	2.6	+ 1.4

NOTE: Percentages have been rounded.
SOURCE: U.S. Department of Education, National Center for Education Statistics, <u>Digest of Education Statistics</u>, annual tabulations of degree completion data.

Associate Degree Patterns

Unlike certificates, associate degrees represent the completion of a postsecondary program comprising more than a narrow set of courses focused on a short-term job requirement. Most of the work done in associate degree programs carries academic credit and can be transferred to a four-year program. This does not mean that associate degree earners actually transfer in large numbers, however, for a feature of the loose organization of U.S. postsecondary education is that possession of a lower-level degree is not always necessary in order to enter a higher-level program. In addition to the opportunity to enter a four-year program without the formality of earning a less-than-four-year credential, there is the fact that most students who enroll in two-year institutions do so to accomplish a specific career- or life-enhancing goal. Once this goal is reached, and they can advance in their career or begin a new interest, they leave -- with or without a credential. This situation helps to explain why enrollments at two-year institutions continue to climb, yet certificate and degree production declines (2).

Data on associate degree majors for the 1984-1987 period are presented in Table 2, and show that, like certificates, there has been a recent declining trend in the number of all associate degrees awarded, although not as much as for the other less-than-four-year credentials. While occupational majors have been common at this level, there has also been a significant number of degree earners who receive liberal arts awards. Most of these so-called liberal arts awards, however, have been in the area of general studies, since associate degrees by their nature do not produce subject-specific academic majors. What is really happening here is that students are completing the equivalent of the first two years of a four-year liberal arts program, consisting of what American educators call the "distribution" or "general" requirements. These are the introductory-level courses in English, mathematics, the sciences, and the social sciences that must be completed prior to concentrating in a major field.

Within the occupational area, most associate degrees are earned in the fields of engineering technology, health, and business, although the numbers of all three majors have recently been declining. At this level, the health awards consist of degrees awarded to registered nurses and other technical and advanced support personnel, such as records specialists and diagnostic and treatment assistants, as well as laboratory technicians. Business awards include such subjects as specialized secretarial skills (legal, medical, executive, etc.), office management, and two-year programs in specialties such as accounting, real estate, sales, and the like. Engineering technology programs involve the study of advanced technical processes and systems, and are closely regulated by the external authorities that license engineers and their assistants.

Both the associate degree data in Table 2 and the certificate data in Table 1 show that students in U.S. less-than-four-year programs tend to be vocationally oriented and usually prepare themselves for occupations in business, health, and (slightly less frequently) technical fields. What little liberal arts education exists is often oriented toward marketable skills (such as art, psychology, and physical science) or toward entry into a bachelor's degree program (general studies). When our attention shifts to four-year degrees and beyond, we will see that this pattern, aside from level

TABLE 2:
Associate Degrees Awarded by Field, 1984-1987

NUMERICAL TOTALS					
Field	1983-84	1984-85	1985-86	1986-87	84-87
ALL FIELDS	452,416	454,712	446,047	437,137	- 3.4
LIB. ARTS (TOT)	131,395	128,800	130,433	131,676	+ 0.2
General	116,237	114,921	117,258	118,003	+ 1.5
Arts	5,337	5,031	4,857	5,356	+ 0.4
Humanities	1,130	1,175	1,132	1,053	- 6.8
Soc.Sci./Psy.	3,822	3,570	3,479	3,631	- 5.0
Bio. Sciences	1,209	1,121	998	907	-25.0
Phys. Sciences	2,877	2,193	2,107	2,059	-28.4
Mathematics	783	789	602	667	-14.8
OCCUPAT. (TOT)	321,021	323,375	314,580	305,315	- 4.9
Eng/Technology	50,762	52,825	50,212	49,604	- 2.3
Computer Sci.	12,824	12,677	10,704	9,098	-29.0
Trades	22,989	22,077	24,467	24,294	+ 5.7
Agric/Nat.Res.	6,879	6,554	5,741	5,428	-21.1
Health Fields	68,270	68,453	66,559	62,545	- 8.4
Public Service	16,222	16,479	16,666	16,730	+ 3.1
Home Economics	9,247	9,611	9,469	9,311	+ 0.7
Business	119,244	119,933	116,460	114,496	- 4.0
Communications	3,752	4,116	3,984	3,537	- 5.7
Education	7,652	7,580	7,391	7,309	- 4.5
Other Occupat.	3,180	3,070	2,927	2,963	- 6.8
UNDESIGNATED	0	2,537	1,034	146	---

(Table 2 continued next page.)

Table 2, Continued:

FIELDS AS PERCENTAGES OF ANNUAL TOTALS					
Field	1983-84	1984-85	1985-86	1986-87	84-87
ALL FIELDS	100.0	100.0	100.0	100.0	N/A
LIB. ARTS (TOT)	29.0	28.3	29.2	30.1	+ 1.1
General	25.7	25.3	26.3	27.0	+ 1.3
Arts	1.2	1.1	1.1	1.2	0.0
Humanities	0.3	0.3	0.3	0.2	- 0.1
Soc.Sci./Psy.	0.8	0.8	0.8	0.8	0.0
Bio. Sciences	0.3	0.3	0.2	0.2	- 0.1
Phys. Sciences	0.6	0.5	0.5	0.5	- 0.1
Mathematics	0.2	0.2	0.1	0.2	0.0
OCCUPAT. (TOT)	71.0	71.7	70.8	69.9	- 1.1
Eng/Technology	11.2	11.6	11.3	11.3	+ 0.1
Computer Sci.	2.8	2.8	2.4	2.1	- 0.7
Trades	5.1	4.9	5.5	5.6	+ 0.5
Agric/Nat.Res.	1.5	1.4	1.3	1.2	- 0.3
Health Fields	15.1	15.1	14.9	14.3	- 8.0
Public Service	3.6	3.6	3.7	3.8	+ 0.2
Home Economics	2.0	2.1	2.1	2.1	+ 0.1
Business	26.4	26.4	26.1	26.2	- 0.2
Communications	0.8	0.9	0.9	0.8	0.0
Education	1.7	1.7	1.7	1.7	0.0
Other Occupat.	0.7	0.7	0.7	0.7	0.0

NOTE: Percentages have been rounded.
SOURCE: U.S. Department of Education, National Center for Education Statistics, *Digest of Education Statistics*, annual tabulations of degree completion data.

distinctions, has remarkable resiliency. The general pattern of a large and increasing shift toward occupational preparation, and a trend away from the liberal arts subjects (with a few exceptions), has cut across most degree levels during the 1977-1987 period.

BACHELOR'S DEGREE TRENDS

The bachelor's degree is the most common postsecondary degree offered in the U.S., and represents the level of education one must possess in order to be eligible for many occupations, as well as to qualify for admission to first-professional and graduate degree programs. Students in bachelor's degree programs have been studied much more closely than those at any other educational level save the doctorate. The resulting data permit the experiences of students in bachelor's degree programs to be examined in greater detail than is possible for students enrolled in less-than-four-year programs. This examination begins with initial interests as to major and follows through to graduation and beyond.

Initial Interest in Major Fields

The Cooperative Institutional Research Program (CIRP) Study, conducted annual by the University of California at Los Angeles and co-sponsored by the American Council on Education, asks enrolling freshmen to indicate their preferred choice of major. This survey is conducted only among full-time freshmen enrollees, so it excludes part-time students, and it is given to a group of respondents who are not often prepared to give an informed answer, since by definition they are only beginning their postsecondary educations and have not had an opportunity to become informed and self-aware academic decisionmakers. Nevertheless, the CIRP data are useful as an index of trends in the popularity of different fields among entering students, which in turn provides an indication of how they, their peers and families view the various options available as they transition from high school to college.

Table 3 presents 1977-1987 data from the CIRP Study, in terms of the percentages of all respondents who indicated a particular field to be their first choice as a major. It is immediately obvious that occupational majors have been more popular than liberal arts majors throughout the decade, a trend that parallels that noted for degree completions at the less-than-four-year level. Equally noteworthy is the indication that liberal arts programs may be becoming more popular; confirmation of this upswing will, however, have to wait for several years until the respondents can be expected to have graduated, and trends in degree completion data examined. Within the liberal arts the most popular fields have been the social sciences and psychology (divided about half and half when the data are broken out). Interest in majors in any of the science and mathematics fields appears to have declined until very recently, a pattern paralleled in the technical occupational fields.

For the approximately two-thirds of traditional freshmen interested in occupational programs, business led the list across the decade, and interest in it steadily gained ground. By contrast, interest in the health professions and engineering, the other two most popular occupational categories, appears to have fallen off even more sharply than for the companion fields in the

TABLE 3:
Percent of All Full-Time, First-Time Freshmen
Indicating an Interest in Various Fields, 1977-1987

FIELD & YEAR	1977	1979	1981	1985	1987	77-87
ALL FIELDS	100.0	100.0	100.0	100.0	100.0	N/A
LIBERAL ARTS	26.9	24.2	23.4	24.1	27.5	+ 0.6
General	---	---	---	0.0	0.0	N/A
Arts	5.0	4.4	4.2	3.2	3.7	- 1.3
Humanities	2.9	3.0	2.9	3.2	4.1	+ 1.2
Soc.Sci./Psy.	8.4	8.0	7.4	9.3	11.0	+ 2.6
Bio. Sciences	6.4	5.0	5.2	5.1	5.6	- 0.8
Phys. Sciences	3.2	3.0	2.8	2.3	2.3	- 0.9
Mathematics	1.0	0.8	0.9	1.0	0.8	- 0.2
OCCUPATIONAL	67.7	70.9	70.5	68.8	64.8	- 2.9
Engineering	12.1	13.2	14.9	14.8	13.8	+ 1.7
Computer Sci.	1.0	1.8	3.3	1.9	1.4	+ 0.4
Technologies	1.0	1.5	2.1	1.5	0.8	- 0.2
Agric./Nat.Res.	3.2	2.5	2.2	1.4	1.0	- 2.2
Health Fields	15.4	13.2	12.7	11.7	9.5	- 5.9
Public Service	1.9	1.7	1.3	1.1	0.9	- 1.0
Home Economics	1.6	1.2	0.8	0.6	0.5	- 1.1
Business	17.5	21.5	20.5	23.3	23.7	+ 6.2
Communications	4.0	5.5	5.3	5.3	5.1	+ 1.1
Education	5.9	4.8	3.8	3.8	4.2	- 1.7
Other Occupat.	4.1	4.0	3.6	3.4	3.9	- 0.2
UNDECIDED	5.3	5.2	6.1	7.0	7.7	+ 2.4

SOURCE: Cooperative Institutional Research Program, American Council on Education/U.C.L.A., Annual Survey of College Freshmen, <u>National Norms</u>.

sciences and mathematics. The CIRP data on interest in the scientific and technical fields are significant because they support the impression -- and the concern -- of policymakers and the media that American youth are not studying these subjects to the degree they once did.

Incomplete as they are, the CIRP data on freshman interest in major fields provide an interesting backdrop to the examination of data on degree completions by field. Such data will be presented in Table 5, but first it is necessary to examine data on how undergraduates actually progress into and through their choices of major, including changes along the way.

Longitudinal Data on Major Fields

The Postsecondary Education Transcript Study (PETS) of the National Longitudinal Study of the High School Class of 1972 provides the only comprehensive data available on the undergraduate academic experiences of U.S. students. The PETS data provides information by field on progress from initial enrollment to degree completion. Three important questions can thus be answered: did these students change their field of study in the course of earning their degrees?, did the time they took to complete their programs vary by field?, and did the frequency of taking graduate school admissions tests also vary by field?

Table 4 presents the findings from the PETS Study pertaining to these questions, for those students who had earned bachelor's degrees some time prior to the year of the Study (1984). As can be seen, the common answer to all three questions is yes.

First of all, the NLS-72 generation appears to have actually majored most frequently in business, education (teacher training), and the social sciences (including psychology). About ten percent chose the sciences and mathematics, and ten percent more majored in related technical occupational fields. This is not quite the sort of pattern that the CIRP freshman interest data predict, and more will be said on this subject in relation to the data in Table 5, below.

Second, it is apparent that the majority of degree earners in every area studied stayed with their initial choice of major, but that a sizeable minority did not. The data indicate that changing field happened most frequently with liberal arts majors, especially in the humanities, social sciences, and physical sciences; and less frequently in most occupational areas -- excepting business and the applied vocational/scientific fields. (The vocational service fields at the four-year level included such subjects as parks and recreation, home economics, business support services, and library science; applied sciences included agriculture, forestry, natural resources conservation, architecture, and science technology.) Considerable variation existed in the time it took students in different programs to finish their degrees. This ranged from a low of around five years for business majors to a high of six years and four months for physical science majors. The liberal arts average was nearly six years (5.91), while the occupational average was five and one-half (5.49). Among the occupational fields, only teacher education majors took as long to finish as did liberal arts majors.

TABLE 4:
Undergraduate Experiences of Bachelor's Degree
Earners Participating in the NLS/72
PETS Study, 1984, by Major Field

MAJOR FIELD OF STUDY	Percent of PETS	Changed Major	Mean Total Time	Took Grad. Test
Visual/Performing Arts	4.6	26.3	5.55	22.1
Humanities	6.1	33.7	5.96	55.7
Social Sciences	17.5	34.1	5.59	46.6
Biological Sciences	6.4	28.9	6.16	73.7
Physical Sci./Math	4.2	31.5	6.29	54.4
Engineering/Comp. Sci.	5.0	20.5	5.34	40.2
Applied Sciences	3.3	26.2	5.81	36.0
Technical/Trades	1.4	17.2	5.43	5.0
Health Sci./Services	7.7	21.7	5.46	46.5
Applied Social Sci.	8.0	35.8	5.21	33.6
Business	16.1	28.0	5.13	34.8
Education	16.5	22.7	6.19	36.0
Vocational Services	1.2	42.8	5.38	36.8
Other	2.2	27.5	6.13	53.2
All Fields	100.0	28.4	5.66	42.1

NOTE: Percent of PETS = Percent of entire PETS sample of bachelor's degree earners who had majored in a particular field; Changed Major = Percent of majors in a field whose transcript indicated at least one change of major during their undergraduate career; Mean Total Time = Average time, for a particular field, that its majors spent in undergraduate education between the ages of 18 and 30; Took Grad Test = Percent of majors in a particular field who took at least one test for admission to graduate school (MCAT, LSAT, GRE, etc.).

SOURCE: Clifford Adelman, *A College Course Map: Taxonomy and Transcript Data*, (Washington: U.S. Government Printing Office, October 1990), p. 252.

The PETS data on field changes and times-to-degree do not show any obvious relationship between the two variables within specific fields, nor was the the number of persons majoring in a field necessarily related to the time it took to finish. The data on the proportion of majors taking graduate admissions tests, however, was (and in this case still is) related quite closely to the character of program offerings and academic behavior in each field. Art majors, and those majoring in technical support fields, for example, do not plan to attend graduate school with the frequency of persons in other subjects. In both cases this has much to do with the culture of the fields, where practice is valued far more than credentialing, where the nature of the subjects is not oriented to research, and where terminal graduate degrees are not very common. Studio and performing artists (as well as instructors) may obtain a master's degree (many do not), but generally only research scholars in history and theory obtain doctorates. No doctoral programs exist in the technical support fields, and only a few master's degree programs. By contrast, most biology and health majors plan to go to graduate school, and the same is true of majors in the humanities, social sciences, and the physical sciences.

Bachelor's Degree Completion Data

Table 5 presents data on bachelor's degrees earned in different fields over the 1977-1987 period, based on the U.S. Department of Education's annual census of institutions. These data reveal patterns over time that lend credence to both the CIRP and NLS-72 (PETS) data previously discussed.

The bachelor's degree data are broadly similar in pattern to the associate degree data, with around two-thirds of all degree earners concentrating in occupational fields, and one-third in the liberal arts. The data do indicate that there may be a slight upsurge of interest in liberal arts majors at the end of the 1977-1987 period, and this observation would support the pattern revealed in the CIRP freshman interest data (see Table 3). Also, the frequency pattern indicates that what was true of the 1972 high school class (see Table 4) remains so: the most common majors are in business, teacher education, and the social sciences.

Table 5 indicates that recent "growth" fields in undergraduate studies have included the high-technology majors (engineering, computer science, engineering technology), business, and communications (which includes journalism, broadcasting, and public relations). General and interdisciplinary liberal arts programs have also been relatively popular -- the only liberal art area to show any consistent growth. By contrast, the proportions of students majoring in education and the social sciences steadily declined until 1987, although fairly large numbers continue to major in these fields. Noteworthy declines have also occurred in the life science fields, in both agriculture, natural resources and the biological sciences.

The data presented in Table 5 are for all students; Table 6 presents data on women who earned bachelor's degrees between 1977 and 1987. Two general observations can be made from these data: women have tended to increase their share of degrees awarded in nearly every field, and, despite this increase, they continue to dominate certain fields and remain poorly represented in

TABLE 5:
Bachelor's Degrees Awarded by Field, 1977-1987

NUMERICAL TOTALS						
Field & Year	1976-77	1978-79	1980-81	1984-85	1986-87	77-87
ALL FIELDS	919,549	921,390	935,140	979,477	991,339	+ 7.8
LIBERAL ARTS	394,656	366,100	347,584	322,530	344,253	-12.8
General	33,912	34,154	34,491	22,687	37,767	+11.4
Arts	41,793	40,969	40,479	37,936	36,223	-13.3
Humanities	64,401	56,735	53,190	53,312	56,633	-12.1
Soc.Sci./Psy.	164,252	150,383	141,178	131,272	139,053	-15.3
Bio. Sciences	53,605	48,846	43,216	38,445	38,114	-28.9
Phys. Sciences	22,497	23,207	23,952	23,732	19,974	-11.2
Mathematics	14,196	11,806	11,078	15,146	16,489	+16.2
OCCUPATIONAL	524,933	555,290	587,556	644,716	647,086	+23.3
Engineering	40,936	53,021	63,287	77,154	73,797	+80.3
Computer Sci.	6,407	8,719	15,121	38,878	39,664	+519.1
Technologies	8,347	9,354	11,713	18,951	19,277	+131.0
Agric./Nat.Res.	21,467	23,134	21,886	18,107	14,991	-30.2
Health Fields	57,122	61,819	63,348	64,513	63,206	+10.7
Public Service	32,716	34,363	33,197	27,505	28,269	-13.6
Home Economics	17,439	18,300	18,370	15,555	14,942	-14.3
Business	150,964	171,764	199,338	233,351	241,156	+59.7
Communications	23,214	26,457	31,282	42,083	45,408	+95.6
Education	143,722	126,109	108,309	88,161	87,115	-60.6
Other Occupat.	22,599	22,250	21,705	20,458	19,261	-14.8
UNDISTRIBUTED	0	0	0	0	0	N/A

(Table 5 continued next page.)

Table 5, Continued:

\multicolumn{7}{	c	}{FIELDS AS PERCENTAGES OF ANNUAL TOTALS}
Field	1976-77	1978-79	1980-81	1984-85	1986-87	77-87
ALL FIELDS	100.0	100.0	100.0	100.0	100.0	N/A
LIBERAL ARTS	42.9	39.7	37.2	32.9	34.7	- 8.2
General	3.7	3.7	3.7	2.3	3.8	+ 0.1
Arts	4.5	4.4	4.3	3.9	3.7	- 0.8
Humanities	7.0	6.2	5.7	5.4	5.7	- 1.3
Soc.Sci./Psy.	17.9	16.3	15.1	13.4	14.0	- 3.9
Bio. Sciences	5.8	5.3	4.6	3.9	3.8	- 2.0
Phys. Sciences	2.4	2.5	2.6	2.4	2.0	- 0.4
Mathematics	1.5	1.3	1.2	1.6	1.7	+ 0.2
OCCUPATIONAL	57.1	60.3	62.8	67.1	65.3	+12.2
Engineering	4.5	5.8	6.8	7.9	7.4	+ 2.9
Computer Sci.	0.7	1.0	1.6	4.0	4.0	+ 3.3
Technologies	0.9	1.0	1.3	1.9	1.9	+ 1.0
Agric./Nat.Res.	2.3	2.5	2.3	1.9	1.5	- 0.8
Health Fields	6.2	6.7	6.8	6.6	6.4	+ 0.2
Public Service	3.6	3.7	3.6	2.8	2.9	- 0.7
Home Economics	1.9	2.0	2.0	1.6	1.5	- 0.4
Business	16.4	18.6	21.3	23.8	24.3	+ 7.9
Communications	2.5	2.9	3.4	4.3	4.6	+ 2.1
Education	15.6	13.7	11.6	9.0	8.8	- 6.8
Other Occupat.	2.5	2.4	2.3	2.1	1.9	- 0.6

SOURCE: U.S. Department of Education, National Center for Education Statistics, <u>Digest of Education Statistics</u>, annual tabulations of degree completion data.

TABLE 6:
The Distribution of Female Bachelor's Degrees, By Field, 1977-1987

| ANNUAL PERCENT OF GRADUATES WHO WERE WOMEN, BY FIELD ||||||||
Field	1976-77	1978-79	1980-81	1984-85	1986-87	77-87
ALL FIELDS	46.3	48.4	49.8	50.8	51.5	+ 5.2
LIBERAL ARTS	46.3	48.7	50.6	53.0	53.6	+ 7.3
General	47.4	52.0	51.1	55.2	55.2	+ 7.8
Arts	61.6	62.7	63.7	62.0	62.0	+ 0.4
Humanities	57.8	58.3	59.2	66.2	66.2	+ 8.4
Soc.Sci./Psy.	44.4	47.5	50.2	51.4	51.7	+ 7.3
Bio. Sciences	36.2	40.3	44.1	47.8	48.4	+12.2
Phys. Sciences	20.3	22.8	24.6	28.0	28.4	+ 8.1
Mathematics	41.8	40.8	42.8	46.2	46.5	+ 4.7
OCCUPATIONAL	46.3	48.2	49.3	49.7	50.4	+ 4.1
Engineering	4.6	8.4	10.3	10.8	12.6	+ 8.0
Computer Sci.	24.0	28.2	32.5	36.8	34.7	+10.7
Technologies	----	----	----	10.2	13.6	N/A
Agric./Nat.Res.	22.3	27.2	30.8	31.0	31.2	+ 8.9
Health Fields	79.2	82.0	83.5	84.9	85.5	+ 6.3
Public Service	44.4	53.0	57.8	54.8	55.2	+10.8
Home Economics	95.9	95.1	95.0	93.5	92.5	- 3.4
Business	23.4	30.6	36.7	45.2	46.5	+23.1
Communications	44.3	49.9	54.7	59.0	60.0	+15.7
Education	72.2	73.2	75.0	75.9	76.2	+ 4.0
Other Occupat.	26.1	28.9	29.8	22.2	22.9	- 3.2

(Table 6 continued next page.)

Table 6, Continued:

FEMALE BACHELOR'S AWARDS BY FIELD AS PERCENTS OF ALL FEMALE AWARDS						
Field	1976-77	1978-79	1980-81	1984-85	1986-87	77-87
ALL FIELDS	100.0	100.0	100.0	100.0	100.0	N/A
LIBERAL ARTS	43.6	40.6	38.5	35.5	36.1	- 7.5
General	3.7	3.8	3.8	3.7	4.1	+ 0.4
Arts	6.0	5.8	5.5	4.7	4.4	- 1.6
Humanities	9.5	8.2	7.5	7.1	7.3	- 2.2
Soc.Sci./Psy.	17.2	16.1	15.3	13.6	14.1	- 3.1
Bio. Sciences	4.6	4.4	4.1	3.7	3.6	- 1.0
Phys. Sciences	1.1	1.2	1.3	1.3	1.1	0.0
Mathematics	1.4	1.1	1.0	1.4	1.5	+ 0.1
OCCUPATIONAL	56.4	59.4	61.5	64.5	63.9	+ 7.5
Engineering	0.5	1.2	1.7	2.2	2.2	+ 1.7
Computer Sci.	0.4	0.6	1.1	2.9	2.7	+ 2.3
Technologies	---	---	---	0.3	0.3	0.0
Agric./Nat.Res.	1.1	1.4	1.4	1.1	0.9	- 0.2
Health Fields	10.7	11.5	11.4	10.9	10.6	- 0.1
Public Service	3.9	4.7	4.6	3.5	3.5	- 0.4
Home Economics	3.9	3.9	3.8	2.9	2.7	- 1.3
Business	8.4	11.9	15.9	21.2	22.0	+13.6
Communications	2.4	3.0	3.7	5.0	5.3	+ 2.9
Education	24.5	20.8	17.6	13.5	13.0	-11.5
Other Occupat.	0.6	0.7	0.7	0.7	0.7	+ 0.1

SOURCE: U.S. Department of Education, National Center for Education Statistics, *Digest of Education Statistics*, annual tabulations of degree completion data.

others. Traditionally "female" undergraduate majors such as health (primarily bachelor's degree nursing programs), teacher education, the non-science liberal arts, and home economics continue to be so, even though the numbers of majors in several of these fields are declining.

Women comprise a rapidly increasing proportion of bachelor's degree holders in the sciences and the high-technology fields, despite the fact that men remain predominant in these majors. This increase in female graduates in technical fields, however, has been exceeded by the numbers completing majors in non-technical fields that had previously been dominated by men. Women are close to becoming a majority of undergraduate business majors, and have become dominant in other majors such as the social sciences (through a steady upsurge in psychology majors), public services (which includes social work and public administration), and communications. The point of repeating these observations from Table 6 is that the pattern of majors for female undergraduates has remained biased away from those that require advanced scientific and mathematical proficiencies. While the data indicate that more women are choosing technical majors than have done so in the past, the involved are still quite small, as are the proportions of the total (3).

The distribution of majors among women undergraduates holds no surprises, and is similar to that for all students (see Table 5), except for the noted tendencies of women to concentrate more heavily in the non-technical fields and the liberal arts than do men.

Bachelor's Degree Majors in the Labor Market.

In Chapter One we observed that the quality of job being obtained with a bachelor's degree is often less than that which might be expected, and we also noted that a sizeable number of bachelor's degree recipients continue their studies, even if they are also working. These two issues, underemployment and graduate study, are brought into sharper focus when the data are broken out by major field. This can be done by using analyses from the U.S. Department of Education's Recent College Graduates (RCG) Survey, a periodic study of bachelor's degree earners conducted one year after they have received their degrees. The most recent RCG Surveys for which data are available were conducted in 1980, 1984 and 1986.

Table 7 presents data from these RCG Surveys arrayed by category of employment and undergraduate major field. These data show the importance of making the distinctions between regular employment, actual unemployment (out of work and seeking a job), and the special categories of graduate study (enrolled in school) and not in the labor force (unable to work or deliberately not looking). Unless one does this, the poor employment record of biological science majors, for example (the "worst" in the Table), might be misinterpreted. It is explained by the breakout: most of these majors go to medical or graduate school immediately rather than seeking full-time jobs.

If the "employed" and "enrolled" data are added together, the figures for effective employment as of 1986 range from a low of 78 percent for humanities and arts majors to a high of 91 percent for engineers, with the liberal arts average just under, and the occupational average just over, the total effective employment rate of 85 percent. The data show that students who graduated in liberal arts subjects were far more likely to go immediately to graduate school than were those with occupational majors, but were also more likely to not be in the labor force at all than were students who had majored in occupational fields.

Table 7 gives some indication of the degree to which individuals with different undergraduate majors differ in their post-graduation experiences, but it does not address the characteristics of the work obtained by graduates. In Chapter One, the observation was made that underemployment, not unemployment, was the chief plague of bachelor's degree holders trying to compete in the labor market. To see how recent college graduates are actually doing in terms of work characteristics, we turn to the data in Table 8. This Table presents information on how 1985-86 graduates -- the most recent year for which RCG Survey data are available -- were doing in terms of job quality. As with the data in Table 7, these data show interesting and wide variations by major field.

Liberal arts graduates, as a group, were much worse off in 1987 than were their occupational counterparts. The only exceptions to this pattern were physical sciences and mathematics majors, whose prospects approached those of engineers and health professionals. Liberal arts majors also tended to be holding only part-time jobs more often than were occupational majors, although it is possible that some of the part-time response was given by persons who were going to graduate school and working at the same time. Teacher education majors were the worst-off among the occupational group, and their poor earnings help to illustrate why this field has been declining in popularity.

TABLE 7:
Trends in the Employment Status of Bachelor's Degree Recipients One Year Later, by Field, 1980 - 1986

Status	Year	All	Hum	Soc	Psy	Bio	PSM	Eng	Hth	PbA	Bus	Ed
Employed	1980	71	56	61	56	46	59	84	77	77	83	76
	1984	73	59	62	58	47	52	85	74	75	85	74
	1986	74	58	60	65	42	75	83	75	75	85	75
Enrolled	1980.	13	17	22	27	35	30	8	6	10	7	7
	1984	9	19	24	23	38	36	10	9	9	4	7
	1986	11	20	23	17	41	13	8	8	8	4	6
Unemployed (Seeking)	1980	6	12	7	7	7	7	4	4	1	4	4
	1984	4	4	3	4	2	2	--	2	5	3	2
	1986	4	6	5	4	3	4	5	2	4	4	3
N.I.L.F.	1980	3	5	4	2	4	2	4	2	5	2	3
	1984	5	6	4	7	7	6	2	3	3	4	4
	1986	4	5	6	7	6	3	2	4	4	3	4
Other	1980	7	11	6	7	9	3	2	12	6	4	9
	1984	5	12	7	10	7	5	2	12	8	3	13
	1986	7	11	6	7	8	5	3	10	9	4	12

NOTE: Percentages have been rounded. Hum = humanities and arts; Soc = social sciences; Psy = psychology; Bio = biological sciences; PSM = physical sciences and mathematics; Eng = engineering; Hth = health fields; PbA = public affairs and services; Bus = business; Ed = teacher education.

SOURCE: Roslyn A. Korb, *Occupational and Educational Consequences of a Baccalaureate Degree*, (Washington: U.S. Government Printing Office, March 1987); and Joanell Porter, *Occupational and Educational Outcomes of 1985-86 Bachelor's Degree Recipients*, (Washington: U.S. Government Printing Office, August 1989).

TABLE 8:
Average Annual Salary and Job Characteristics of Employed 1985-86 Bachelor's Recipients One Year Later, by Field

MAJOR FIELD	SALARY	TYPE OF JOB FULL-T	TYPE OF JOB PART-T	RELATED TO FIELD	SOME CAREER POTEN.	DEGREE NOT NEEDED
ALL FIELDS	20,300	87 %	13 %	78 %	68 %	36 %
ALL LIBERAL ARTS	19,400	81	19	65	58	41
ARTS & HUMANITIES	16,200	74	26	55	49	51
SOCIAL SCIENCES	20,300	82	18	53	60	46
PSYCHOLOGY	17,300	80	20	66	47	50
BIOLOGICAL SCI.	16,400	75	25	67	46	45
PHYSICAL SCI./M.*	22,500	88	12	81	71	26
ALL OCCUPATIONAL	21,300	90	10	85	74	31
ENGINEERING	26,600	93	7	89	80	15
HEALTH FIELDS	22,600	85	15	93	79	31
BUSINESS	21,100	94	6	84	73	37
PUBLIC SERVICES	17,700	84	16	71	63	55
EDUCATION	15,800	84	16	85	72	22
OTHER FIELDS**	17,600	87	13	76	66	42

NOTE: Percentages have been rounded. Table data refer only to respondents who were employed in 1987, thus job-holders = 100 percent. *Physical Sci./M. = Physical Sciences and Mathematics (incl. Computer Science); **Other Fields = agriculture/natural resources, architecture/related fields, area studies, communications, home economics, library science, legal services, military.

SOURCE: Joanell Porter, *Occupational and Educational Outcomes of 1985-86 Bachelor's Degree Recipients*, (Washington: U.S. Government Printing Office, August 1989).

Both Tables illustrate that the job market for new bachelor's degree holders has tended to favor technical over non-technical majors, and occupational majors over those in the liberal arts (especially non-science). Starting salaries for bachelor's degree holders are not high in most fields, and many graduates can expect to face the prospect of dead-end jobs (no career potential) and/or uninteresting and unchallenging work. However, the RCG data also reveal that significant numbers of liberal arts majors enroll in graduate programs of some kind, especially those earning degrees in the sciences and humanities.

FIRST-PROFESSIONAL DEGREE TRENDS.

In Chapter One, the discussion of first-professional degrees indicated that there were important differences within this category in regard to patterns of degree completion. This observation is unsurprising in view of the disparate collection of majors grouped together under this degree category -- ranging from chiropractic and medicine in the health area to law and theology. For this reason, disaggregation of first-professional degree data by specific field of study is a more meaningful way to present these data. And, since first-professional instructional programs are closely tied to -- and often regulated by -- practicing professions and their associations, the data provide a general idea of the flow of persons into each of the individual professional fields included in this category.

Degree Completions

Table 9 presents data on total first-professional degree completions by field. The patterns in these data have been consistent over the 1977-1987 period, and show that half of all first-professional degree completers attend law school, just under one-half attend one of the several professional schools for the medical arts, and roughly ten percent attend theological seminary. Growth in these programs was strong throughout most of the decade under study, but had stopped by 1987.

Several trends revealed in Table 9 correspond to developments in the economics and social context surrounding different professions, and are worth brief mention. The very large increase in degree completions in osteopathy and chiropractic are indicative of the increased interest being paid by Americans to wellness issues and to alternative health remedies. Osteopaths now make up a growing plurality of all U.S. family and general practice physicians, and their emphasis on preventive medicine and wholistic health has been well-received. Chiropractic, unlike osteopathy, is a truly alternative health philosophy, and in the U.S. is a field that requires less formal education than the other health professions (4). These factors, plus the (relatively) low cost of chiropractic treatment and the fact that it qualifies under most health insurance programs, have helped the field experience recent growth. By contrast, the decline in the number of dentistry completions is a consequence of a reduced demand for this specialty. A revolution in treatment technology has been behind this development, and a number of dental schools have recently closed. Law school graduation rates experienced only modest growth and now seem to have stopped, in part due to the saturation of the market for law school graduates.

TABLE 9:
Trends in the Award of First-Professional*
Degrees, by Field, 1977-1987

TOTAL NUMBER OF DEGREES AWARDED						
FIELD	1976-77	1978-79	1980-81	1984-85	1986-87	77-87
ALL	63,949	68,503	71,340	75,063	72,750	+13.8
HEALTH FIELDS	24,379	26,927	28,727	30,266	29,397	+20.6
Medicine	13,461	14,786	15,505	16,041	15,620	+16.0
Osteopathy	852	1,065	1,145	1,489	1,618	+89.9
Chiropractic	1,368	1,671	2,337	2,661	2,655	+94.1
Dentistry	5,138	5,434	5,460	5,339	4,741	- 7.7
Podiatry	486	572	597	582	590	+21.4
Optometry	961	1,046	1,097	1,115	1,082	+12.6
Pharmacy	527	639	664	861	861	+63.4
Veterinary Med.	1,586	1,714	1,922	2,178	2,230	+40.6
LAW	34,104	35,206	36,331	37,491	36,172	+ 6.1
THEOLOGY	5,455	6,370	6,282	7,221	7,181	+31.6
UNCLASSIFIED	23	0	0	85	0	N/A
DEGREE EARNERS BY FIELD AS A PERCENT OF ALL DEGREES						
FIELD	1976-77	1978-79	1980-81	1984-85	1986-87	77-87
ALL	100.0	100.0	100.0	100.0	100.0	N/A
HEALTH FIELDS	38.1	39.3	40.3	40.3	40.4	+ 2.3
Medicine	21.1	21.6	21.7	21.4	21.5	+ 0.4
Osteopathy	1.3	1.6	1.6	2.0	2.2	+ 0.9
Chiropractic	2.1	2.4	3.3	3.6	3.7	+ 1.6
Dentistry	8.0	7.9	7.7	7.1	6.5	- 1.5
Podiatry	0.8	0.8	0.8	0.8	0.8	0.0
Optometry	1.5	1.5	1.5	1.5	1.5	0.0
Pharmacy	0.8	0.9	0.9	1.2	1.2	+ 0.4
Veterinary Med.	2.5	2.5	2.7	2.9	3.1	+ 0.6
LAW	53.3	51.4	50.9	50.0	49.7	- 3.6
THEOLOGY	8.5	9.3	8.8	9.6	9.9	+ 1.4

NOTE: Percentages may not add to 100 due to rounding.

*First-Professional degrees are a collection of degrees awarded for post-bachelor's study in various occupational fields (neither true research doctorates nor master's degrees) that are specifically recognized by the Secretary of Education as comprising a separate data reporting category.

SOURCE: U.S. Department of Education, National Center for Education Statistics, annual HEGIS/IPEDS Degrees Awarded/Completions Surveys tabulations in *Digest of Education Statistics*.

One of the important observations made about first-professional programs in Chapter One was the generally low proportion of women who entered these fields and earned degrees. As was stated, though, this situation varies by specific field, as a glance at the data presented in Table 10 confirms.

The female degree completion rate in most first-professional fields is dismal, just as the aggregate data in Chapter One suggested. The proportion of women graduating at this level has increased dramatically, but even quintupling the number of female graduates (or more, in some cases) has not served to push the totals anywhere near what the proportions should be if they were to reflect female undergraduate performance. In only two first-professional fields, pharmacy and veterinary medicine, have female degree completions approached or exceeded the proportion of enrolled undergraduate students who are female (about 52-53 percent). Part of the reason, at least in the case of the health professions, may be the relatively low number of women who complete undergraduate majors in the sciences (see Table 6). But this explanation is not sufficient to explain the pattern, since the two first-professional fields in which women participate the most -- pharmacy and veterinary medicine -- are highly science-oriented, and one of them, veterinary medicine, has so few places in entering classes in relation to demand as to be one of the most competitive graduate programs in the U.S.

THE MASTER'S DEGREE

Aggregate data for master's degree completions suggest that this degree has been declining in frequency in recent years. As with other educational degree statistics, however, there is some evidence that the decline has now stopped. Nevertheless, this degree remains by far the most common graduate-level credential offered, and earned, in U.S. postsecondary education.

When broken out by field of study, data for master's degree completions reveals a pattern that clearly separates degrees earned in occupational subjects from those earned in the liberal arts. Indeed, no other degree data show such extremes. Table 11 presents master's degree completion data for the years 1977-1987.

The picture presented by these data show that U.S. master's degree earners are heavily concentrated in two fields, education and business, that together account for nearly 50 percent of all degrees at this level. The fields of engineering, health (mainly nursing, medical technology, and public health), public services (chiefly social work and public administration), and the social sciences account for another one-quarter of the total. This leaves all other fields providing only some 25 percent of U.S. master's degrees. And these figures, quoted for the 1987 data in Table 11, continue a pattern that existed throughout the decade under study. The number of fields in which the master's degree production rate has declined are numerous and include nearly all of the liberal arts fields except the physical sciences, and most of the occupational fields other than those mentioned above. In particular, library science master's degrees have declined by half, and several library science programs have been closed during this period. Significant increases in degree production have been confined to the dominant fields of engineering, business, and health, and to the small but growing fields of computer science and communications. Fall-off in the number of education and social science

TABLE 10:
Trends in the Award of First-Professional*
Degrees to Women, by Field, 1977-1987

WOMEN AS A PERCENT OF ALL DEGREE EARNERS, BY FIELD						
FIELD	1976-77	1978-79	1980-81	1984-85	1986-87	77-87
ALL	18.7	23.6	26.8	33.2	35.0	+109.6
HEALTH FIELDS	15.4	19.6	22.2	27.5	31.6	+146.5
Medicine	19.1	23.0	24.7	28.7	32.0	+94.5
Osteopathy	8.8	15.7	16.4	23.7	25.5	+449.3
Chiropractic	8.5	10.4	16.7	22.1	23.7	+442.2
Dentistry	7.3	11.8	13.2	18.5	24.0	+204.0
Podiatry	3.3	7.2	11.6	20.3	20.9	+668.8
Optometry	10.9	13.0	18.9	27.1	35.6	+266.7
Pharmacy	27.5	36.0	42.6	36.9	59.2	+251.7
Veterinary Med.	22.8	28.9	35.2	47.9	48.4	+198.3
LAW	22.5	28.5	32.4	37.2	40.1	+89.3
THEOLOGY	9.9	13.4	15.0	17.9	18.5	+144.7
DISTRIBUTION OF FEMALE DEGREE EARNERS, BY FIELD						
Field	1976-77	1978-79	1980-81	1984-85	1986-87	77-87
ALL FIELDS	100.0	100.0	100.0	100.0	100.0	N/A
HEALTH FIELDS	31.4	32.7	33.2	35.3	37.0	+5.6
Medicine	21.5	21.1	20.0	19.6	19.9	-1.6
Osteopathy	0.6	1.0	1.0	1.5	1.6	+1.0
Chiropractic	1.0	1.1	2.0	2.5	2.5	+1.5
Dentistry	3.1	4.0	3.8	4.2	4.5	+1.4
Podiatry	0.1	0.3	0.4	0.5	0.5	+0.4
Optometry	0.9	0.8	1.1	1.3	1.5	+0.6
Pharmacy	1.2	1.4	1.5	1.4	2.0	+0.8
Veterinary Med.	3.0	3.1	3.5	4.4	4.3	+1.3
LAW	64.0	62.0	61.5	59.1	57.8	-6.2
THEOLOGY	4.5	5.3	4.9	5.5	5.3	+0.8

NOTE: Percentages may not add to 100 due to rounding.

SOURCE: U.S. Department of Education, National Center for Education Statistics, annual HEGIS/IPEDS Degrees Awarded/Completions Surveys tabulations in Digest of Education Statistics.

master's degrees has been quite large and follows a trend away from these fields noted at the bachelor's level.

One conclusion to be drawn from these figures is that U.S. master's degrees are increasingly professional credentials rather than academic ones, and that most master's degree holders are teachers (as they have been for many years), M.B.A.s, and engineers. It should be pointed out that academic master's degrees are no longer an expected step on the way to a doctorate in many disciplines, especially in the social and natural sciences. In many of these fields, master's degrees are frequently awarded as consolation prizes for failing to advance to candidacy for the doctorate. Nor do academic master's degrees any longer qualify their holders for tenure-track positions on faculties, save for a few fields such as the fine and performing arts. These developments have diminished the popularity of the master's degree outside those occupational fields where it remains, or has become, the standard credential for practicing professionals.

Female Recipients of Master's Degrees

The distribution of master's degrees across fields further suggests that a large number of degree earners are female. As Table 12 shows, this supposition is indeed correct. Women have come to be a majority of all earners of master's degrees, the only graduate-level credential for which this is the case. Table 12 demonstrates that women especially dominate master's degree production in the non-scientific liberal arts, a pattern reminiscent of that at the bachelor's degree level. A comparison of Tables 11 and 12 illustrates that women are, as of the late 1980s, completing master's degrees in most non-science liberal arts fields at rates that come close to their proportion of the undergraduate student population, even as the total number of degrees awarded in these fields shrinks. Relatively significant gains have been achieved in the sciences and technical occupational fields, but the absolute numbers of women earning degrees in these subjects is still very low (17.6 percent of all female master's degree earners as of 1987).

More critically, women have been overwhelmingly concentrated in one field -- education -- and have significantly increased their degree completion rates in only one other, business. Education alone accounted for over 55 percent of all female master's degree earners in 1977, and education (despite a steep decline) and business together accounted for over 52 percent in 1987. Even more than men, women seek master's degrees mainly in those few occupational subjects where the degree is an expected credential.

The data also indicate that virtually no changes have taken place in recent years at this level in the pattern of the fields dominated by men and women, regardless of whether the field in question is experiencing growth or decline. Women remain the primary earners of master's degrees in the arts, the health fields, home economics, education, and library science; while men remain dominant in the sciences and mathematics, the technical occupations (other than health), and business. The only fields in which real transformations have taken place are public services and communications, where women have moved from a clear minority of degree earners to a clear majority in both cases.

TABLE 11:
Master's Degrees Awarded by Field, 1977-1987

TOTAL NUMBER OF DEGREES AWARDED						
Field	1976-77	1978-79	1980-81	1984-85	1986-87	77-87
ALL FIELDS	317,164	301,079	295,739	284,263	289,557	- 8.7
LIBERAL ARTS	67,170	60,948	57,842	55,307	55,029	-18.1
General	4,498	4,585	4,519	4,364	4,167	- 7.4
Arts	8,636	8,524	8,629	8,714	8,506	- 1.5
Humanities	14,200	11,711	10,652	9,704	9,828	-30.8
Soc.Sci./Psy.	23,696	20,810	19,853	18,788	18,601	-21.5
Bio. Sciences	7,114	6,831	5,978	5,059	4,954	-30.4
Phys. Sciences	5,331	5,451	5,284	5,796	5,652	+ 6.0
Mathematics	3,695	3,036	2,567	2,882	3,321	-10.1
OCCUPATIONAL	249,994	240,130	238,257	230,944	234,504	- 6.2
Engineering	15,961	15,227	16,386	20,926	22,081	+38.3
Computer Sci.	2,798	3,055	4,218	7,101	8,491	+203.5
Agric./Nat.Res.	3,724	3,994	4,003	3,928	3,523	- 5.4
Health Fields	12,323	14,781	16,004	17,383	18,426	+49.5
Public Service	21,172	21,676	21,894	19,076	19,994	- 5.6
Home Economics	2,334	2,510	2,570	2,383	2,070	-11.3
Business	46,420	50,372	57,898	67,527	67,496	+45.4
Communications	3,091	2,882	3,105	3,669	3,913	+26.6
Education	126,825	111,995	98,938	76,137	75,501	-40.5
Library Sci.	7,572	5,906	4,859	3,893	3,815	-49.6
Other Occupat.	7,774	7,732	8,382	8,921	9,194	+18.3
UNDISTRIBUTED	0	0	0	0	0	N/A

(Table 11 continued next page.)

Table 11, Continued:

DEGREE EARNERS BY FIELD AS A PERCENT OF ALL DEGREES						
Field	1976-77	1978-79	1980-81	1984-85	1986-87	77-87
ALL FIELDS	100.0	100.0	100.0	100.0	100.0	N/A
LIBERAL ARTS	21.2	20.2	19.6	19.5	19.0	- 2.2
General	1.4	1.5	1.5	1.5	1.4	0.0
Arts	2.7	2.8	2.9	3.1	2.9	+ 0.2
Humanities	4.5	3.9	3.6	3.4	3.4	- 1.1
Soc.Sci./Psy.	7.5	6.9	6.7	6.6	6.4	- 1.1
Bio. Sciences	2.2	2.3	2.0	1.8	1.7	- 0.5
Phys. Sciences	1.7	1.8	1.8	2.0	2.0	+ 0.3
Mathematics	1.2	1.0	0.9	1.0	1.2	0.0
OCCUPATIONAL	78.8	79.8	80.4	80.5	81.0	+ 2.2
Engineering	5.0	5.1	5.5	7.4	7.6	+ 2.6
Computer Sci.	0.9	1.0	1.4	2.5	2.9	+ 2.0
Agric./Nat.Res.	1.2	1.3	1.4	1.4	1.2	0.0
Health Fields	3.9	4.9	5.4	6.1	6.4	+ 2.5
Public Service	6.7	7.2	7.4	6.7	6.9	+ 0.2
Home Economics	0.7	0.8	0.9	0.8	0.7	0.0
Business	14.6	16.7	19.6	23.8	23.3	+ 8.7
Communications	1.0	1.0	1.1	1.3	1.4	+ 0.4
Education	40.0	37.2	33.5	26.8	26.1	-13.9
Library Sci.	2.4	2.0	1.6	1.4	1.3	- 1.1
Other Occupat.	2.5	2.6	2.8	3.1	3.2	+ 0.7

NOTE: Percentages may not add to 100 due to rounding.
SOURCE: U.S. Department of Education, National Center for Education Statistics, annual HEGIS/IPEDS Degrees Awarded/Completions Surveys tabulations in Digest of Education Statistics.

TABLE 12:
Trends in the Award of Master's Degrees to Women, 1977-1987

WOMEN AS A PERCENT OF ALL DEGREE EARNERS, BY FIELD						
Field	1976-77	1978-79	1980-81	1984-85	1986-87	77-87
ALL FIELDS	47.3	49.5	50.5	50.3	51.2	+3.9
LIBERAL ARTS	41.9	44.0	45.3	48.4	48.3	+6.4
General	37.3	39.1	40.0	55.7	46.7	+9.4
Arts	51.2	53.9	53.0	55.5	55.8	+4.6
Humanities	55.6	55.7	54.8	53.9	52.3	-3.3
Soc.Sci./Psy.	38.2	42.5	45.8	49.8	50.8	+12.6
Bio. Sciences	33.7	37.6	38.9	47.7	48.7	+15.0
Phys. Sciences	16.7	18.3	20.7	23.3	25.0	+8.3
Mathematics	35.2	34.7	34.1	34.9	39.1	+3.9
OCCUPATIONAL	48.8	51.0	51.9	50.8	51.9	+3.1
Engineering	4.5	6.2	8.3	10.8	12.6	+8.1
Computer Sci.	17.0	19.2	23.3	28.9	29.4	+12.4
Agric./Nat.Res.	14.7	20.2	23.5	27.5	30.1	+15.4
Health Fields	67.9	71.0	73.9	76.3	78.9	+11.0
Public Service	42.8	50.7	52.2	57.3	58.3	+15.5
Home Economics	91.1	91.2	90.2	88.7	87.6	-3.5
Business	14.4	19.3	25.2	31.1	33.0	+18.6
Communications	44.4	48.6	53.4	58.3	59.2	+14.8
Education	65.8	68.6	71.5	72.5	74.0	+8.2
Library Sci.	79.6	81.9	82.7	80.5	79.1	-0.5
Other Occupat.	22.5	28.5	29.2	33.8	32.9	+10.4

(Table 12 continued next page.)

Table 12, Continued:

DISTRIBUTION OF FEMALE DEGREE EARNERS, BY FIELD						
Field	1976-77	1978-79	1980-81	1984-85	1986-87	77-87
ALL FIELDS	100.0	100.0	100.0	100.0	100.0	N/A
LIBERAL ARTS	19.8	19.2	18.8	19.7	19.5	-0.3
General	1.1	1.2	1.2	1.4	1.3	+0.2
Arts	3.0	3.1	3.1	3.4	3.2	+0.2
Humanities	6.6	5.8	5.5	5.1	5.2	-1.4
Soc.Sci./Psy.	6.1	6.0	6.1	6.6	6.4	+0.3
Bio. Sciences	1.6	1.7	1.6	1.7	1.6	0.0
Phys. Sciences	0.6	0.7	0.7	0.9	1.0	+0.4
Mathematics	0.9	0.7	0.6	0.7	0.9	0.0
OCCUPATIONAL	80.2	80.8	81.2	80.3	80.5	+0.3
Engineering	0.5	0.6	0.9	1.6	1.9	+1.4
Computer Sci.	0.3	0.4	0.7	1.4	1.7	+1.4
Agric./Nat.Res.	0.4	0.5	0.6	0.8	0.7	+0.3
Health Fields	5.9	7.4	8.2	9.2	9.8	+3.9
Public Service	6.0	7.4	7.7	7.7	8.1	+2.1
Home Economics	1.4	1.5	1.6	1.5	1.2	-0.2
Business	4.5	6.5	9.8	14.7	15.1	+10.6
Communications	0.9	0.9	1.1	1.5	1.6	+0.7
Education	55.8	51.6	47.3	39.0	37.7	-18.1
Library Sci.	4.0	3.3	2.7	2.2	2.0	-2.0
Other Occupat.	4.9	6.0	6.2	7.9	7.3	+2.4

NOTE: Percentages may not add to 100 due to rounding.
SOURCE: U.S. Department of Education, National Center for Education Statistics, annual HEGIS/IPEDS Degrees Awarded/Completions Surveys tabulations in Digest of Education Statistics.

Foreign Students at the Master's Degree Level.

It is at the graduate degree level, beginning with master's degree programs, where sizeable numbers of non-U.S. students enroll in U.S. postsecondary education. Much recent attention has been devoted to the phenomenon of foreign student enrollment in doctorate-level study, and this issue will be addressed in the next section of this Chapter. At the master's degree level the number of foreign students and degree earners is not so great, but it is still significant.

Data collection procedures in the United States treat foreign students as a minority population in order to facilitate separate reporting. As of 1987, this "minority" was earning a significant percentage (more than any single true minority of the U.S. student population) of master's degrees in every field except two, public services and education, in which black students earned more degrees. And they were earning a plurality (more than all other minority groups put together) of all master's degrees in every field of the liberal arts except general/multidisciplinary studies (5).

TRENDS IN DOCTORAL FIELDS OF STUDY

A great deal of information exists regarding the U.S. doctorate, enabling researchers to examine factors such as time-to-degree, degree completions, characteristics of degree holders, and employment experience, both in the aggregate and by field. This discussion, then, follows the aggregate data discussed in Chapter One, taking the examination down to the fields in which doctoral students earn degrees. The database used for this analysis is the Survey of Earned Doctorates, an annual study conducted on behalf of several Federal agencies by the National Research Council.

Time to the Doctorate.

One concern expressed by contemporary researchers and educational organizations has been the gradually increasing amount of time that it takes to earn the Ph.D. or equivalent degree (S.J.D./J.S.D., D.Sc., Th.D., etc.). While incremental, this increase has nevertheless amounted to an extra year or more, with attendant implications for students and others interested in the cost-effectiveness of graduate-level education. In Chapter One, we examined the aggregate trend for doctoral programs over time, and noted that researchers subdivide the time-to-degree question into four component variables: the amount of time between completing undergraduate studies and enrolling in a doctoral program; the amount of time spent registered as a formal doctoral student; the amount of time spent not registered (stop-out time) but while en route to the degree; and the sum of these, the total time taken to obtain the doctorate. The aggregate data for all doctoral programs indicate that the noted increase in total time to a degree is primarily due to an increase in the registered time, implying that changes in curriculum and other academic issues are responsible for the increase, not delays in starting a program or stop-out time.

Table 13 presents time-to-the-doctorate data for different fields of study. The data presented are median times expressed in years. These data

TABLE 13:
Trends in Time to the Doctorate from the Date of the Bachelor's Degree, by Field, 1977-1987

FIELD	MEDIAN TOTAL TIME (MTTD)					MEDIAN REGISTERED TIME (MRTD)				
	1977	1979	1981	1985	1987	1977	1979	1981	1985	1987
All	8.7	9.0	9.4	10.4	10.4	6.1	6.2	6.4	6.8	6.9
Humanities	9.9	10.3	10.8	12.1	12.0	7.1	7.5	7.7	8.2	8.4
Soc.Sci/Psy	8.0	8.5	9.0	10.0	10.3	5.9	6.2	6.5	7.2	7.2
Bio. Sci.	7.0	7.0	7.0	8.1	8.1	5.8	5.8	6.0	6.4	6.5
Phys. Sci.	6.9	6.6	6.7	7.1	7.1	5.7	5.6	5.7	6.0	5.9
Mathematics	6.9	7.1	6.9	7.3	7.9	5.8	5.9	5.9	6.0	6.3
Engineering	7.5	7.6	7.9	8.1	8.1	5.6	5.5	5.6	5.9	5.8
Computer S.	---	7.5	7.7	9.1	9.1	---	5.8	6.2	6.5	6.6
Agri. Sci.	8.2	8.1	8.0	9.2	9.5	5.4	5.3	5.6	6.0	6.3
Health Sci.	7.3	8.1	8.3	11.9	12.2	5.6	5.9	6.0	6.9	7.0
Business	---	---	---	11.9	11.3	---	---	---	7.0	6.8
Education	12.5	12.7	13.5	15.7	16.2	6.4	6.6	7.0	7.8	7.9
Other Prof.	10.7	10.7	11.1	13.7	13.8	6.2	6.4	6.6	7.7	7.7

CHANGE IN YEARS, 1977-1987, FOR MEDIAN TOTAL AND REGISTERED TIMES

77-87 Time Change	FIELD OF DOCTORATE											
	All	Hum	Soc	Bio	Phy	Mat	Eng	*CpS	AgS	MdS	*Bus	Edu	Oth
MTTD	+1.7	+2.1	+2.3	+1.1	+0.2	+1.0	+0.6	+1.6	+1.3	+4.9	-0.6	+3.7	+3.1
MRTD	+0.8	+1.3	+1.3	+0.7	+0.2	+0.5	+0.2	+1.8	+0.9	+1.4	-0.2	+1.5	+1.5

NOTE: MTTD = Median Total Time to Doctorate; MRTD = Median Registered Time to Doctorate (time actually spent as a registered graduate student). Fields marked (*) were not reported some years. Percentages are rounded.

SOURCE: National Research Council/National Academy of Sciences, Survey of Earned Doctorates, Annual Summary Reports.

clearly show that the situation regarding time-to-degree varies by field. The largest increases by far have been in the health sciences and education, with the humanities and social sciences not far behind. It is noteworthy, however, that these fields experienced an almost uniform increase in registered time to the doctorate -- around one and one-half years each. While this is a significant increase, it would put these fields in line with the aggregate increase were it not for the additional time recorded. These fields are exceptional in that stop-out time, primarily, and time prior to enrollment, secondarily, appear to have been responsible for much of the increased total time (6). Although the descriptive data presented in this Report do no more than hint at an explanation for these exceptional increases, it is possible to speculate. Liberal arts graduate students indicated that they obtain part-time employment more frequently than students in other fields (see Tables 7 and 8), and evidence exists to show that many graduate students in the health and education fields are older than the norm (7), all of which suggests that students in these fields may have financial and career priorities that combine to delay their progress toward the doctorate.

One further point that is worth noting is the fact that the time required to achieve a doctorate -- regardless of increases or decreases across the years -- has tended to be absolutely longer in some fields than others. Comparing the amount of registered time required, students in non-technical fields (liberal arts, business, and education) take on average 1.3 more years to complete their formal studies and research than do their counterparts in the technical fields (the sciences, engineering, agriculture, and health). The extremes as of 1987 were the humanities (over eight years of registered work, not counting other time) and engineering (less than six years, not counting other time). The fact that the non-technical fields are the leaders in degree length, and not the reverse, is an interesting phenomenon that deserves further study.

Changes in Major Field.

One phenomenon that occurs rather frequently in U.S. postsecondary education, and that can affect time to degree among other variables, is that of changing the field of study. The section above on undergraduate studies examined the data that we possess about field-of-study changes among bachelor's degree recipients (see Table 4). These data, from the NLS-72 longitudinal study, showed that some 31 percent of liberal arts majors and 27 percent of occupational majors, on average, had changed their major prior to finishing the bachelor's degree. The data on this phenomenon for doctorate earners is more extensive, since the question is asked of all respondents to the annual Survey of Earned Doctorates Questionnaire. These results, for the 1977-1987 period, are presented in Table 14.

These data indicate that just under half of all earners of U.S. doctorates tend to concentrate in a field other than the one in which they majored on the undergraduate level, and that the tendency to do this has increased in recent years. The trend to do so has been strongest among those who earn doctorates in the humanities and the technical occupations; less so among those in the biological and health sciences.

TABLE 14:
Doctorate Recipients Who Earned Their Undergraduate Degree in a Different Field,
1977 - 1987

FIELD	PERCENT WHO CHANGED FIELDS, BY YEAR					Change 77-87
	1977	1979	1981	1985	1987	
ALL	44.5	46.2	46.7	44.1	45.1	+ 0.6
Humanities	36.5	37.7	39.0	41.2	41.5	+ 5.0
Soc.Sci/Psy	41.8	43.6	40.9	41.5	43.6	+ 1.8
Bio. Sci.	60.3	61.2	60.7	40.6	44.8	- 15.5
Phys. Sci.	23.5	21.9	23.4	25.0	27.4	+ 3.9
Mathematics	23.8	18.6	19.8	26.7	27.0	+ 3.2
Engineering	20.0	22.1	25.9	25.8	24.8	+ 4.8
Computer S.	----	91.4	86.2	80.4	79.8	- 11.6
Agri. Sci.	40.7	41.5	44.2	41.4	40.8	+ 0.1
Health Sci.	77.5	75.0	73.3	47.8	47.0	- 30.5
Business	----	----	----	61.2	64.5	+ 3.3
Education	60.3	61.4	61.1	61.3	62.2	+ 1.9
Other Prof.	62.2	62.5	65.4	75.8	76.4	+ 14.2

NOTE: Percentages are rounded.

SOURCE: National Research Council/National Academy of Sciences, Survey of Earned Doctorates, Annual Summary Reports.

Trend data aside, the highest proportions of doctorate earners actually changing fields are in computer science, business, and education. Overall, approximately 37 percent, on average, of liberal arts degree earners had changed fields as of 1987, as compared with 57 percent of those in occupational fields. We repeat these data here in order to show a pattern. Field-changing appears to be most common at the doctorate level in subjects which are either closely related (such as between the theoretical and applied sciences and technologies) or that do not require a tightly sequenced undergraduate preparation in the same field (such as business and education).

Field-changing is not so common a practice in many other countries, but this has to do as much with the organization of postsecondary education as with different academic cultures. U.S. undergraduate study, as pointed out, is both preparation for further study and a general capstone to what is often higher-level secondary education in other societies. In this sense it differs from the first-university degree sequence offered elsewhere, which often comprises a concentrated and advanced preparation for the practice of a profession or qualification for doctoral preliminary examinations. In the United States this type of specialized study really begins at the graduate level (and often in the transitional senior year of college for ambitious and qualified undergraduates). This sequence means that many students not only do, but are required to, change their fields when they enter graduate school, because the specific subject that is their goal simply is not offered at the more general undergraduate level. Coupled with this sequencing is the fact that advanced research in the U.S. has crossed disciplinary lines for many years, but has only recently begun to do so elsewhere. These factors together add up to the high rates of field-changing that characterize U.S. doctoral-level studies.

Completing the Doctorate.

Completion data for the doctorate are presented in Table 15. It will be noted that the list of fields included in the Table has undergone slight changes. These changes reflect the fact that certain fields are mainly offered at specific levels of instruction, or are studied with enough frequency to produce significant counts of degrees only at certain levels. In the case of the doctorate, psychology is separated from the social sciences, and a separate category appears for doctorates in theology. Professional certification to practice clinical psychology and its cousins (counseling psychology, school psychology) in the U.S. generally requires possession of a doctorate, so the count for psychology degrees is large enough at this level -- and different enough in meaning from other social science programs -- to warrant separate treatment. Likewise, doctorates in theoloy and related studies, which are awarded in seminaries more often than in academic departments of religious studies, are distinct enough from other degrees in the humanities and large enough in number to also get a separate listing.

The data on doctorate completions show significant changes in the distribution pattern of major fields as compared with the bachelor's and master's degree levels. At the doctorate level, liberal arts fields still accounted for over 50 percent of all degree awards as of 1987, the only degree level at which this was true. The observable trend is for liberal arts degrees to decline in number, and they are likely to now be approaching a minority, but may still account for a larger proportion of all degrees than at other levels.

Within specific fields the doctorate data also run counter to trends at other levels. A much larger proportion of doctoral students, for example, earn degrees in the scientific and technological fields than is the case at lower postsecondary degree levels, indicating that a relatively high percentage of the students in these fields go on to the doctorate. If one includes data on agriculture (an applied science field at this level) and the health sciences, students in the sciences, mathematics, and the technical professions accounted for over 45 percent of all doctorates as of 1987. This contrasts with the figures of 23 percent of all master's degrees and just under 29 percent of all bachelor's degrees. By comparison, some fields with large degree production at lower levels, such as business, the health fields, and the social sciences, do not dominate degree production at the doctoral level.

Other trends in the doctoral data are not so different from the trends observed elsewhere in this Report. The general decline in degree completions in the non-scientific liberal arts fields is also reflected at the doctoral level, especially in the humanities and social sciences (excepting psychology). Education doctorates also appear to be decreasing at a rate similar to that for

Table 15

Doctorates Awarded by Field, 1977-1987

Field	1976-77	1978-79	1980-81	1984-85	1986-87	77-87
ALL FIELDS	31,672	31,200	31,319	31,201	32,278	+ 1.9
LIBERAL ARTS	18,012	17,335	17,035	17,007	17,534	- 2.6
General	48	52	45	45	53	+10.4
Arts	641	681	628	676	725	+13.1
Humanities	2,931	2,600	2,395	2,177	2,155	-26.5
Social Sciences	3,988	3,655	3,418	3,115	3,142	-21.2
Psychology	2,827	2,918	3,177	2,948	3,009	+ 6.4
Bio. Sciences	3,172	3,317	3,397	3,766	3,824	+20.6
Phys. Sciences	3,410	3,321	3,208	3,531	3,837	+12.5
Mathematics	995	791	767	749	789	-20.7
OCCUPATIONAL	13,660	13,865	14,284	14,194	14,744	+ 7.9
Engineering	2,641	2,494	2,528	3,165	3,716	+40.7
Computer Sci.	---	209	232	311	450	+115.3
Agric./Nat.Res.	924	1,008	1,150	1,258	1,112	+20.4
Health Fields	817	890	1,054	724	806	- 1.3
Public Service	363	340	384	352	319	-12.1
Home Economics	76	88	85	90	67	-11.8
Business	667	712	622	793	980	+46.9
Communications	305	284	239	266	309	+ 1.3
Education	7,581	7,533	7,669	6,884	6,536	-13.8
Theology	155	191	201	229	253	+63.2
Other Occupat.	87	90	85	126	135	+55.2
UNDISTRIBUTED	44	26	35	36	61	+38.6

Table 15, Continued

DEGREES AWARDED BY FIELD AS A PERCENT OF ALL DEGREES AWARDED

Field	1976-77	1978-79	1980-81	1984-85	1986-87	77-87
ALL FIELDS	100.0	100.0	100.0	100.0	100.0	N/A
LIBERAL ARTS	56.9	55.6	54.4	54.5	54.3	- 2.6
General	0.2	0.2	0.1	0.1	0.2	0.0
Arts	2.0	2.2	2.0	2.2	2.3	+ 0.3
Humanities	9.3	8.3	7.7	7.0	6.7	- 2.6
Social Sciences	12.6	11.7	10.9	10.0	9.7	- 2.9
Psychology	8.9	9.4	10.1	9.5	9.3	+ 0.4
Bio. Sciences	10.0	10.6	10.9	12.1	11.9	+ 1.9
Phys. Sciences	10.8	10.6	10.2	11.3	11.9	+ 1.1
Mathematics	3.1	2.5	2.5	2.4	2.4	- 0.7
OCCUPATIONAL	43.1	44.4	45.6	45.5	45.7	+ 2.6
Engineering	8.3	8.0	8.1	10.1	11.5	+ 3.2
Computer Sci.	---	0.7	0.7	1.0	1.4	+ 0.7
Agric./Nat.Res.	2.9	3.2	3.7	4.0	3.5	+ 0.6
Health Fields	2.6	2.9	3.4	2.3	2.5	- 0.1
Public Service	1.2	1.1	1.2	1.1	1.0	- 0.2
Home Economics	0.2	0.3	0.3	0.3	0.2	0.0
Business	2.1	2.3	2.0	2.5	3.0	+ 0.9
Communications	1.0	0.9	0.8	0.9	1.0	0.0
Education	23.9	24.1	24.5	21.9	20.3	- 3.6
Theology	0.5	0.6	0.6	0.7	0.8	+ 0.3
Other Occupat.	0.3	0.3	0.3	0.4	0.4	+ 0.1

NOTE: Percentages are rounded.
SOURCE: National Research Council/National Academy of Sciences, Survey of Earned Doctorates, Annual <u>Summary Reports</u>.

this field at other levels, although the numbers are so large that the field still accounts for nearly half of all non-science/technology doctorates. And, as observed at other levels, the proportions of degree earners in high-technology fields (engineering and computer science) are rising swiftly, although still relatively small in terms of absolute numbers.

These trend data appear to be rather encouraging, showing as they do that U.S. graduate students tend to concentrate in fields for which there is high demand, yet still revealing healthy interest in other important fields of enquiry such as the arts and religion. A somewhat different picture emerges, however, when one considers who it is that majors in some of these fields. If this latter question is addressed, we quickly discover that the picture is very promising when broken out by gender, but quite mixed when broken out by citizenship.

Female Doctorate Recipients.

Women started the decade under study earning approximately one-fourth of all U.S. doctorates, and by 1987 had increased their share to just over one-third. This development, while encouraging, shows that females still tend to finish graduate degree programs at much lower rates than do men. Most of the data presented in Table 16, though, indicate that women have been making progress at the Ph.D. level, and that this improvement is especially noteworthy in fields that have not been traditionally "female" in composition. (The data presented in the Table are for all female recipients of U.S. doctorates, not just U.S. citizens.)

The first part of Table 16 shows that the production of female doctorates has been growing faster in the occupational fields than in the liberal arts disciplines, but that the most astounding growth in productivity in both categories -- an average of over 100 percent per field between 1977 and 1987 -- has taken place in the sciences and the technical occupations. This increase in numbers of scientific and technical degree completions, however, as at other levels, has occurred from a very small base number and thus does not represent anywhere close to a majority (or even a large plurality) in most of these fields. Equally impressive growth in productivity has occurred in business and theology, but with the same caveat about numbers as opposed to percentages of the total. By comparison, women appear to be leaving the humanities (just as are men -- the entire field has been shrinking across all degree levels), but their slower rate of abandonment has resulted in the female proportion of all humanities doctorates actually climbing.

The data also show that two fields at the doctorate level -- psychology and education -- have changed from male-dominated to female-dominated professions during the 1977-1987 period. At least in the case of education, this development confirms a trend that has been the case at lower degree levels for a longer time, and which eventually had to be expressed in statistics for the doctorate. The shift in psychology is primarily due to increased female interest in the practicioner-oriented subfields of clinical and counseling psychology, rather than in laboratory research (8).

Table 16

Awards of the Doctorate to Women, 1977-1987

WOMEN AS A PERCENT OF ALL DEGREE EARNERS BY FIELD					
Field	1976-77	1978-79	1980-81	1984-85	1986-87	77-87
ALL FIELDS	24.8	28.6	31.5	34.3	35.2	+44.9
LIBERAL ARTS	24.9	28.1	30.1	33.0	34.7	+36.1
General	33.3	50.0	31.0	42.2	35.9	+18.8
Arts	32.3	37.7	40.1	40.5	40.6	+42.0
Humanities	41.6	42.7	45.3	47.0	48.9	-13.5
Social Sciences	21.2	25.4	26.7	31.9	31.6	+17.1
Psychology	36.2	40.6	43.9	48.9	53.2	+56.8
Bio. Sciences	23.0	26.8	29.0	32.6	35.3	+85.2
Phys. Sciences	8.9	10.6	11.4	16.3	16.7	+87.6
Mathematics	13.4	15.4	15.5	16.0	17.5	+ 3.8
OCCUPATIONAL	24.7	29.2	33.2	35.4	35.8	+56.7
Engineering	2.8	2.5	3.9	6.3	6.5	+227.0
Computer Sci.	---	12.9	11.2	10.6	14.4	+140.7
Agric./Nat.Res.	6.8	9.0	12.8	15.3	17.4	+206.4
Health Fields	28.9	32.0	37.4	60.0	59.2	+102.1
Public Service	28.1	28.8	35.9	47.4	44.5	+39.2
Home Economics	82.9	85.2	82.4	85.6	89.6	- 4.8
Business	6.0	12.8	14.5	18.2	23.4	+472.5
Communications	28.2	32.0	41.0	41.7	46.3	+66.3
Education	34.9	42.1	47.1	52.0	55.1	+36.2
Theology	7.1	8.9	11.0	15.7	14.2	+227.3
Other Occupat.	48.3	36.7	48.2	47.6	51.1	+64.3

Table 16, Continued

DISTRIBUTION OF FEMALE DEGREE EARNERS, BY FIELD

Field	1976-77	1978-79	1980-81	1984-85	1986-87	77-87
ALL FIELDS	100.0	100.0	100.0	100.0	100.0	N/A
LIBERAL ARTS	57.0	54.6	52.0	52.5	53.5	- 3.5
General	0.2	0.3	0.1	0.2	0.2	0.0
Arts	2.6	2.9	2.6	2.6	2.6	0.0
Humanities	15.5	12.4	11.0	9.6	9.3	- 6.2
Social Sciences	10.8	10.4	9.3	9.3	8.7	- 2.1
Psychology	13.0	13.3	14.1	13.5	14.1	+ 1.1
Bio. Sciences	9.3	10.0	10.0	11.5	11.9	+ 2.6
Phys. Sciences	3.9	3.9	3.7	5.4	5.6	+ 1.7
Mathematics	1.7	1.4	1.2	1.1	1.2	- 0.5
OCCUPATIONAL	43.0	45.4	48.1	47.0	46.5	+ 3.5
Engineering	0.9	0.7	1.0	1.9	2.1	+ 1.2
Computer Sci.	---	0.3	0.3	0.3	0.6	+ 0.3
Agric./Nat.Res.	0.8	1.0	1.5	1.8	1.7	+ 0.9
Health Fields	3.0	3.2	4.0	4.1	4.2	+ 1.2
Public Service	1.3	1.1	1.4	1.6	1.3	0.0
Home Economics	0.8	0.8	0.7	0.7	0.5	- 0.3
Business	0.5	1.0	0.9	1.4	2.0	+ 1.5
Communications	1.1	1.0	1.0	1.0	1.3	+ 0.2
Education	33.7	35.6	36.6	33.3	31.7	- 2.0
Theology	0.1	0.2	0.2	0.3	0.3	+ 0.2
Other Occupat.	0.5	0.4	0.4	0.6	0.6	+ 0.1

NOTE: Percentages are rounded.
SOURCE: National Research Council/National Academy of Sciences, Survey of Earned Doctorates, Annual Summary Reports.

Data on the distribution of fields of study in which women earn doctorates further highlights the patterns revealed in the first part of Table 16. Data presented in the second part of the Table show that the science and technology shift described above amounted to a six percent change in the proportion of women completing degrees in these fields. The effect of the changes in the pattern of female doctorates has been to reduce the number of fields in which women tend to concentrate in large numbers. In 1977 women in the U.S. were most likely to earn doctorates in the humanities, the social sciences, psychology, and education. As of 1987 this had changed; only psychology and education remained, but these fields had been joined by the biological sciences. A definite shift away from the non-science liberal arts was thus confirmed. The other changes noted, while important within the context of those fields, involved too few individual cases to affect the overall pattern.

Foreign Recipients of U.S. Doctorates

Although there is a long way to go before women in the U.S. exhibit a doctorate-earning pattern that is well-distributed across all fields, and while this eventuality may not -- even then -- resemble the pattern for men, the data so far available show that considerable progress has been made as regards moving away from a non-scientific and non-technical pattern of majors. When attention shifts to a comparison between U.S. citizens and permanent residents who earn U.S. doctorates, and foreign students (non-resident aliens) who do so, a different picture emerges. Such data highlight the considerable popularity of U.S. graduate programs among citizens of other countries, but also point up some of the problems that currently beset U.S. postsecondary education and the U.S. economy.

The data presented in Table 17 illustrate the rapid and significant increase in foreign students in U.S. doctoral programs. Were the figures to include resident aliens (non-citizens granted permanent residency status), to which category belong many students who have entered the U.S. with refugee or asylum status, the increase would be even more impressive. In any case, foreign students as defined here account for nearly one-fifth of all doctorates awarded by U.S. postsecondary institutions, with the number approaching one-half of all awards in some fields. Since the fields in which foreign students are most heavily represented include the sciences and engineering, and since foreign student doctorate awards in these fields have virtually doubled over the decade under study, it is unsurprising that this development has occasioned considerable study. What is truly significant about this trend is that it reveals how little of the recent increase in interest in these fields is due to U.S. students taking advanced degrees in the subjects. This, in turn, has future implications for the U.S. workforce and the economy.

Foreign graduate students do not, it seems, come to the United States to study the non-science liberal arts disciplines, although there has been fairly consistent interest in the social sciences -- primarily economics. Until recently, there was also a considerable degree of interest in the graduate study of education. Psychology, by contrast, is a popular field among U.S. graduate students but not among foreign students who study here. The vast majority of foreign graduate students, however, 62 percent in 1977 through 68.5 percent in 1987, have pursued degrees in the scientific and technical

Table 17

Awards of U.S. Doctorates to Foreign Students, 1977-1987

FOREIGN STUDENTS AS A PERCENT OF ALL U.S. DEGREE EARNERS, BY FIELD						
Field	1976-77	1978-79	1980-81	1984-85	1986-87	77-87
ALL FIELDS	10.9	11.5	12.5	16.7	17.3	+62.3
LIBERAL ARTS	9.6	9.2	10.2	13.7	15.3	+55.6
General	8.3	9.6	8.9	8.9	26.4	+250.0
Arts	5.1	3.7	4.1	5.3	5.8	+27.3
Humanities	4.9	5.1	7.0	8.6	11.0	+65.0
Social Sciences	12.3	12.4	14.0	18.8	18.4	+18.0
Psychology	2.3	2.2	2.4	2.7	2.7	+25.0
Bio. Sciences	9.4	8.0	7.4	11.2	12.8	+64.1
Phys. Sciences	14.9	14.6	16.3	20.8	24.0	+81.5
Mathematics	18.8	20.2	26.6	36.5	41.3	+74.3
OCCUPATIONAL	12.6	14.3	15.4	20.4	19.7	+68.9
Engineering	29.3	32.7	37.3	44.7	41.2	+98.2
Computer Sci.	---	15.3	17.2	28.6	31.6	+343.8
Agric./Nat.Res.	33.4	33.0	33.7	32.0	29.9	+ 7.4
Health Fields	7.6	10.0	8.4	13.4	11.9	+54.8
Public Service	11.0	12.7	11.5	9.9	12.6	0.0
Home Economics	7.9	6.8	7.1	6.7	13.4	+50.0
Business	15.6	17.1	14.8	21.3	23.3	+119.2
Communications	4.6	8.8	8.8	18.1	12.3	+171.4
Education	5.1	6.5	6.9	8.4	6.4	+ 9.1
Theology	5.8	5.8	7.0	8.3	9.9	+177.8
Other Occupat.	16.1	21.1	24.7	28.6	23.0	+121.4

fields already mentioned, and have done so with remarkable consistency over time (9). Exceptions to the "rule of science" in foreign participation in U.S. doctoral programs include business and theology. Both fields are ones in which U.S. institutions have established reputations, and private sponsors are numerous.

AFTER THE DOCTORATE

The Survey of Earned Doctorates data allow us to analyze the career plans of doctorate recipients by field of study. Table 18 presents the findings for the 1977-1987 period, and compares the situation in each field with that for the aggregated total of all doctorate recipients.

As can be seen, the aggregate results have been fairly consistent over time. Around 65 percent of new Ph.D.s have reported firm contracts for employment as of graduation, about one-fourth have been pursuing promising job leads but have not finalized their situations, and the rest have no definite plans at all and are in a state equivalent to the bachelor's degree recipient who is "unemployed and looking for work".

When broken out by field, these data show interesting variations. Across the board, the proportion of doctorate recipients who have no plans has increased over the decade under study, with the largest increases occurring among occupational fields. The data are not very encouraging at any point. Only two fields, the humanities and physical sciences, registered an increase in actual employment over 1977-1987, and only four -- business, engineering, computer science, and the social sciences -- reported even improved prospects.

Humanities graduates faced a grim situation in 1977 -- just over 50 percent employed as of graduation -- that appeared to improve somewhat by 1987, while the employment outlook for doctorate recipients in the technical fields apparently got worse. Such results may appear counterintuitive at first blush. An explanation for the latter situation, though, suggests itself in the form of the large numbers of foreign students taking degrees in these subjects. Non-citizens are not eligible for jobs involving any work on Federal Government-related contracts, which comprise much of the U.S. high-technology industry's business, and some foreign students may also have uncertain plans regarding employment back home -- or going home, for that matter.

Table 18

Trends in the Employment Status of Doctorate Recipients, 1977 - 1987

Year & Status		All	Hum	Soc	Bio	Phy	Mat	Eng	*CpS	AgS	MdS	*Bus	Edu	Oth
77	D	66	54	66	71	69	63	68	--	67	70	--	68	80
79	E	68	54	66	73	75	67	73	76	67	75	--	66	79
81	F I N	69	60	68	72	75	72	68	76	68	72	--	69	79
85	I T	66	59	63	72	70	68	62	69	63	67	80	69	68
87	E	65	59	61	71	70	62	59	66	63	68	74	67	68
77-87		-1	+5	-5	0	+1	-1	-9	-10	-4	-2	-6	-1	-12
77	S	26	35	26	24	24	29	25	--	28	22	--	26	14
79	E E	25	36	26	20	19	25	22	19	26	18	--	28	15
81	K I	24	32	25	22	19	22	23	20	27	23	--	25	15
85	N G	26	33	29	23	23	24	27	23	30	23	11	25	21
87		25	30	27	22	21	27	29	24	27	21	14	24	20
77-87		-1	-5	+1	-2	-3	-2	+4	+5	-1	-1	+3	-2	+6
77	U	8	11	8	6	7	8	6	--	6	8	--	6	6
79	N K	7	10	8	7	6	8	6	5	6	7	--	7	6
81	N O	6	8	7	6	6	6	7	3	6	5	--	6	6
85	W N	8	9	9	6	7	8	11	7	7	10	9	7	11
87		10	12	11	7	9	11	12	10	10	11	11	9	12
77-87		+2	+1	+3	+1	+2	+3	+6	+5	+4	+3	+2	+3	+6

NOTE: Percentages are rounded.

SOURCE: National Research Council/National Academy of Sciences, Survey of Earned Doctorates, Annual.

CONCLUSIONS

The data on the flow of U.S. postsecondary students through the system, when broken out by field of study, reveals several points worth highlighting. Among them are the following:

- Degree completions, and presumably enrollments, in the non-science liberal arts disciplines have tended to decline in recent years across undergraduate and graduate levels;

- Degree completions in the scientific and technical fields are generally on the rise, but still represent a minority of all awards;

- At the graduate level, especially the doctorate, between one-quarter and one-half of all science and technical degrees (depending on the field) are awarded to foreign students;

- Women have steadily increased their share of degrees at all levels, and have made small but significant shifts in their choices of majors away from traditional non-science fields and toward more frequent study of the sciences and the technical occupations;

- Employment prospects for undergraduates who enter the labor market directly after graduation indicate that non-science liberal arts majors have a slightly more difficult time finding rewarding work at competitive salaries than other majors, but that this difference is not overwhelming and that all undergraduates share the problem to some extent;

- High proportions of undergraduate majors in the non-science liberal arts fields and in the sciences continue on to graduate school, and this must be considered in evaluating true levels of employment for these majors;

- Graduate students' employment prospects, for doctorate recipients, have been only fair for most majors in recent years, and the number of new Ph.D.s without any job prospects has been rising in every field over the 1977-1987 period.

These findings are not always good news, especially in regard to the labor market. They appear to suggest that Americans with more education -- beyond the bachelor's degree -- can improve their career opportunities, but that further education has its limits in a market where many traditional jobs for holders of advanced degrees are already filled, and new avenues of employment are not opening up rapidly enough. On the other hand, the attractiveness of an American education for many foreign graduate students is undeniable and a testament -- at least in part -- to the strengths of an often-maligned educational system, but employment prospects for such products of U.S. institutions may be no less uncertain than for domestic citizens.

More data, especially longitudinal studies and follow-ups, are needed in order to discover whether the uninspiring jobs picture for new postsecondary degree holders improves after a while, or does not. Until these data are available, however, we must make do with what knowledge we can glean from occasional glimpses of the post-education landscape.

NOTES:

1. The data presented in Table 1 refer to students who complete programs while enrolled in non-profit, regionally accredited public and private institutions. A large number of students are enrolled in certificate programs in private for-profit trade schools, but this universe of postsecondary schools is not currently surveyed on a comprehensive basis. Postsecondary trade schools usually offer only one program, or at most a few related ones, in occupational areas that require licensure and some training. Examples include schools of barbering and cosmetology, cooking and food preparation, health care assistance, sales (usually a specialty like real estate), computer and electronics servicing, etc.

2. For a detailed explanation of the real function of two-year institutions in U.S. postsecondary education, based on an analysis of who enrolls and what happens to them in their academic careers, see Clifford Adelman, "Using Transcripts to Validate Institutional Mission: The Role of Community Colleges in the Postsecondary Experience of a Generation", Office of Research Working Paper No. 90-523, (Washington: Office of Educational Research and Improvement, February 1990).

3. The tendency of women to major in non-technical subjects appears to have little or nothing to do with their actual ability to perform well academically in rigorously quantitative disciplines. When they major in such fields, women often outperform men -- as they also do in the other subjects. For a more detailed look at the undergraduate academic performance of women, see Clifford Adelman, _Women at Thirtysomething: Paradoxes of Attainment_, (Washington: U.S. Government Printing Office, June 1991), pp. 3-18.

4. Chiropractic schools do not require completion of a bachelor's degree prior to entry, but only two years of postsecondary education. Thus, first-professional degrees in this field often signify barely the equivalent of a bachelor's degree.

5. For the raw data upon which these observations rest see Henry Gordon and Patricia Q. Brown, _Degrees Conferred in Institutions of Higher Education, by Race/Ethnicity and Sex: 1976-77 through 1986-87_, (Washington: U.S. Government Printing Office, October 1990); and William H. Freund, _Race/Ethnicity Trends in Degrees Conferred by Institutions of Higher Education: 1978-79 through 1988-89_, (Washington: U.S. Government Printing Office, January 1991).

6. See Tuckman, _et al_, _On Time to the Doctorate_, pp. 93-104 and 115-117; plus annual breakouts of doctorate recipient characteristics in the Survey of Earned Doctorates _Summaries_.

7. See the age data in the characteristics breakouts for annual tabulations of Survey of Earned Doctorates data, as reported in the annual Summary Reports. These reported data indicate that the median age of non-science/technology doctorate recipients increased from 34.6 years to 37.7 years over 1977-1987, while that of science/technology doctorate recipients increased from 30 years to 31.5 over the same period. As of 1987, the median ages of doctorate recipients in the specific fields in question were: health sciences, 35.6 years; education, 39.8 years; humanities, 35 years; and social sciences, 33.5 years.

8. Susan T. Hill, "Ph.D.s Awarded to U.S. Citizens and Permanent Residents by Race, Gender, Fine Field of Study, and Year of Degree", unpublished tabulations, National Science Foundation, 1991. When broken out by subfield (fine field), psychology data show that some 42 percent of all psychology doctorates were in clinical and counseling psychology in 1977; as of 1987 this percentage had climbed to 55.5. Women accounted for 36 percent of the clinical and counseling doctorates in 1977 and 55 percent in 1987. At the same time, the proportion of all female doctorates in psychology earned in these two subfields went from 41 percent in 1977 to 77 percent in 1987.

9. In part, this consistency may be attributable to student assistance policies that encourage foreign students, and the home and local sponsors responsible for them, to concentrate on subjects of use to their countries' economic and technological development. Non-science students may not receive direct sponsorship assistance as frequently, or in such large amounts, and educational opportunities in their areas of interest may be available at home at a level competitive with, or in advance of, that which might be offered in the U.S.

ALSO AVAILABLE

Alternatives to Universities (1991)
(91 90 05 1) ISBN 92-64-13530-8   FF90 £12.00 US$22.00 DM35

Financing Higher Education. Current Patterns (1990)
(91 90 04 1) ISBN 92-64-13422-0   FF100 £12.00 US$21.00 DM39

Reviews of National Policies for Education

Reviews of National Policies for Education. Higher Education in California (1990)
(91 90 02 1) ISBN 92-64-13412-3   FF140 £17.00 US$30.00 DM55

Prices charged at the OECD Bookshop.
THE OECD CATALOGUE OF PUBLICATIONS and supplements will be sent free of charge
on request addressed either to OECD Publications Service,
or to the OECD Distributor in your country.

ÉGALEMENT DISPONIBLES

Examens des politiques nationales d'éducation
Examens des politiques nationales d'éducation. L'Enseignement supérieur en Californie (1990)
(91 90 02 2) ISBN 92-64-23412-8   FF140   £17.00   US$30.00   DM55
Le Financement de l'enseignement supérieur. Tendances actuelles (1990)
(91 90 04 2) ISBN 92-64-23422-5   FF100   £12.00   US$21.00   DM39
Nouvelles formes d'enseignement supérieur (1991)
(91 90 05 2) ISBN 92-64-23530-2   FF90   £12.00   US$22.00   DM35

Prix de vente au public dans la librairie du siège de l'OCDE.
LE CATALOGUE DES PUBLICATIONS de l'OCDE et ses suppléments seront envoyés
gratuitement sur demande adressée soit à l'OCDE, Service des Publications,
soit au distributeur des publications de l'OCDE de votre pays.

MAIN SALES OUTLETS OF OECD PUBLICATIONS – PRINCIPAUX POINTS DE VENTE DES PUBLICATIONS DE L'OCDE

Argentina – Argentine
Carlos Hirsch S.R.L.
Galería Güemes, Florida 165, 4° Piso
1333 Buenos Aires   Tel. (1) 331.1787 y 331.2391
                          Telefax: (1) 331.1787

Australia – Australie
D.A. Book (Aust.) Pty. Ltd.
648 Whitehorse Road, P.O.B 163
Mitcham, Victoria 3132   Tel. (03) 873.4411
                          Telefax: (03) 873.5679

Austria – Autriche
OECD Publications and Information Centre
Schedestrasse 7
D-W 5300 Bonn 1 (Germany) Tel. (49.228) 21.60.45
                          Telefax: (49.228) 26.11.04

Gerold & Co.
Graben 31
Wien I   Tel. (0222) 533.50.14

Belgium – Belgique
Jean De Lannoy
Avenue du Roi 202
B-1060 Bruxelles   Tel. (02) 538.51.69/538.08.41
                          Telefax: (02) 538.08.41

Canada
Renouf Publishing Company Ltd.
1294 Algoma Road
Ottawa, ON K1B 3W8   Tel. (613) 741.4333
                          Telefax: (613) 741.5439
Stores:
61 Sparks Street
Ottawa, ON K1P 5R1   Tel. (613) 238.8985
211 Yonge Street
Toronto, ON M5B 1M4   Tel. (416) 363.3171

Federal Publications
165 University Avenue
Toronto, ON M5H 3B8   Tel. (416) 581.1552
                          Telefax: (416)581.1743

Les Éditions La Liberté Inc.
3020 Chemin Sainte-Foy
Sainte-Foy, PQ G1X 3V6   Tel. (418) 658.3763
                          Telefax: (418) 658.3763

China – Chine
China National Publications Import
Export Corporation (CNPIEC)
P.O. Box 88
Beijing   Tel. 44.0731
                          Telefax: 401.5661

Denmark – Danemark
Munksgaard Export and Subscription Service
35, Nørre Søgade, P.O. Box 2148
DK-1016 København K   Tel. (33) 12.85.70
                          Telefax: (33) 12.93.87

Finland – Finlande
Akateeminen Kirjakauppa
Keskuskatu 1, P.O. Box 128
00100 Helsinki   Tel. (358 0) 12141
                          Telefax: (358 0) 121.4441

France
OECD/OCDE
Mail Orders/Commandes par correspondance:
2, rue André-Pascal
75775 Paris Cédex 16   Tel. (33-1) 45.24.82.00
                          Telefax: (33-1) 45.24.85.00
                          or (33-1) 45.24.81.76
                          Telex: 620 160 OCDE

Bookshop/Librairie:
33, rue Octave-Feuillet
75016 Paris   Tel. (33-1) 45.24.81.67
                          (33-1) 45.24.81.81

Librairie de l'Université
12a, rue Nazareth
13100 Aix-en-Provence   Tel. 42.26.18.08
                          Telefax: 42.26.63.26

Germany – Allemagne
OECD Publications and Information Centre
Schedestrasse 7
D-W 5300 Bonn 1   Tel. (0228) 21.60.45
                          Telefax: (0228) 26.11.04

Greece – Grèce
Librairie Kauffmann
Mavrokordatou 9
106 78 Athens   Tel. 322.21.60
                          Telefax: 363.39.67

Hong Kong
Swindon Book Co. Ltd.
13 - 15 Lock Road
Kowloon, Hong Kong   Tel. 366.80.31
                          Telefax: 739.49.75

Iceland – Islande
Mál Mog Menning
Laugavegi 18, Pósthólf 392
121 Reykjavik   Tel. 162.35.23

India – Inde
Oxford Book and Stationery Co.
Scindia House
New Delhi 110001   Tel.(11) 331.5896/5308
                          Telefax: (11) 332.5993

17 Park Street
Calcutta 700016   Tel. 240832

Indonesia – Indonésie
Pdii-Lipi
P.O. Box 269/JKSMG/88
Jakarta 12790   Tel. 583467
                          Telex: 62 875

Ireland – Irlande
TDC Publishers – Library Suppliers
12 North Frederick Street
Dublin 1   Tel. 74.48.35/74.96.77
                          Telefax: 74.84.16

Israel
Electronic Publications only
Publications électroniques seulement
Sophist Systems Ltd.
71 Allenby Street
Tel-Aviv 65134   Tel. 3-29.00.21
                          Telefax: 3-29.92.39

Italy – Italie
Libreria Commissionaria Sansoni
Via Duca di Calabria 1/1
50125 Firenze   Tel. (055) 64.54.15
                          Telefax: (055) 64.12.57

Via Bartolini 29
20155 Milano   Tel. (02) 36.50.83

Editrice e Libreria Herder
Piazza Montecitorio 120
00186 Roma   Tel. 679.46.28
                          Telex: NATEL I 621427

Libreria Hoepli
Via Hoepli 5
20121 Milano   Tel. (02) 86.54.46
                          Telefax: (02) 805.28.86

Libreria Scientifica
Dott. Lucio de Biasio 'Aeiou'
Via Meravigli 16
20123 Milano   Tel. (02) 805.68.98
                          Telefax: (02) 80.01.75

Japan – Japon
OECD Publications and Information Centre
Landic Akasaka Building
2-3-4 Akasaka, Minato-ku
Tokyo 107   Tel. (81.3) 3586.2016
                          Telefax: (81.3) 3584.7929

Korea – Corée
Kyobo Book Centre Co. Ltd.
P.O. Box 1658, Kwang Hwa Moon
Seoul   Tel. 730.78.91
                          Telefax: 735.00.30

Malaysia – Malaisie
Co-operative Bookshop Ltd.
University of Malaya
P.O. Box 1127, Jalan Pantai Baru
59700 Kuala Lumpur
Malaysia   Tel. 756.5000/756.5425
                          Telefax: 757.3661

Netherlands – Pays-Bas
SDU Uitgeverij
Christoffel Plantijnstraat 2
Postbus 20014
2500 EA's-Gravenhage   Tel. (070 3) 78.99.11
Voor bestellingen: Tel. (070 3) 78.98.80
                          Telefax: (070 3) 47.63.51

New Zealand – Nouvelle-Zélande
GP Publications Ltd.
Customer Services
33 The Esplanade - P.O. Box 38-900
Petone, Wellington   Tel. (04) 5685.555
                          Telefax: (04) 5685.333

Norway – Norvège
Narvesen Info Center - NIC
Bertrand Narvesens vei 2
P.O. Box 6125 Etterstad
0602 Oslo 6   Tel. (02) 57.33.00
                          Telefax: (02) 68.19.01

Pakistan
Mirza Book Agency
65 Shahrah Quaid-E-Azam
Lahore 3   Tel. 66.839
                          Telex: 44886 UBL PK. Attn: MIRZA BK

Portugal
Livraria Portugal
Rua do Carmo 70-74
Apart. 2681
1117 Lisboa Codex   Tel.: (01) 347.49.82/3/4/5
                          Telefax: (01) 347.02.64

Singapore – Singapour
Information Publications Pte. Ltd.
Pei-Fu Industrial Building
24 New Industrial Road No. 02-06
Singapore 1953   Tel. 283.1786/283.1798
                          Telefax: 284.8875

Spain – Espagne
Mundi-Prensa Libros S.A.
Castelló 37, Apartado 1223
Madrid 28001   Tel. (91) 431.33.99
                          Telefax: (91) 575.39.98

Libreria Internacional AEDOS
Consejo de Ciento 391
08009 - Barcelona   Tel. (93) 488.34.92
                          Telefax: (93) 487.76.59

Llibreria de la Generalitat
Palau Moja
Rambla dels Estudis, 118
08002 - Barcelona   Tel. (93) 318.80.12 (Subscripcions)
                          (93) 302.67.23 (Publicacions)
                          Telefax: (93) 412.18.54

Sri Lanka
Centre for Policy Research
c/o Colombo Agencies Ltd.
No. 300-304, Galle Road
Colombo 3   Tel. (1) 574240, 573551-2
                          Telefax: (1) 575394, 510711

Sweden – Suède
Fritzes Fackboksföretaget
Box 16356
Regeringsgatan 12
103 27 Stockholm   Tel. (08) 23.89.00
                          Telefax: (08) 20.50.21

Subscription Agency/Abonnements:
Wennergren-Williams AB
Nordenflychtsvägen 74
Box 30004
104 25 Stockholm   Tel. (08) 13.67.00
                          Telefax: (08) 618.62.32

Switzerland – Suisse
OECD Publications and Information Centre
Schedestrasse 7
D-W 5300 Bonn 1 (Germany) Tel. (49.228) 21.60.45
                          Telefax: (49.228) 26.11.04

Suisse romande
Maditec S.A.
Chemin des Palettes 4
1020 Renens/Lausanne   Tel. (021) 635.08.65
                          Telefax: (021) 635.07.80

Librairie Payot
6 rue Grenus
1211 Genève 11   Tel. (022) 731.89.50
                          Telex: 28356

Subscription Agency - Service des Abonnements
Naville S.A.
7, rue Lévrier
1201 Genève   Tél.: (022) 732.24.00
                          Telefax: (022) 738.87.13

Taiwan – Formose
Good Faith Worldwide Int'l. Co. Ltd.
9th Floor, No. 118, Sec. 2
Chung Hsiao E. Road
Taipei   Tel. (02) 391.7396/391.7397
                          Telefax: (02) 394.9176

Thailand – Thaïlande
Suksit Siam Co. Ltd.
113, 115 Fuang Nakhon Rd.
Opp. Wat Rajbopith
Bangkok 10200   Tel. (662) 251.1630
                          Telefax: (662) 236.7783

Turkey – Turquie
Kültur Yayinlari Is-Türk Ltd. Sti.
Atatürk Bulvari No. 191/Kat. 21
Kavaklidere/Ankara   Tel. 25.07.60
Dolmabahce Cad. No. 29
Besiktas/Istanbul   Tel. 160.71.88
                          Telex: 43482B

United Kingdom – Royaume-Uni
HMSO
Gen. enquiries   Tel. (071) 873 0011
Postal orders only:
P.O. Box 276, London SW8 5DT
Personal Callers HMSO Bookshop
49 High Holborn, London WC1V 6HB
                          Telefax: 071 873 2000
Branches at: Belfast, Birmingham, Bristol, Edinburgh,
                                                Manchester

United States – États-Unis
OECD Publications and Information Centre
2001 L Street N.W., Suite 700
Washington, D.C. 20036-4910 Tel. (202) 785.6323
                            Telefax: (202) 785.0350

Venezuela
Libreria del Este
Avda F. Miranda 52, Aptdo. 60337
Edificio Galipán
Caracas 106   Tel. 951.1705/951.2307/951.1297
                          Telegram: Libreste Caracas

Yugoslavia – Yougoslavie
Jugoslovenska Knjiga
Knez Mihajlova 2, P.O. Box 36
Beograd   Tel. (011) 621.992
                          Telefax: (011) 625.970

Orders and inquiries from countries where Distributors have not yet been appointed should be sent to: OECD Publications Service, 2 rue André-Pascal, 75775 Paris Cédex 16, France.

Les commandes provenant de pays où l'OCDE n'a pas encore désigné de distributeur devraient être adressées à : OCDE, Service des Publications, 2, rue André-Pascal, 75775 Paris Cédex 16, France.

OECD PUBLICATIONS, 2 rue André-Pascal, 75775 PARIS CEDEX 16
PRINTED IN FRANCE
(02 92 02 3) ISBN 92-64-03525-7 - No. 45954 1992